D1596813

Circuits of the Sacred

A Faggotology
in the
Black Latinx Caribbean

WRITING MATTERS! a series edited by
Saidiya Hartman, Monica Huerta, Erica Rand, and Kathleen Stewart

Circuits of the Sacred

CARLOS
ULISES
DECENA

Duke University Press · Durham and London · 2023

© 2023 Duke University Press
All rights reserved
Printed in the United States of America on acid-free paper ∞
Designed by Aimee C. Harrison
Typeset in Garamond Premier Pro, Avenir LT Std, and
SangBleu Kingdom by Westchester Publishing Services

Library of Congress Cataloging-in-Publication Data
Names: Decena, Carlos Ulises, [date] author.
Title: Circuits of the sacred : a faggotology in the Black Latinx Caribbean / Carlos
Ulises Decena.
Other titles: Writing matters! (Duke University Press)
Description: Durham : Duke University Press, 2023. | Series: Writing matters! | Includes
bibliographical references and index.
Identifiers: LCCN 2022039177 (print)
LCCN 2022039178 (ebook)
ISBN 9781478019442 (paperback)
ISBN 9781478016809 (hardcover)
ISBN 9781478024071 (ebook)
Subjects: LCSH: Decena, Carlos Ulises, 1974– | Gays, Black—Caribbean Area. | Black
people—Caribbean Area—Religion. | Gay immigrants—Caribbean Area. | Queer theory. |
Feminist theory. | Caribbean Area—Emigration and immigration—Social aspects. |
BISAC: SOCIAL SCIENCE / Ethnic Studies / Caribbean & Latin American Studies |
SOCIAL SCIENCE / LGBTQ Studies / Gay Studies
Classification: LCC HQ76.3.C27 D44 2023 (print) | LCC HQ76.3.C27 (ebook) |
DDC 306.760109729—dc23/eng/20221018
LC record available at https://lccn.loc.gov/2022039177
LC ebook record available at https://lccn.loc.gov/2022039178

Cover art: Rotimi Fani-Kayode, *Under the Surplice*, 1987. © Rotimi Fani-Kayode.
Courtesy of Autograph, London.

A mis tres Jotas: Jordan Joaquín, Joshua Ulysses, y Joaquín Alfredo

En honor a Robyn Magalit Rodriguez y a su hijo,
Amado Khaya Canham Rodriguez,
minamahal na umalis kaagad sa amin (the beloved who left us too soon)

Contents

Gratitudes

For the breath of life that animates my journey with and beyond the creature of ink and paper you now read, I am grateful for the ancestors and divinities holding space for me. May this instrument bring many closer to what freedom can be.

I am privileged to work at a public university where many of us believe and practice learning for ourselves, for others, and for the many who can dream and aspire through our work, our teaching, and the gift of accompanying one another and our students. My colleagues in Latino and Caribbean Studies and Women's, Gender, and Sexuality Studies have held space for the visions articulated through this study for more than a decade. I am especially appreciative for the mentorship, friendship, and companionship of Ethel Brooks, Zaire Dinzey-Flores, Nelson Maldonado-Torres, Michelle Stephens, Deb Vargas, and Omaris Zamora. Nelson deserves special recognition for supporting my thinking about this study through an appearance and exchange with students in one of his graduate seminars and for sponsoring the workshop on my manuscript with Roberto Strongman and Edgar Rivera-Colón. Thank you to Omaris and Zaire and to all the colleagues in attendance for accompanying me in working through some of the ideas in this book at the Black Latinx Americas Labs before the COVID-19 pandemic hit. This book has enjoyed the companionship and mentorship of many friends connected to Rutgers University throughout the years, including colleagues in the Institute for Research on Women's 2020–21 Seminar, led by Arlene Stein and Sarah Tobias, and the Tepoztlán Institute for the Transnational History of the

Américas' 2021 virtual meeting. Mary Hawkesworth provided invaluable and rigorous feedback on the manuscript as a whole. Emerging scholars who have collaborated with me, listened to me, and redirected me as needed include Camilla Belliard-Quiroga, Alok Vaid-Menon, and Rafael Vizcaino. Yomaira Figueroa-Vásquez mentored me through an important rewrite of the intro-duction of the book—what a marvel to be mentored by one of your own mentees! Judith Rodriguez has become a dear friend and fierce interlocutor with this text; it is sharper and richer because she has given the most trans-formative feedback I have ever enjoyed receiving for my work; I only hope I might model for others the kind, loving, and rigorous engagement that Judith has shared with me. Hyacinth Miller has been a companion and interlocutor about and beyond this book; your presence and mentorship have meant the world to me. Madai Poole and Maria Ealey have been steadfast supporters and ingenious collaborators in working through all bureaucratic challenges of our collective institutional life. But perhaps the biggest shout-outs here go to Carlos iro Burgos, who worked with me steadfastly throughout the draft-ing and revising process and whose own growth and evolution as a scholar activist I have accompanied. This study benefits from his unerring writer's ear, his ability to model steadiness and peace even in the thick of crisis, his gentle and big-hearted sense of humor, and his belief that men of color can hold space for one another to grow into fuller expressions of the men we have been taught to be. Gracias.

I am a devoted unionist, and part of what has made Rutgers a genuine home for me has been the community I have found with fellow hell-raisers. For your presence, companionship, and guidance, I am grateful to Sandra Rocío Castro, Saskia Cipriani, Carlos Fernández, Michelle Shostack, and Silismar Suriel. My union peeps keep me hoping, dreaming, and actively working to realize a better workplace for everyone, and I am grateful for the comradeship of Becky Givan, Patrick Nowlan, BJ Walker, Sherry Wolf, and Todd Wolfson. Donna Murch deserves a special shout-out for her political intuition, as well as her boundless intellectual generosity. And we just have a hell of a lot of fun when we get to hang out. I hope we get to write a book together some day, but my heart swells with pride to know that we are friends.

As the manuscript evolved, it earned some friends and taught me lessons about what honest collegiality is supposed to be. In this regard, I extend my gratitude to Richard Morrison for offering sobering critical editorial feedback at the time I needed it. Salvador Vidal-Ortiz also provided invaluable feed-back and the sustained gift of friendship. I am happy to be in the company of Ken Wissoker and the Duke University Press team in bringing this study to the world, and I am gratified to see this work published in the Writing Matters! series. Particular kudos goes to Erica Rand, whose advocacy for this work included challenging me to see more than I could see on my own. I am also indebted to the external readers for their rigorous engagement with this work, for their belief in its promise, and for their continued challenge for me to push it to be closer to realize its potential. Joshua Gutterman Tranen, Liz Smith, Annie Lubinsky, and Aimee Harrison: thank you for your responsiveness and clearheaded guidance in the production process. Leonard Rosenbaum continues to amaze me with his editorial skill and responsiveness. Thank you for the attention you brought to preparing the text for production and indexing.

I came to think and write this book in and through community and love for the parts of myself I had been taught to hate. I credit and thank Ana-Maurine Lara and Alaí Reyes-Santos for the Transnational Black Feminist Retreat that changed everything for me and (I know) for several others of us who were there. For my introduction into Regla de Ocha, I am indebted to Maritza Barranco Rodríguez and all members of the Ilé de Abbebe Oshún in Santo Domingo-Havana. I am also grateful for the spiritual companionship and mentorship of Jaime Gaviria, and I look forward to writing a book together.

Friends and interlocutors of this book include folks I literally met while revising. They took on reading and offering their thoughts on specific sections of the book, and it has grown the richer for it: Luis Menéndez-Antuña, Vinicius Marinho, and Santiago Slabodsky. My love and comradeship with the poet and critic Octavio González grew through helpings of Zoom conversations and the way he brings a generous heart to his incisive engagement with this book and with me. Over the years, my soul has been fed with steady helpings of the extraordinary work of Caroline Bergvall, Alexis Pauline Gumbs, Caridad Souza, and Gina Athena Ulysse, and I had the good fortune to getting them to lay eyes on this text and talk with me about it. For stunning and formative readings, I am also grateful to Elizabeth Pérez and Roberto Strongman at a Zoom talk hosted by the Chicano Studies Institute at the University of California, Santa Barbara. Director Inés Casillas deserves special mention for her leadership and invitation. Questions, suggestions, and comments emerging from interaction with all these smart interlocutors were important in how this text evolved. Nelson Maldonado-Torres, Yolanda Martinez-San Miguel, and Michelle Stephens are towering figures in their fields, amazing mentors, and priceless colleagues. Their generosity as demanding readers and perspicacious interlocutors has also shaped this text. I am grateful to Yolanda for her mentorship and support throughout the decades we have known each other and for having invited me to visit and present sections of the book before her colleagues at the University of Miami and to her colleagues for engaging and supporting my work: Jafari S. Allen, Donnette Francis, Gema Perez Sanchez, and George Yúdice. Alan Filreis, my mentor of almost three decades, read and engaged this book with his characteristically relentless intensity, and I credit our emotional and intellectual reencounter for the crystallization of the signature term of this text: *faggotology*. Thank you.

Edgar Rivera-Colón appears more than once in the gratitudes because he has traveled with me and with this text for several of its iterations. I think one of the reasons I got the job at Rutgers almost twenty years ago was so I would meet Edgar. He is at once my toughest critic and most generous intellectual companion, my spiritual adviser and the friend who can put you in your place when that needs to happen. You have believed in this text and in our pastoral mission with the little queens coming up. Ours is work that feeds la obra, and I hope that this text, born out of many of our conversations throughout the years, will also become a friend and companion in your ministry.

I have enjoyed companionship and friendship that makes family not something you are but something you practice. My family includes dear mentors such as Stuart Curran, Alan Filreis, and Joseph Wittreich, and friends of a lifetime Shauna Ahern, Aaron Ampie, Ethel Brooks, Yudy Cairo, Erica Edwards, Maceo Edwards, Rosario and Rosita Fernández and clan, Corinne Minard and her daughters Paloma and Ilona García-Minard, Katherine Grau, Marina Grau, the Labour clan (Agueda, Luana, and Diego), Fátima Portorreal Liriano, Pablo Mella, Julissa Reynoso, Robyn Rodriguez, Deb Vargas, Katyuska Vazquez, and my cousins in the Decena clan (Pablo, Carlos Alberto, Dorca Gilbertson, Gloria, Ginette, Gisselle) and the Fernández clan (Rhina Esmeralda, Giselle Oliva, Angela Celeste). Little by little, I enjoy reencountering my blood brothers Edwin and Omar as adults, as well as my viejos Xiomara and Dario.

The only thing greater than coming into this life to do work that opens paths for others is the opportunity to accompany human beings through their journeys, and this is where my home front continually feeds my zeal to imagine a world more capacious, more open, than the one I inherited. It's sometimes shocking for me to take stock of the fact that I am a man who is married to another man and that our love and companionship have made space for the lives of the two young men we are honored to call our sons. I look forward to the day when Jordan Joaquín or Joshua Ulysses will come back from a college class and argue with me about a point made in this book, in an article, or in anything else I get to produce in print. May this offering be as much of a gift to them as it might be for other queerlings in the future so they might teach me and all of us how they see the horizon for freedom and the full realization of our humanity.

Joaquín Alfredo Labour-Acosta has taught me so much about what it means to mobilize power, resources, and sacrifice in support of others. This book represents a very personal take on what it means to have one's work irradiate, open, and expand the horizon for the ones coming. But the love of humanity that fires up this query comes from the same love that defines our life together, and this is a love he models for himself, for our sons, and for me.

I can only speak for myself. But what I
write and how I write is done in order to
save my own life. And I mean that literally.

BARBARA CHRISTIAN,
"THE RACE FOR THEORY"

Orígenes
(Origins)

PART 0

Pensar Maricón (Faggotology)

An Introduction

CIRCUITS OF THE SACRED DOCUMENTS HOW ONE BODY MOVES, IMAGINES, WITNESSES, AND REMEMBERS, ILLUSTRATING HOW BLACKNESS TRANSMOGRIFIES IN ONE PERSON'S JOURNEY AS A CHILD, AS AN IMMIGRANT IN THE UNITED STATES, AND AS A UNIVERSITY STUDENT AND PROFESSIONAL. I aim for audiences to experience reading and thinking as a transit analogous to writing and remembering, a gathering attuned to all dimensions of embodied life. This black Caribbean study is a conversation on spirit in working-class queer feminisms. It is an exploration of how our fleshy bodies operate as instruments for sensation, pain, struggle, joy, and pleasure. Modeling a pensar maricón, or what I call a faggotology, I center excessive black latinidades, lo sucio, los sucios, y las sucias.[1] Together, we swish along and touch the divine through the abhorrent.

This writing makes space for the ancestors we want to be for the black working-class locas, maricones, jotería of the future.[2]

We do not need a verb to validate our existence.

Ou pa chwazi sa ou vle le w'ap fè yon rasanblaj ou ranmanse tout bagay. Catalyst. *Você não pode ficar escolhendo do lixo, deve recolher tudo.* Keyword. *On ne choisi pas entre les choses quand on fait un rasanblaj. On ramasse tout.* Method. *No escogemos de aquí y allá entre los desechos: debemos ensamblar todo junto.* Practice. You don't pick and choose when you make rasanblaj, you gather everything. Project.

GINA ATHENA ULYSSE, "INTRODUCTION," *EMISFÉRICA*

CIERRA LOS OJOS (CLOSE YOUR EYES).

My back was turned to a bridge to the force of the universe that chose this head before I slid into the world as a newborn, forgetting that even though the orishas all loved me, only one of them crowned my third eye (ori).[3]

My charge? Entrust my body to mentors and strangers. Like floating in water. Boyar.

Upon prompting, I turned around. I knocked on a door; I said what I wanted; and the world went aflutter. Hands touched me. My clothes tore, brushing by my skin as they withdrew their caress.

Scissors cut hair; herb-scented water slid through me. People paid tribute and asked for blessings. Some prayed in Cuban Lucumí/Yoruba. The officiating priest, who led the bath and cut my hair, sang. One by one, voices named their ancestors, loved ones who had passed, mentors.

Felt hands on top of hands.

Love was in the air, in the smell, in the touching hands, and in the feel of the room. The iyawo's ori and body were the object being consecrated, the head of a maturing gay man turned into an infant of the gods born in stone, their consecrated head now sibling to stones through sacrifice. But this was not about the iyawo. This was an offering to the gods. Gratitude to the gods; blessings in breath, in saliva, in words, in touch. People giving thanks for their health and wishing the iyawo health.

I was not I. To the strangers in that room, this was the iyawo—bride of the orisha.[4]

Hands joined and instructions ceased. Chanting, singing. More chanting and all hands on one head. Drums.

Later, my eyes opened again.

Abre los ojos.

MADRINA (GODMOTHER) SAID that la morfología del cuerpo cambia (the morphology of the body changes). I savored the phrase after it jumped off the lips of this Cuban iya and journalist in Santo Domingo, who had become my third mother, and my first black mother.[5]

As I embarked on this pilgrimage, a friend told me that I seemed more "whole": en paz conmigo mismo (at peace with myself).

But *wholeness* suggests *enclosure*. My body was not for me to own or close but, rather, an instrument of contact with sentience.

The morphological turn is outward, to imbibe the world, an opening.

I felt more *hole* than whole, as years put distance between my friend's view and my interpretation.

I am at peace with being a hole. A black (w)hole, all in the opening, the raja (tearing)—unavailable to vision but there, like the weather, an idea from the black feminist historian of science Evelyn Hammonds that has stayed with me for years.[6] "Black hole dark matter is special for another reason," writes the black feminist physicist Chanda Prescod-Weinstein. "It's the only scenario where I might agree that 'dark' is a good descriptor because they tend to absorb light and not give it off."[7] Could Olodumare be the black (w)hole whose force I could feel, touch, breathe, and smell but not see? The god whose grace I willed to forget until madrina hugged me for the first time?

Ceremonies involved friends and strangers in love, faith, and physical intimacy with other strangers. Your pores opened. Your body tingled, eagerly awaiting brush, touch, saliva. Their touch. Their smell. Their density and heat. Their breath—its funk on your head.

My black gay male sensibility snuck into the analogies I drew on to sense what was happening. Sexual practice was off the table, but the whole path was electrified by the sensorial erotic. Rhythm, mixture of wills and bodily fluids, and the proximity of other bodies to mine connected to anonymous intimacy, sex with strangers, dark rooms, orgies, and gangbangs. Like the philosopher Georges Bataille, I sensed the religious and the erotic as "part and parcel of the same movement," though my drift in "movement" is closer to classical music, as a "principal division of a longer musical work, self-sufficient in terms of key, tempo, and structure."[8] As Doña Cristiana Viuda Lajara (my first piano teacher) said, music is la combinación de los sonidos y el tiempo (the combination of sounds and time).

The comparisons are offensive, even heretical. Doña Cristiana would be horrified, and perhaps so would my madrina and other Santería elders. Yet this queerling writing walks with Santería/Lucumí, with gratitude and respect, to gather the insurgent, rebellious, and affirmative traditions in working-class, black Latinx, and queer life. This is the task.

Circuits of the Sacred is fè yon rasanblaj. It performs a gathering of everything for black Caribbean study, arguing that black queer paths to the divine swerve from the transparent "I" of the academic and drift toward the intuitive, the sensorial, and the disreputable. Consistent with Ashon Crawley's vision, *Circuits of the Sacred* leans on blackness as "but one critical and urgently necessary disruption to the epistemology, the theology-philosophy, that produces a world, a set of protocols, wherein black flesh cannot easily breathe."[9] As rasanblaj, *Circuits of the Sacred* disrupts, expands, and unmoors blackness and black study from the myopia of US-centered coordinates to account for transit in and through the Caribbean. To elaborate its claims, *Circuits of the Sacred* turns to memoir, ethnography, analysis, and creative writing to reckon with racially marked upward mobility and deracination, gay male coming of age, and sustained family loyalty. This book chronicles episodes drawn from my path to initiation in Santería, inclusive of my year of initiation and encompassing ethnographic work in New Jersey; metropolitan Santo Domingo, San Cristóbal, and San Juan de la Maguana (Dominican Republic); and Havana from 2013 until 2019.

Circuit

I argue that blackness is a circuit, demanding a reckoning with contradictory grids of intelligibility for racial markings, geopolitical histories, and structural arrangements that insist on black-presenting people and black women as the most precarious yet foundational to all labor implicated in religious and other becomings. I elaborate the "circuit" metaphor as a multipronged and multi-sensorial field, linking nodes that otherwise appear separate. While discussing *circuits of desire*, Yukiko Hanawa stresses the need to see the local in the global when interrogating sexualities across regions and areas. "It is neither possible nor desirable to insist upon some *pure* local episteme: we must consider the *circuits of desire*," she writes, pressing critical imaginations to unpack processes, exchanges, and forces coalescing around sexual and other formations in Asia and shaping their making and evolution.[10] In her ethnography on BDSM in San Francisco, Margot Weiss encourages her readers to consider multiple nodes in the making of pleasure and collectivities among the practitioners with whom she works.[11] "Like an electrical circuit, which works when current flows between individual nodes, the circuits of BDSM work when connections are created between realms that are imagined as isolated and opposed.... The elaborate circuitry of BDSM energizes any particular BDSM scene, but it also provides the productive charge that constitutes the BDSM scene itself."[12] Hanawa and Weiss emphasize a coming together of nodes that energize one another while tasking their readers to consider complex mediations and contradictions in their assembly. My study centers the circuit to illustrate a gathering of forces, grids of intelligibility, and structural alignments and contradictions that animate how Caribbean immigrant blackness is lived.

An expansive view of *blackness* is the frame to what follows. Each chapter of this study is a nodal point that amasses observations, insights, stories, anecdotes, and theories and that elaborates evolving and contradictory articulations of blackness. By displacing the narrative "I" by shifting pronouns, genres, narrative styles, and storytelling techniques, I invite readers to (1) join, feel, hear, and touch the voices of the text and the text's narrative nodes; and (2) hear through these nodes the ancestors and spirits that they bring and that the narrators could not anticipate or imagine.

Listening, feeling, and opening to the sacred in spirit work, voices, words, and worlds challenged me to question the authority of academics, invested in their ability to proffer expertise and assert confidence and evidence where either (1) neither confidence nor evidence could be fully had; or (2) they could be had only in passing. In other words, the scholar's speaking "I" (what Denise Ferreira da Silva calls the "transparent I" of reason) would not suffice. As da Silva explains, "In writings of the black subject, one consistently meets a transparent I, buried under historical (cultural or ideological) debris, waiting for critical strategies that would clean up the negative self-representations it absorbs from prevailing racist discourse."[13] Instead of cleaning up the debris described by da Silva, I dwell in it.

Let us gather in excess of the transparent I. Orisha energies live in sacred stones but require other fundamentos, or "foundational" utensils associated with that deity, plus the ritual work of consecrating the mystical objects, spaces, and receptacles, to settle at one's altar. For the ensemble to dwell there requires the pieces and the rituals, the aché of the priests, and the blessing of the orishas propitiating the birth.[14] Additional requirements may be involved, such as the rule that priests may "birth" Orisha in others only if they have received the consecrated deity themselves. The pieces move or "electrify" as objects, actors, and rituals come together.[15] This text is built not so much on a flight of Whitmanian fancy ("I am large, I contain multitudes") than as a composition that energizes a circuitry for lives of mind and spirit.[16]

A view of blackness as a circuit is useful in black Latinx studies, as this emerging field addresses the white supremacist conditionings of latinidad while also proffering cartographies of blackness in, through, and beyond the United States.[17] When discussing the dangers of agglutinating different contexts, politics, and geo-imperial histories of blackness into one label, Yomaira Figueroa-Vásquez cautions: "The move to label all of these subjects as Black peoples, without a nuanced understanding of the stakes and limits of what that means in each of their homelands and diasporic context would produce violent cartographies that flatten and distort their subjective experiences."[18] I perform a gathering to theorize and map blackness in and through one Dominican queer immigrant identity and story to demonstrate as worthy the quest for creative expression as theory and practice of collective psychic survival. This study grapples with the price higher education exacts from the professionals it produces, complicitous as universities are in producing and reproducing alienation in us. Like Barbara Christian, I write to save my life. I hope that, regardless of what conditions shape the arrival of their eyes to these pages, readers will find space to dwell in this book's affirmations of black queer life.

Upon becoming a tenured professor as the first college graduate from a working-class black Dominican immigrant family, I considered the contradictions of my achievements and the toxicities of academic institutions.[19] Despite what looked (at first glance) like a story of an immigrant of color achieving his "American dream," why did my quotidian life feel empty? How could I achieve while my family struggled with deteriorating health, poverty, addiction, and deportation? And what price did I pay for "making it"? Socialization and training as a man, immigrant, and scholar of color taught me to temper and discipline aspects of myself seen as an affront to the white supremacy of the institutions from which I write, read, and think. This left my soul desolate.

How did I survive as a black Dominican working-class faggot? Is *survival* even the right word for my accomplishment, or could it be something closer to *survivance*—"an active sense of presence over absence, deracination, and oblivion; survivance is the continuance of stories, not mere reaction. . . . Survivance is greater than the right of a survivable name"?[20] As this book grew over a decade, I realized that writing it honestly required grappling with the ways different parts of my life—pre- and post-immigration, high school and college, in the professoriate, and in the pursuit of religious initiation and life as an openly gay and black Latino man—could be examined and reflected on together. Gathering and analyzing disparate moments in one journey allows for the discernment of the broader outlines of the journey, the fundamentos that energize one life. *Survivance* is oriented to black Latinx immigrant coordinates (not to be confused with those of Native America): it hinges on refusing to pick and choose parts of myself, in turning toward and tuning into interior work on the dimensions I have been taught to hate. Following the Haitian American feminist anthropologist and theorist Gina Athena Ulysse, I fè yon rasanblaj (gather everything), though I dwell in the felicitous (if unintended) use of the word *desechos* (remains) in the Spanish and *lixo* (trash) in the Portuguese translation of Ulysse's definition of *rasanblaj*.[21] As a Dominican in diaspora, I theorize and dream through the guiding mind of a Haitian American colleague and sister. Given the centrality of antagonism toward Haiti and Haitians in the Dominican context, which has intensified since a time when I learned anti-Haitianism in history books as a child, *Circuits of the Sacred* will strike some as a heretical text. This particular reading would be welcome: heresy is central to dwell in blackness as the cut, wound, and raja with specific historical and geopolitical coordinates on the island of my biological birth.[22]

Circuits of the Sacred: A Faggotology in the Black Latinx Caribbean is a gathering of remains, desechos, lixo, lacras, wretched refuse.[23]

Muerteando Methods

Circuits of the Sacred insists that our lusty, funky, and stank quests to freak through our bodies couple eros with the mystical. My take on "the sacred" follows the black feminist M. Jacqui Alexander's thinking about what makes up the divine as it "knits together the quotidian in a way that compels attunement to its vagaries, making this the very process through which we come to know its existence. It is, therefore, the same process through which we come to know ourselves."[24] Informed by ethnography, this study is inspired by scholarship that centers small-scale yet consequential dimensions of quotidian labor and life. For instance, Elizabeth Pérez focuses on micropractices— "routine and intimate sequences of operations that can be broken down into more minute units of activity."[25] She explains that this focus "answers the need to look beyond valorized genres of ritual action to see the centrality of micropractices in fashioning sacred selves, spaces, and societies."[26] In this way, Pérez's work is consistent with the increased attention feminists have paid to anecdotal theory.[27] My impulse throughout is to draw on the ethnographic and to challenge its zeal for empirical verifiability through recourse to memoir, crónica, and experimental and speculative writing, pushing toward a capacious and open mapping of that which cannot be fully known.

My take on what are viable moments, sites, and narrated traces of the sensorium for analysis throughout *Circuits of the Sacred* is inspired by Pérez, as well as by Susan Howe's poem "Melville's Marginalia."[28] In the preface, Howe explains that after the negative commercial reception of the novels *Moby-Dick* and *Pierre*, Herman Melville became increasingly isolated and turned to reading and writing: "Melville read with a pencil in his hand. Marks he made in the margins of his books are often a conversation with the dead."[29] In a poetic turn, Howe breaks the thread of her preface and proffers her own marginalia, in verse: "Margins speak of fringes of consciousness of marginal associations. / What is the shadow reflex of art I am in the margins of doubt."[30] In writing about Melville, Howe's poem doubles the conversation that this canonical writer was having with the dead: "One day while searching through Melville criticism at the Temple University Library I noticed two maroon dictionary-size volumes, lying haphazardly, out of reach, almost out of sight on the topmost shelf. That's how I found *Melville's Marginalia* or *Melville's Marginalia* found me."[31]

Los muertos son ideas (The dead are ideas). This is what a young Babalawo told me in Havana.

Circuits of the Sacred is an extended conversation with the dead. It is part of a generational trend in feminisms of color by emerging and established scholars thinking toward a future where other scholars of marginalized backgrounds might emerge, establish themselves, and survive the academy.

This book is a journey, a pilgrimage, to geographic, psychic, and intellectual sites. *Circuits of the Sacred* rehearses and practices the itinerary of my pilgrimage across countries, regions, and languages. It moves through Spanish, English, and the Yoruba terms I learned phonetically in prayer and religious life. It slides through anecdotes, refrains, and remembrances of the Havana of my birth in santo; the Santo Domingo that birthed and reared me; and the Philadelphia, New York, and New Jersey where I came of age and became a racialized subject and a black Latinx and feminist queer man.

As it activates and energizes otherwise disparate nodes of relationality, this study illustrates what Roberto Strongman calls *transcripturality*: "cultural creation—painting, photography, film, and particularly writing—in an altered or exalted state of consciousness that mirrors trance possession and prompts or suggests a similar experience in the receiver of such a work of art."[32] Though there are moments in the study where the voice makes implicit or explicit invitations to psychoanalytic reading, *Circuits of the Sacred* gestures to but does not pursue this path for analysis. This is a deliberate choice to eschew normative misapprehensions of spiritual or religious experience as psychologically problematic.[33] Through the deployment of multiple pronouns to decenter a singular voice, this study takes up, valorizes, and stages "altered states" as they connect to trance possession and dissociative forms of "acting out" associated with black latinidad, locura, and mariconería.[34] Beyond the shift in perspectives it stages, *Circuits of the Sacred* insists on scholarship as a form of channeling for writers, readers, and texts valorizing the radicality of black madness.

My job is to channel becoming. Thinking with the anthropologist Todd Ramón Ochoa, the morphogenesis of narrative in *Circuits of the Sacred* "happens at the interface of the dead and the subject or object in which it is actualized. . . . The dead are divinity's verb, or potential—not existing prior to it, but generating life in Divinity itself."[35] Marginalia prompt my conversations with the ambient dead, lingering at the corner while awaiting ceremonies, hanging out, recalling the beauty of falling petals of flowers on my head and shoulders, the joy of dancing with madrina. The dead are also carriers of the words I read and the stars of gay male 1970s and '80s porn, whose bodies and acts I celebrated in awe and lusty delight, despite warnings by my elders that most of these men died from AIDS. Here I also follow and take inspiration from Ochoa: "It is the dead that inspire action in Palo and Ocha/ Santo, and the dead that are the generative spark behind all that is beautiful and emergent in them.... The ambient dead is a climate of transformation, complete with zones of woe and marvel, flashes of inspired intuition, and thunderclaps of astonishment that echo in the cavities of our bodies to wake us from our petrified thoughts."[36] In other words, the writer might score points as the "author" of this work; he is also responsible for all errors in this text. Yet *Circuits of the Sacred* is an exercise in talk, walk, and dance with spirit; it is an extended dialogue with, alongside, and through turning intellectual labor into a mystical quest—writing, thinking and speaking with and through the dead (muerteando). After all, don't intellectuals talk to the living and the dead?

I don't believe that identifying as queer increases my ability to channel what's coming. That's the woke ruse of identity politics, the "individual method" of our multicultural neoliberal elites, as Asad Haider recently noted, echoing earlier critiques of the class politics of queer feminisms from Rosemary Hennessy and Michael Hames-García (among others).[37] Let's open up to the flaming queen as your eyes meet the ink and paper of this word body, as we walk together, as we touch one another in our transit and stranger intimacy.

Faggotology

Circuits of the Sacred is a mystical bottoming, a *pensar maricón*, a *faggotology*. I am inspired in this pursuit by what Peter Savastano calls *spiritology*: "I have invented the word 'spiritology,' as one alternative to 'theology' in order to signify the 'spiritual' as energy and/or a 'force' that is non-anthropomorphic, fluid and polymorphic.... I use both 'theology' and 'spiritology' interchangeably so as to destabilize theology from its epistemologically privileged position in the nomenclature of gay male spirituality."[38] With Crawley, Savastano, and Marcella Althaus-Reid, these writings exceed theology and dwell in polymorphous perversity. As Crawley puts it, "What is dematerialized in theology is the materiality of funk, the materiality of unworn cloth.... Perhaps we need to become indecent and queer *against* theology."[39] Faggotology reverses the dynamic and influence of queer thinking in theology. *Circuits of the Sacred* is the work of a black Latinx writer and critic in dialogue with feminist and queer theology, black and Latinx radical critical theories, and Afro-Caribbean anthropology. Instead of informing theology through feminist and queer-of-color scholarship, *Circuits of the Sacred* engages Afro-Caribbean religions and liberation theologies *from* the vantage point of radical feminism and queer-of-color thinking. The text speaks to religious studies and anthropology while also directing itself to scholar activists in feminism and in queer-of-color collectives. A pensar maricón also pries open the political, intellectual, and sensorial coordinates of black study to a hemispheric black diasporic sensibility, connecting it to the literatures of ferocious Latin American writing queens such as the Cubans Severo Sarduy, Reinaldo Arenas, and Virgilio Piñera; the Chilean Pedro Lemebel; and the Argentine Manuel Puig.

Circuits of the Sacred also offers a critical perspective on the class dimensions of racialized politics in feminist, black, and queer-of-color communities. Many of us did not come out to see our sex, bodies, and political and spiritual imaginations stunted by mainstreaming, neoliberal formations inclusive of sanitized respectabilities and calcified identities. Some of us who read, write, live, think, and fornicate also did not pursue this path to witness our bodies limited by the shiny objects that keep us away from "thinking sex," imagining and reimagining the choreographies, geographies, and possibilities of pleasure and relationality, as Gayle Rubin advised us to do at one of the founding moments of queer studies. If we are to have sainthood as maricones, let's have it as Yves F. Lubin, the Haitian American fierce queen writer and performance artist known by the pseudonym Assotto Saint, liked to have it: "Assotto is the Creole pronunciation of a fascinating-sounding drum in the voodoo [*sic*] religion.... Saint is derived from Toussaint L'Ouverture, one of my heroes. By using the *nom de guerre* of Saint, I also wanted to add a sacrilegious twist to my life by grandly sanctifying the low-life bitch that I am."[40] With a nod to the assotto drums to imbibe the musicality of this text, I pay respect to Assotto Saint as ancestor and to the lwas of the Vodun pantheon.[41]

This text interrupts the desire to know, explain, and master.[42] Instead, the lowlife bitch narrator steers in the direction of an openness that can produce ruptures—rajas that hurt but that might also hurt good, hurt hot enough to make you hard/wet: contradictions as we sit with the tingle, licking the cut or the sphincter that dilates as we press a finger or tongue or as we swallow and hold the shocks and thrusts of expressive puncture. Thinking and feeling like a flaming faggot is intellectually, politically, and spiritually productive, for the sake not of the queen who speaks, but of the queerness in nosotres.

The yo (I) who tells stories, analyzes, and curates what follows has a voice within the US academic tenure system due to work, degrees, publications, titles longer than his name, and recognition: a small collection of objects, symbolic and material. Following the Argentine philosopher and anthropologist Rodolfo Kusch, our narrator has confused the freedom of ser (to be) with the zeal to ser alguien (to be someone), just like the urban Argentine and Latin American elites Kusch critiqued for their urban, metropolitan, and Europhilic orientation.[43] And that afán de ser alguien (zeal to be somebody) left desolate the yo who writes. The journey to the "transparent I" resulted in violence to self, deracination, and dilapidation. Writing to liberate more than one person starts with discerning what material accomplishments, degrees, and other objects of reason are for, and what price we pay for becoming someone.

Ser alguien will not cure my mother's dementia or her broken hip that healed in misalignment due to postfracture neglect, nor will it stop the addictions that have plagued my biological family. Ser alguien also will not stop the horror of realizing, on the day my compañero Alfredo and I picked up one of our sons after his birth ten days earlier, that nobody would be coming for several of the other babies crying in that nursery in Newark, New Jersey. Ser alguien might help me support my students with letters of recommendation, but it will not assist me in walking with them to arrive at their judgment of why they do intellectual work or to realize that intellectual work matters only to the degree that it helps us hustle, think, feel, fuck, and walk toward freedom.

The point of this writing, then, is to collaborate in figuring out "how we get free."[44]

In writing through what you encounter in these pages, it became clear to me that recalling moments along this path also triggered details of the larger canvas of a life remembered. The result is a fragmented and extended conversation with the child, adolescent, and adult who was as he (1) talked to his dead and living mentors, relatives, beloved elders, contemporary friends, colleagues, and companions in the profession; and (2) relished sparkles of fleshy contact with love, intimacy, or transitory spark. The muertos of that child re-membered are mine and yours. They also hover in crevices of this narrative, in a shelf or pocket somewhere in this text, awaiting for you to open for them, to listen. I hope that you will catch a glimpse of their world-making force.

Arrivals

When I first thought that Santería could be the focus of a research study that resulted in this queerling in academic drag, existing models of how one might pursue this constituted a voluminous body of scholarship, much of it foundational to Caribbean studies and anthropology.[45] The names associated with the early study of Santería and sibling traditions were those of the towering figures Lydia Cabrera, Maya Deren, Zora Neale Hurston, Ruth Landes, and Fernando Ortiz. A foray into more recent works on the subject, which provided critiques of and revisions to questions I had at the outset of this writing, linked sexuality and religiosity as they swirled within and across Yoruba-influenced religious practices in the Américas.

Perspectives that paralleled mine inform contributions to the interdisciplinary social science on Afro-Caribbean religions. Some students, observers, and specialists cast Santería (a.k.a. Regla de Ocha) and other Afro-Caribbean religions as more "tolerant" of queer bodies (inclusive of LGBTQ folks, as well as socially and sexually atypical people in general). But a newer generation of scholars (e.g., Aisha Beliso-De Jesús, Roberto Strongman, and Salvador Vidal-Ortiz) echoed and expanded on established scholarship by J. Lorand Matory, Stefan Palmié, and others. Some believe Regla de Ocha is more "tolerant" and "open" to queers than are Afro-Cuban traditions such as Ifá, Regla de Palo, and the Abakuá secret society. However, evidence within Santería suggests ambivalence. Vidal-Ortiz's ethnographic research in the New York metropolitan area, for example, explored the relationship between LGBTQ practitioners and Santería traditions, division of labor in houses of worship, and restrictions regarding who leads ceremonies and who performs consecrations.[46] In *Queering Black Atlantic Religions* (2019), Strongman maps out and explores the operations of queerness in Haitian Vodou, Brazilian Candomblé, and Cuban Santería, suggesting that these traditions appeal to gender and sexual dissenters because of their vision of the human subject as not being limited by its encasement in the Cartesian cogito.[47] Strongman is inspired in this interpretation by Matory's view of Afro-Atlantic religions in their critique of the Cartesian body as immutable, contained, and individual; instead, Matory argues that Afro-Atlantic religions view the body as a vessel that can be occupied and disposed of during trance possession.[48] Strongman's work expands Matory's insight by exploring "just how the notion of the body as vessel allows for queer resubjectifications that are rare or impossible under the containment model provided by Descartes."[49] Strongman builds on a large-scale close reading of a polyglot ethnographic archive by pioneering figures in the study of Black Atlantic religion; practicing and writing in English, Spanish, French, Portuguese, German, and Kreyòl; and straddling the Américas, Africa, and Europe to support the view of what he calls a *transcorporeal* Afro-diasporic self. Strongman believes that this self is "multiple, external, and removable" and that it rests on corporeal surfaces, irrespective of the gendered embodiments that might be most readily associated with those surfaces.[50]

Other views of queerness in Ocha suggest further challenges to notions of its tolerance of queers and queerness. Even while remaining open to the presence and supposed "openness" of Santería to sexual and gender diversities, Beliso-De Jesús, an anthropologist, embeds her discussion of the political dimensions of gender and queer dissent in houses of worship within a critique of the operations of patriarchy and heteronormativity *within* Santería. She suggests that the ethnographic record shows, at best, ambivalence. "Even as Santería is perceived of as seemingly more 'open' to gays, lesbians, and women," she writes, "there are also important heteronormativities and patriarchies that make it extremely difficult for divergent sexualities."[51]

While considering nuances and ambivalences concerning queerness and queer people in Santería, it is crucial to attend to the messiness of religious practice and belonging in the early twenty-first century. My engagement and insights drawn from initiation are debatable, given how Yoruba traditions have been commoditized and encased in religious transnational tourisms. The faggotology this study conceptualizes and practices emerges from movement and discernment of *Santería as idea* with a commoditized, complex, and contradictory life under transnational neoliberalism as related yet distinct from Santería/Lucumí as "a bona fide religion with a theology and practice."[52] Still, suggesting that I "found" Santería cedes to my scholarly voice more ground than it deserves. In fact, Santería found me.

Presenting the sequence of events in this way lets readers grasp how much the text of *Circuits of the Sacred* allows for the transit scholarly analysis deployed to make space for conocimiento.[53] After years of Catholic religious devotion as a child in the Dominican Republic, I turned my back on religious matters after my family migrated to the United States. My family was part of what was then a small but growing community of Dominicans migrating to Philadelphia and cities of the Northeast (and elsewhere in the United States) other than New York City.[54] My education, training, and professional advancement allowed me to live, work, and thrive without engaging in a direct appeal to a higher power, given my isolation from fellow Dominicans and other people of color. I grew to doubt that the God of my childhood was operating in my life. I became irritated by how much Dominican colloquial phrasing turns on God's will—for example, we're going on vacation si Dios lo permite (if God allows); that job will happen si Dios quiere (if God wants). At my angriest, I claimed to be atheist, but that affirmation became untenable with most of the nonacademics around me, so I settled on claiming to be agnostic.

My adolescent anger and resistance to organized faith was connected to how immigrant assimilation and (gay) coming out afforded me access to privileged institutions of higher learning, elite literature and culture, and networks of peers disinclined to talk openly about spirituality. Spirit mattered, but people in my upwardly mobile class cohort would not call or recognize spirituality as such or ever utter the word *God*. Their engagement with inner life came through in commodified forms of contemplative practice that promoted conformity to white middle-class deportment. Accordingly, I tried yoga and meditation. These traditions (and the overwhelming middle- and upper-class whiteness of the spaces where they are practiced) challenged me. Any talk of God, spirit, or the divine was like farting, burping, and snoring while doing yoga—everyone hears and some smell, but the stench wafts through like just another muerto. I was trained to notice and move the focus back to the breath, no matter the intensity of the ass trumpet, the duration of the funk wave moving in the space, or the fact that you are sitting there and breathing in the funk of the neighbor who did not shower and put their imprint on your nose.

Circuits of the Sacred is a belated tribute and response to a Transnational Black Feminist Retreat in Santo Domingo that I attended in 2013 and that was organized and facilitated by Ana-Maurine Lara and Alaí Reyes-Santos. My "arrival" to faggotology was informed by my literary training and absorption of elite writing traditions in Anglo, Latin American, and world literatures. These debts are reflected in the writing throughout *Circuits of the Sacred*. Another set of foundations for the journey was prompted by my encounter, reading, thinking, and teaching of the writings of Gloria Anzaldúa, Audre Lorde, and M. Jacqui Alexander. The routes here are calibrated through my sustained engagement with the thinking, flesh-to-flesh encounters, and spirit work of gay male and radical lesbian artists, writers, mentors, and ancestors in Santo Domingo, Philadelphia, New York, New Jersey, and Havana. I crossed the bridge to the English language through the guiding presence and hand of James Baldwin. My loca fleshy consciousness found its erotic expression through the writings, films, and activist and artistic praxis of mentors and elders such as David Acosta and Frances Negrón-Muntaner and ancestras Marlon Riggs, Essex Hemphill, Joseph Beam, and Assotto Saint. I also note the thorny questions that Anzaldúa, Maria Lugones, and Frantz Fanon raise for the pursuit of black Latinx queer critique. I make no apology for the trouble these ancestors represent for those of us aspiring to werk black Latinx study. Nevertheless, I find valuable contributions (for what I undertake later) in the larger canvas that is the work of these thinkers while recognizing the shortcomings, recurring patterns, and ambivalences that generate debate across fields, especially concerning blackness, black women, and homosexuality.[55]

Reading as Listening

One early reader of this study joked that I was building a three-dimensional cathedral on a two-dimensional surface and that the density of this book's architecture might be hard to visualize.

Instead of visualizing, listen.

Listen to the voices in *Circuits of the Sacred* the way you might lend your ear to contrapuntal music in a contemporary string quartet. In this soundscape, the pressures and releases that have acculturated our ears to the comforts of tonal harmonies are dislocated in combinations that acculturate one's ear to dissonance. Tonal European composers, particularly those considered canonical, have trained the listening habits of audiences to experience sound combinations as pleasant if they subscribe to learned expectations of tension, melody, harmony, and resolution. Twentieth-century atonality renders explicit that what we hear in any combination of notes, in chords and instrumental arrangements, is how sounds work *through* one another—interrupting, grating, and producing vibrations that might be pleasant or unpleasant, agreeable or disagreeable, depending on how we receive and organize them.

Listen to what you read in this book in this manner; listen to it in your mind's ear. Listen to it as Omi Tinsley listens to the songs of divine Ezili in her *Ezili's Mirrors*. The book form might present us with temporal arrangements of which moment/anecdote/crónica/analysis/story comes when. Yet this book aspires to be a "transcorporeal" body like those Strongman describes as modular, flexible, and mobile.

Listening to this archipelago of sounds is no writerly conceit. I ask you to consider sound metaphors to alter what might be available to us through visual metaphors for "soul work."[56] I concur with Beliso-De Jesús in finding utility in the feminist theorist Karen Barad's conceptualization of *diffraction* for a reading, writing, and spiritual practice in Santería and other Afro-diasporic traditions.[57] Drawing from visual metaphors, Barad explains that *diffractive* events take place when combinations of light and surface produce visible manifestations of how they come together, grind, combine, and move through one another: "For example, the rainbow effect commonly observed on the surface of a compact disc is a diffraction phenomenon. The concentric rings of grooves that contain the digital information act as a diffraction grating spreading the white light (sunlight) into a spectrum of colors."[58] How do moments of critical exegesis spread or narrow the reach of sound in the moments that came before and will come after? How does insight sound through the vibrations of the evocative writing in its expressive ability to activate nodes in a circuit?

How might a moment interpreted one way appear different to the reader upon learning later that another element, insight, or message subtended it? What if we imagined flashes of insight or narrative threads as waves, capable of sweeping through our mind's eye and ear, hit the pit of our stomach, the base of our genitals, and other body hot spots, on top of one another and occupying the same space temporally, synchronically, and asynchronically? Barad explains that, in physics, "only waves produce diffraction patterns."[59] *Diffraction grating* in Barad becomes what Beliso-De Jesús presents as *reading diffractively*—tuning our bodies to the affective work of concepts. As Beliso-De Jesús explains, to read in this way turns the intellectual labor out to expose its affective dimensions: "Scapes are therefore shifted into affectivities and intensities (instead of only representations of imagined communities)."[60] Still, let us simmer in Barad a bit more, floating on waves: "A diffraction grating is simply an apparatus or material configuration that gives rise to a superposition of waves. A reflecting apparatus (e.g., mirrors) produce[s] images of objects (that are relatively faithful to the objects) placed a distance from the apparatus. In contrast, diffraction gratings are instruments that produce patterns that mark differences in the relative characters . . . of individual waves as they combine."[61] What if objects that appear in front of the mirror are diffraction gratings produced by combinations of light, shadow, surface, and gaze? Although this encouragement to hear in what we see and see in what we hear is a clunky mixing (or messing) of metaphors, it goes to a core protocol for the reading praxis promoted by *Circuits of the Sacred*: allow the ideas to move through this text, find you, and surprise you.

Peregrinas: Contours of the Journey

The "pilgrimage" that the title of the book calls forth moves through different levels of liberatory work in company forged through a practice of *tantear* for meaning, for the limits of possibility; putting our hands to our ears to hear better, to hear the meaning in the enclosures and openings of our praxis. I say *different levels* to try to accommodate levels of comprehension and incomprehension, as well as levels of opening ourselves to each other, levels of intimacy, and large and sometimes dispersed solidarity.

MARÍA LUGONES, *PILGRIMAGES/PEREGRINAJES*

Maria Lugones offers this passage to readers of her book *Pilgrimages/Peregrinajes* (2003). I echo her sensorial maps of intimacy in *Circuits of the Sacred*. I particularly appreciate how tanteo gets done in Lugones's formulation. In a footnote, she explains that she uses "'tantear' both in the sense of exploring someone's inclinations about a particular issue and in the sense of 'tantear en la oscuridad,' putting one's hands in front of oneself as one is walking in the dark, tactilely feeling one's way."[62] We might not be the only ones putting hands to "our" ears to hear, to hear better, to touch and feel one another's pulse as reader and writer, as friends and allies. I am not alone as I sit in front of the platform that allows for a discharge of energy and movement, marking letters to compose words. I am touched, and I can touch. I hear, and I am heard. Can you feel my words moving through the iris of your eye/I across this paper, this meeting point, this eje (axis) between us, like the veil through which our muertos tease, talk, and touch us?

My piano teacher said that before I could achieve the quality we were working toward, I had to hear sounds in my head. Then I moved toward that which we were trying to entwine one another in hearing together, through the co-flexing of our imagination muscles, a kinesthetic sensing that allowed our ears to collaborate in the tanteo for the right nuance. I invite the collaborative experience of building toward black futures and futures of freedom, for us to listen at our points of contact with one another through the membrane of the page.

In ritual fashion, a narrative tribute to the ancestors follows this introduction and closes the "Orígenes (Origins)" part of the study. Titled "Re-membered Life: A Composition for Egun," this piece is an homage to the black Dominican working-class child. Through a description of my early socialization in Santo Domingo, this narrative is a topography of the barrio that describes the forces of discipline mobilized through commentary, instructions, and the child's increased awareness of and distance from other black queens. This introduction also highlights how the sissy survived through an activation of allegiance and mentorship of teachers and older women, leaning on religion and prayer and finding (in classical music) alternative sites of being beyond his immediate surroundings. "Re-membered Life" pays tribute to ancestral forces, and it casts the queer child as an ancestral figure. The chapter also pays homage to the black faggots and femmes whose presence guided a young man's sense of the interdictions of manhood in urban working-class Santo Domingo of the 1980s.

What follows is divided into three parts.

Part I, "Caminos," counterpoises a narrative bridge to an analytical chapter, addressing immigration and higher education. The sequencing of the "Caminos" chapters stages an about-face that is as much experiential as it is epistemological. The deracination of the quest for upward mobility and exile from the struggling biological family in "Bridge Crónica: A Triptych, with Elegguá" is countered in "Experiencing the Evidence" through an opening to the sensorium and a dialogue with a text in the scholar's training and access to the transparent "I" of antifoundationalist critique. Chapter 2, "Bridge Crónica," continues the "re-membering" that began in chapter 1 through an elaboration of the distortions of blackness produced through the inhabitation and access to elite institutions. These anecdotes illustrate the mixture of forces that deracinate queer black subjects and the ongoing linkages and discomforts that structure kinship and working-class loyalty. A ritual tribute to Elegguá (the deity that grants permission to all paths), the chapter charts divergence but insists on the urgency and discomforts of sustained love and loyalty.

Chapter 3, "Experiencing the Evidence," challenges the way feminists and queers have addressed "personal experience" in our work. It charts my shift away from the predations of a normative reasoning that disavows blackness, excess, and the body. This shift allowed my senses to reengage with the world. Instead of thinking about the "evidence of experience," I probe the possibility of "experiencing the evidence," arguing that normative projects of research are steeped in the pursuit of the mastery of the transparent "I" and that such pursuit unfolds in and through the disavowal of blackness and embodied life. Rejecting the notion that "personal" and "individual" are always the same, I envision our bodies as socially mediated instruments to access and apprehend the world—to feel, hear, and think. Moving beyond the transparent "I" of reason provides hints of where one meets the other, where we touch one another, and where we hear and touch the body of the other. "Experiencing the Evidence" is staged in dialogue with narrative materials and in conversation with the historian Joan W. Scott and the science fiction writer and critic Samuel R. Delany, moving toward an enlarged and embodied epistemological frame through the kinesthetic. A faggotology can help bring our sentient capacities into closer contact with historicities embedded in small flashes of insight in the present tense.

Part II, "Dos Puentes, Tránsitos," works toward faggotology by focusing on the impossibility of the transparent "I," mapping instead how circuitries illustrate the body as a transitive vessel that can be heard, touched, and occupied by forces beyond its sovereign will, in transnational settings, as well as in scenes of subjectivation. Chapter 4, "Loving Stones: A Transnational Patakí," works through the situatedness of Santería and sibling traditions (as well as those who walk those paths) in circuits of transnational exchange, contradictory geopolitical histories, and projects of belonging despite differential access to resources and asymmetries of power. Mobilizing a loose formulation of the Santería patakí (morality tale), I argue that absences push us to grapple with the uncomfortable politics of transnational religious belonging. Locating the workings of what cannot be fully known in a narrative about the loss and travel of sacred stones, the chapter argues that the relationship to the commodity form is one of the ways Santería repurposes commodity fetishism, registering an overcoming and retention of racialized coloniality. I engage Karl Marx, M. Jacqui Alexander, and J. Lorand Matory to challenge conventional views of commodity fetishism while describing the complexity of transnational Santería practice, community, and belonging.

The knot of the transnational in the circuit that is blackness is part of the broader mappings of diaspora in "Loving Stones." But those knots also present in smaller sites for the making of subjects, where we have yet more opportunities to meditate on what we learn from silence and absence. Chapter 5, "¡Santo! Repurposed Flesh and the Suspension of the Mirror in Santería Initiation," juxtaposes two narratives that chart the movement and interruption of the gaze of the other in the ideation of the religious subject. I present two narratives side by side. Interrogating the introjection of the imago at the site of its gendered and racialized formation in "Mirrors," I explore withdrawal from the mirror in "Looking for Santo," thereby critically scrutinizing the mirror, gaze, and circuits that structure subject formations. I analyze subject forms made possible through the call to blessing (not by the "I" of the ego but, rather, through the vessel of the *santo*). The side-by-side narrative structure (a short story about learning to dance in counterpoint to crónica sketches from religious initiation) tasks the reader with grasping the diffractive relay in becoming a man in relation to santo becoming. Both point to something ineffable that the body cannot witness but that the body can carry and that can be recognized only in the other and by the other. However, becoming a legible man demands the authorizing and approving gaze, while the santo shifts the dynamic as it also tasks the other who calls to ask for a blessing.

Chapters 1–5 of the book are nodal points, gatherings activated in and through narrative in the service of a tanteo through blackness as a circuit in preparation for faggotology.

Part III, "Trances," the final section of the book, puts faggotology into practice, arguing for the power that derives from vulnerability in our sensorial, mystical, and erotic openness to the dense funk of the other in pursuit of the anonymous and impersonal infinity of the divine. It consists of a long narrative (which I call a "suite") to entreat readers to read as listening, imagining each part of the piece as writing and musical movement. Chapter 6, "Indecent Conocimientos: A Suite Rasanblaj in Funny Keys," performs faggotology by combining ethnography and film analysis with creative writing and crónica to raise questions about sex, intimacy, and the divine for queer men. This suite is a meditation that starts from questions of trance possession in tourist economies, exploring and mapping the racial, class, and gender politics of labor and extraction. The second movement, "Adagio," offers a short-story treatment of stranger intimacy to thematize the way passion affords glimpses of connectivities laden with forms of conocimiento. The final movement, a crónica of coming of age as a gay man in the late 1990s, centers generational shifts among cis gay men to emphasize the degree to which the zeal to "be safe" foreclosed past and present cohorts of men from deeper discussions about sex as soul work. The closing section of the chapter underscores the need for continued thinking and bridge building to link sex, the perverse, and the divine, given how much may be learned by thinking and taking seriously the open and vulnerable body, the (w)hole, at the center of faggotology.

The closing "Epístola al Futuro/An Epistle to the Future," a letter to my children and to black queer children of the future, is a perverse appropriation of the Pauline epistolary tradition and an opening of the faggotological as foundation and bridge for livable and breathable black futures for todes. It completes the cycle of the study by turning the ritual homage to ancestors into a gift to progeny, offering a queer gospel for black lives.

Re-membered Life

A Composition for Egun

WHEN I WAS LITTLE, I PRAYED A LOT. I WAS A MARICONCITO, A SISSY, WHO FOUND IN THE CHURCH AND THE LIVES OF SAN JUAN BOSCO, DOMINGO SAVIO, AND LA VIRGEN MARÍA A SPACE THAT DID NOT EXIST IN MY HOME OR NEIGHBORHOOD. Everywhere I worked on how to move in my body, which was held hostage in the pupil of the other, and for the other. Mine was not the perilous "tough" Baltimore that Ta-Nehisi Coates describes in his memoir, *Between the World and Me*.[1] But my movement through my working-class barrio (neighborhood) was shaped by the possibility of experiencing the discipline of normativity whipping all children into shape. I visited with friends, but for the most part I went out to run errands for my mother, who sensed the danger of sending me out for too long and instructed me on how best to go from home to the colmado (bodega), to school, and back.

No te partas (literally, "don't break"; figuratively, "act like a man").

She couldn't have said it like that.

Partirse, to break, must have been an expression I picked up coming and going from Doña Aurora's

Moyugba egun: Abdul Emir Sudan Hasan, Julius Eastman, Anacaona, Enriquillo, Hatuey, Rotimi Fani-Kayode, árbol del frente, árbol del malecón, Andrew Dowe, Fanny Acosta, Doña Cristiana Viuda Lajara, Lionel Cantú, Horacio Roque Ramírez, Lora Romero, Lauren Berlant, José Esteban Muñoz, Juan Flores, Micky Bretón, Alanna Lockward, Fradique Lizardo, Pedro René Contín Aybar, Bambino, Mat, Gloria Anzaldúa, Frantz Fanon, Sonia Pierre, Assotto Saint, Marlon Riggs, Essex Hemphill, James Baldwin, Barbara Christian, Melvin Dixon, Marcel Proust, Thomas Mann, Primo Levi, Yukio Mishima, Walter Benjamin, Zora Neale Hurston, Liborio Mateo, Mercedes Sosa, Marcella Althaus-Reid, Tony De Moya, Reinaldo Arenas, Severo Sarduy, Virgilio Piñera, Francisca, Rhina Celeste Báez Pimentel (Niní), Francisco Fernández (abuelo Francisco), Pablo Decena (abuelo Pablo),

Belén Lugo (Mamá Nena), la Comisión Eclesiástica, Santa Teresa de Jesús, Doña Cristiana Viuda Lajara, Sor Juana Inés de la Cruz, Juan Carlos Moya, Comisión del Antiguo Egipto, Comisión Indígena, todes las trans que mueren asesinadas con hambre de justicia y a todos los mariconcitos que caen ante el abuso y el corte de sus alas, a todes les maricones, tortilleras y cueros de mi barrio de infancia, a toda la jotería que muere por la osadía de ser.

Maferefún. A todos los espíritus de luz que me acompañan a mi, Carlos Ulises Decena, a mi esposo, Joaquín Alfredo Labour-Acosta, a nuestros hijos Jordan Joaquín y Joshua Ulysses Labour-Decena, y a Candy.

Ibaé.

Our foreparents imagined our families out of whole cloth. They imagined each individual one of us. They imagined me. They had to. It is the only way I am here, today, a mother and a wife, a community organizer and Queer, an artist and dreamer learning to find hope while navigating the shadows of hell even as I know it might have been otherwise.

PATRISSE KHAN-CULLORS AND ASHA BANDELE, *WHEN THEY CALL YOU A TERRORIST*

Re-membering gay Latinos, then, is not an act of nostalgic recovery. . . . We invoke gay Latino studies as an act of re-membering, as a gesture toward what has been and what might still be possible, even if it is only provisionally named.

MICHAEL HAMES-GARCÍA AND ERNESTO JAVIER MARTÍNEZ, "INTRODUCTION"

bodega. Maybe I picked it up from my cousins, or maybe the expression was floated loudly enough by one of the tígueres so I would hear as I walked while the person pretended to be talking to themselves—a master class in Dominican indirection, with the crushing brutality of banal heteronormativity.[2]

Por aquí hay muchos muchachitos que se parten. (There are lots of swishy little boys around here.)

You know this comment is about you, but the person just opens their mouth to release venom into the air

And if you turn

And if you twitch

And if your body registers its impact,

then the statement and its sequelae stay with you: a scarlet "M" burned into your aura, corralling you into a designation.

Maricón. That's you, and the tíguere or the doña did not even have to use the word.

To turn Frantz Fanon's phrase "to speak is to exist absolutely for the other" toward what I describe, the disciplinary power of indirection resides in how it sanctions class, race, and gender normativity in the overall texture of the social—legitimizing "not breaking" as mandate while punishing femininity as vulnerability.[3] Indirect speech acts cement asymmetrical force fields that all bodies navigate. Thus, such acts might be released "into the air" as warnings to be metabolized unevenly by all bodies within spitting distance from their source.

Mami was concerned about how I moved, but she would have said, "No camines así. ¡Camina bien!" (Don't walk like that. Walk correctly!). This may have been where her love for me held her back from decreeing that my boy's frame did not, and could not, signify manhood. But she figured out ways to signal her disapproval of my attempts, with a scowl punctuated by denying me access to her eyes.

No te partas. As if memory were a membrane, "no te partas" is tattooed in the recollection of who I was. A remembrance of that child brings me back to Fanon's discussion of racial structuration, with a twist drawn out from heteronormativity and gender dissent in an already black and working-class setting: "A slow construction of my self as a body in a spatial and temporal world—such seems to be the schema. It is not imposed on me; it is rather a definitive structuring of my self and the world—definitive because it creates a genuine dialectic between my body and the world."[4] The guiding hands and words of my parents could take me only so far, being that it was for me to discern the topographies of my surroundings, a "structuration" that I was to approximate and that I ingested as codes, interdictions, and enclosures—a whole grammar for being and moving in my world, a morphology of the closed body: a strai(gh)tjacket.[5]

I was a model student at Colegio Don Bosco, a private school across the street from my home. People at school and in the barrio were also intimidated enough by my dad to know better than to mess with me. Papo, my physical education teacher, often picked me to lead the whole grade of up to ninety students in the gymnastics routine he developed for the end-of-the-school-year event. I stood in front of everyone else in the yard while Papo instructed on the sequence of movements we were to execute.

I avoided looking at boys directly for more than a second or two. My trick to look at male bodies then was to play with the angles I could access through mirrors I spotted across school, in men's rooms, and in other places. If I was lucky and a body that I was curious about showed up, I found the right angle to look at legs, the arch of the back, the tight waist, and hips. Through furtive peeks, I witnessed my classmates' growing bodies for years. It was as a Boy Scout that I first enjoyed looking (still, only for a few seconds) at naked bodies of full-grown men when we went on camping trips.

After practice in educación física class at the end of a school day, my eyes settled for an extra beat on an athletic boy. His hair must have been dirty blond or brown. I was interested in him for a while, and I had built an archive of mental notes about his prowess on the basketball court, the sass of his gait, and his chest.

He looked at me and talked to his basketball buddy, loudly enough so that I could hear. He had participated in the gymnastics routine. I had been, as usual, leading the movements.

"¿Ese? Ese es raro." That one? He's raro (strange, queer).

Maybe he wasn't reacting with the fear and alarm of the white child in Fanon. "*Maman*, look, a Negro; I'm scared!"[6] Still, his "Ese es raro," delivered with the deadpan monotone of a proto-macho jock, fell on me like a brick of cement. I was not laughing.

This moment stayed with me, but I must have done exactly what I watched my mother and grandmother do when someone threw an unwanted compliment at them on the street: I moved on and refused to concede my introjection of that call. To get through that moment and let it pass, I had to keep moving, a form of fighting back I associated with the women in my life. This thirteen-year-old mariconcito kept it moving. Como que no era conmigo la cosa (as if what he said had nothing to do with me).

Still, the hail from the hot jock of my prepubescence crystalized how I epidermalized a proto-queer black body in working-class Santo Domingo, where the referents for mariconería in my barrio were overwhelmingly black female and femme-presenting. I grew up in the late 1970s and early 1980s, and though anti-Haitianism was central to the history books I read, I don't recall anti-Haitian sentiment as structuring everyday life. My immediate referents for working-class blackness were all Dominican.[7] There was Pedro, the pitch-black older neighborhood maricón, widely respected and often seen hanging out in the colmadones with older men in the barrio. There was also Margarita, the young black queen who sashayed by the basketball court at the corner of my house and who weathered the insults of the children and tígueres. Oh, she was fierce. I heard stories about her getting beaten, and I was even invited to join a party to get her to see our dicks and then whoop her ass—an invitation I said a panicked "no" to, sensing that I would get such a raging hard-on that I would get swept into the beating. Camilo, the refined hairdresser and older brother of the J family, a queen whom people mumbled about but rarely insulted openly, because Camilo's younger brothers had a reputation as warrior men in the neighborhood. Then there was JCM—my best friend and the son of one of the barrio's reigning marimachos: a black single mother who had more tigueraje than all the barrio tígueres combined, who hung out at the colmadón at the corner of her house and who had little to do with her son. JCM never talked about his mom. I knew she was his mother, but on the rare occasions I saw him with an adult (e.g., when we were eight and received our first communion together), JCM was accompanied by his grandmother. After that, he came by my house almost daily with a tray, selling ten-cent coconut pastries made by his grandma. Sometimes I would buy one, and I can still taste their lingering touch of warm vanilla on my tongue. Their taste also brings back an image of JCM's open hand as he held it out to me, whenever I had the ten cents—a hand with the glisten of midday sweat, being that he stopped by for a break during his shift. He wore flip-flops. I enjoyed the visits because he kept me abreast of neighborhood gossip. As we grew into adolescence, those visits bordered on the erotic.

For a while after I came out, I joked about the high density of faggotry in my 'hood. Alta densidad pajaril por centímetro cuadrado. And as I write, other neighborhood locas return to the eye of my mind: J—the fiercest and most outrageous of them all, and someone I could only look at and admire from afar, being that he pranced around being his full-on maricón libre, dressed in women's clothes. I remember a white-presenting mariconcito—the son of a seamstress who might also have had a disability, though my memory is fuzzy.

I remember the niño raro que fui as the queer child fighting to get by. I might become yet one more of these locas—black queens whose fierceness my child's mind cast as tragic. I walked by them and listened to conversations about them, finding it hard to imagine a future beyond the violence visited on Margarita, Pedro, Camilo, J, JCM, and the others. Still, they laughed, joked, and enjoyed being themselves, hinting at freedoms I could not see.

Luck and circumstance connected me to other paths to the interior life. In 1986, as I walked down Calle Dr. Delgado, going toward the Boy Scouts Association, I saw the face of a friend through the window of a house. He was white and was seated facing the wall, concentrated on something. I knew that he lived in the well-to-do neighborhood of Gazcue and that this was not his house, so I walked across the street to find out what he was up to. I peered through the window and realized, then, that he was playing "Für Elise" on the piano, which captured my fancy. I wanted to learn the piano so I could play this. I waved at his teacher; she ignored me until my friend stopped playing. I called out his name and asked for permission to come in and listen. The teacher, Doña Cristiana Viuda Lajara, told me to come in, sit, and be quiet. However, at the end of the lesson I went up to her and asked to become her student. "Tú tienes cara de merenguero," she said. You have the face of a merengue musician. Over and over she said that this was not music for me. Her soft and humorous comment was coupled with a scan of my clothes. I said that I would talk to my father about taking lessons and that this music *was* what I was interested in learning to play. I saw plenty of merengueros, entertaining at dizzying speeds on the keyboards they played in musical acts on national television. But this was different. After becoming my piano teacher, Doña Cristiana eventually conceded that classical music *was*, indeed, for me, even though I now see that her initial assessment of my suitability for this music was based on her surface reading of the twelve-year-old in front of her. My friend from the Boy Scouts, also named Carlos, was white and blond. I was neither.

My parents were unsure of what to make of my desire to be a musician. I lobbied my dad for a month (with the promise that I would apply myself to the typewriter and English-language courses I was also taking after school) to convince him to talk to Doña Cristiana and agree to pay for me to take piano lessons. They knew I was diligent and purposeful in my after-school rosaries with the neighborhood viejas in the Legión de María. My dad must have recognized me for the queen I would become. He spent a night in jail once for breaking the nose of a neighbor who tried to fondle me. He also confronted a guy on the street who had the audacity to call me *maricón*. Justifying piano lessons to friends and relatives was easier than explaining the rosaries, the hanging out with doñas, the reading, and the obsessive praying. And I put all the expressiveness into the instrument: I would not gesticulate with my hands, dance, or do anything else that showed the plumas (feathers) I was growing.

I wasn't white like the other Carlos, but I was close enough to have a new world open to me. I must have felt then that the *Ave Marías* and the sound worlds of Bach and Beethoven, removed as they were from the soundscapes of my childhood and early adolescence, allowed me to experience alternatives to what could become my life. Doña Cristiana let me practice on her piano when she was not teaching a lesson, and one of the doñas in the Legión allowed me to come to her house (a few blocks away) to practice on her piano. Another señora, with whom I prayed in the Legión, was the librarian at Radio Televisión Dominicana (Dominican Radio and Television Station). She invited me to come by and listen to their LP collection. Later I read Borges, but it was by befriending this lady that I had first access to dead people's music and to the joys of libraries. I was besotted, hanging out with the dead.

One weekend a charismatic preacher appeared to a crowd of hundreds of people at a public event on the Don Bosco grounds. On Saturday evening, he promised those in attendance that their dreams would be realized in miracles, as in the Bible. I have no clue how I got in there, or how anyone got the curas in Don Bosco to approve the hosting of this "miracle worker" on their school grounds, but I remember what I prayed for: I asked God Almighty to help me stop desiring my compañeros de colegio and to stop wanting to see, touch, smell, and lick G's armpits. For a moment in prayer, I felt something, perhaps the electricity moving through that large crowd as everyone closed their eyes on that warm evening. A few beats later, I opened my eyes, turning inward and announcing to myself that my craving for other boys was over.

CHAPTER ONE

This moment of fervent devotion delivered me, from myself.
Then I spotted the sinewy figure of a short-sleeved devotee.
A jolt hit the base of my balls.
My miracle would not be.

A MOJUGBA IS A PRAYER/homage/invocation/praise song to ancestral and other forces. I juxtaposed an homage to egun with stories of the sissy boy I remember, some of the paths I took to grow a sense of myself beyond what was immediately available where I grew up, a connection to organized religion, to music that few of my peers listened to, and to black queer people near me, also egun in my path. Perhaps it is in the invocation of the circuitries and textures of recalled socialities that I also pay homage to the young life I once held and pay respect to my black working-class faggot and dyke elders who dared to experience freedom and joy. This is a piecing together of memory to bridge to a past that is of use, a "repopulating" of one Latino gay male body to re-member. A faggotology starts from an homage to the child who was, the ancestor in that other country that was my childhood.[8] This memory bridge reestablishes a link and a space for the divine in that young human and holds space for the freedom longing that structured the journey to the person who looks back. I gather and hold the remains, the "desechos" of my queer child as mystical foundation.[9] Mojugba to you, re-membered child, growing sideways and getting by. You are loved.

Love and respect to the locas de mi barrio. You did not imagine me by first and last name, but I echo Patrice Khan-Cullors in the certainty that you had to have imagined the coming of queer children like me. Why else am I here, dreaming with and for the queer black children to come?

Ibaé.

Mojuba: an expansive memory refusing to be housed in any single place, bound by the limits of time, enclosed within the outlines of a map, encased in the physicality of body, or imprisoned as exhibit in a museum. A refusal that takes its inheritance from the Crossing, which earlier prophets had been forced to undertake from the overcrowded passage-ways in a place called Gorée, the door of no return, still packed centuries later with the scent of jostled grief so thick that no passage of human time could absorb it. It hangs there, this grief, until today, an indelible imprint of the Crossing, fastened by a pool of tears below, constantly replenished by the tremors of human living.

M. JACQUI ALEXANDER,
PEDAGOGIES OF CROSSING

He had left his queer thought-world and come back to a world of motion and men. . . . He grew slowly to feel almost for the first time the Veil that lay between him and the white world; he first noticed now the oppression that had not seemed oppression before, differences that erstwhile seemed natural, restraints and slights that in his boyhood days had gone unnoticed or been greeted with a laugh.

W. E. B. DU BOIS, "OF THE COMING OF JOHN,"
THE SOULS OF BLACK FOLK

Caminos

PART I

Bridge Crónica

A Triptych, with Elegguá

A *PATH* IS A PHYSICAL EXTENSION THROUGH WHICH ONE'S BODY MOVES, "A WAY OR TRACK FORMED BY THE CONTINUED TREADING OF PEDESTRIANS OR ANIMALS, RATHER THAN ONE DELIBERATELY PLANNED AND MADE."[1] The dictionary describes a trace that is made "al andar," as one walks, as the Spanish poet Antonio Machado puts it in the verses popularized by the Catalan songwriter-singer Joan Manuel Serrat.[2] The habitual reference to one's camino ("path") in Santería/Lucumí captures individual circumstances and how the tradition impacts one's life. As the anthropologist Aisha Beliso-De Jesús explains: "Practitioners often reference their present as part of their own personal camino (*ona*), the spiritual and physical roads that they travel through in life. . . . The mystical roads, caminos of life, are zones where practitioners link their lives to multiple worlds. Caminos bring together one's own land space, *ará*, with the spiritual landscapes, *ará onú*, which are thought of as the interconnected land of spirits."[3] Caminos are discussed regarding one's consecrated deities, each of whom engages the practitioner through signs, histories, characteristics, recommendations, prohibitions,

You stop in the middle of the field and, under your breath, ask the spirits—animals, plants, y tus muertos—to help you string together a bridge of words.

GLORIA E. ANZALDÚA, *LIGHT IN THE DARK*

Tu camino de conocimiento requires that you encounter your shadow side and confront what you've programmed yourself (and have been programmed by your cultures) to avoid (desconocer), to confront the training and habits distorting how you see reality and inhibiting the full use of your facultades.

GLORIA E. ANZALDÚA, *LIGHT IN THE DARK*

and stories. This is compounded by divinations that draw on oracular letras, or signs with advice, refrains, and stories that reference a person, situation, or ritual. When requesting a reading from a Babalawo (*consulta* or *registro*) or a consultation (*dafa* or *osode*), the priest will ask the deity Orunmila about you by uttering your full legal name. He will also name your sign of Ifá, or the name of the signs that result from divination following the ceremony where one's head orisha is determined; your religious name, acquired upon initiation; and the overall sign of initiation, or the signo de santo, which is drawn from a combination of signs established in initiation.

The signs have meanings mobilized in liturgical, ritual, and ceremonial practice. What addresses the uniqueness of one's circumstances is the combination of these signs and the force fields their circuitry produces, which is juxtaposed in divination to fulfill requirements for ritual or to ensure that ceremony has been properly carried out. One elder shared with me that this combination, in a person, cannot be repeated. Thus, one's camino is analogized to a fingerprint in its nongeneralizability.

"Re-membered Life," the previous chapter, paid homage to the ancestors and to the queer child as being an ancestor seeking to grow through prayer, soundscapes built mostly by dead white men, fantasies of escape from the child's immediate surroundings, and studied avoidance of associations with working-class black queer bodies. The tryptic of writings later in this chapter accounts for how the immigrant scholar actualized a sentimental education in whiteness, which translates into upward mobility and a desconocimiento of black people and of his own working-class blackness. As is typical of Anzaldúan thought, the Chicana thinker provides terms to offer more than their equivalence in translation: "to avoid" (*desconocer*). For now, *desconocer* will stand in as *avoidance*, as well as a disavowal of knowing, or to act as if one does not know. A faggotology built on the caminos opened by Elegguá becomes an Anzaldúan "bridge of words" that takes the "I" who narrates to task for that which has been avoided or intentionally unknown in the pursuit of what Rodolfo Kusch calls *el afán de ser alguien* (the quest to be somebody).[4]

Turning toward blackness in the service of faggotology demands attunement to the contradictory registers at which it operates. My route to blackness through the immigrant latinidad of the Dominican American scholar attends to layered caminos as they energize one another: the "black behind the ear" of the Dominican, the structural reward of antiblackness and immigrant innocence and complicity, the whiteness of gayness, and the deracination of the scholar of color in higher education.[5] A swivel through what Anzaldúa describes as one's "camino de conocimiento" obtains from turning outward the markings on the path to view anew its circuitry, reckon with the damage, and propitiate a different morphology.

Uno

The eye of the scholar's mind returns to Edwin's graduation day. There is a picture of it in the pile of photographs he has stashed away. This happened in the late 1990s, when phones did not yet store family archives. To everyone celebrating, Edwin was finally giving his public defender and the judge reasons to stay out of prison after being charged (at eighteen) with drug possession with intent to distribute. That the young man was alive was, in itself, cause for celebration: at least two of Edwin's buddies from Philadelphia's Sterner Street had been shot dead before they turned eighteen.

On the afternoon of Edwin's graduation, the scholar came to support his brother. As he writes, he is unsure of how willingly or happily he did this, being that relations between the brothers had cooled since the family migrated to Philadelphia in 1989, and especially after the scholar's Jewish librarian, Dr. B, took him under her wing. Among her contributions, Dr. B had enough foresight to feed him what he craved: books, films, classical music concerts, rides to piano lessons, and every other incentive for the scholar to become a renaissance man. Though he still lived in West Philadelphia and his family lived in "Badlands" North Philly, the scholar's visits to the parental home became rare. But the abyss had begun to grow years before he moved out, with the lock and key he put in his own bedroom at his parents' house. Against the world of his working-class Dominican and immigrant upbringing (where hand-me-downs and sharing were common), he learned not to share his clothes and books. He had begun to think that being born into this family was an accident, as he recognized less and less of who he was becoming in contrast with the house to which he returned at night. He increasingly thought that "his people" were those with whom he shared a taste for the fetish objects of US upper-middle-class culture. His move to live on the University of Pennsylvania campus completed a physical departure from the deteriorating working-class community of Edison High School in North Philly in 1991, inoculating him from teen pregnancy and the crack epidemic.

Edwin's prosecution was ongoing. The judge proposed that Edwin finish high school and enroll in the military, with an offer to throw out the case. At the time, becoming yet another black body in the military-industrial complex, disposable in the service of empire, appeared to the scholar a better choice than prison. But Edwin did not want this.

Everyone in the Philadelphia branch of the Decenas clan had an opinion: what to do about the case, and what was missing in the moves that were being made by Edwin's family. This made dealing with Doña Xiomara an exercise in seeing the kin whom the scholar preferred not to see. While they lived in Santo Domingo, visits with the Decenas were mandatory, and the scholar abhorred them. The scholar may have been disciplined by his relatives because of his mannerisms, his inability to dance, or his weight, but Edwin experienced discipline on a whole different level. He was the most recognizably black of the three boys, which contributed to the aggressive physical punishments he received and the discourse about how Xiomara and Dario's second son would amount to "no good." The opinions of Edwin's relatives in Philadelphia invariably built on this family lore regarding who Edwin became. The scholar listened and either nodded or stayed quiet, for his mother's sake. He was always getting back on the train while his mother countenanced whatever complaints came through about his uppity attitude, disregard for his elders, and lack of gratitude for all the Decena family did to bring him to the United States.

Edwin's graduation was a big deal, and his brothers talked with each other before heading to the Edison High School football field. This was their first chat as full-grown men. They sat on a stoop, and Edwin talked to the scholar about his situation and the pending court date until the scholar interrupted him. The older brother had no tolerance for what sounded like Edwin's self-pitying account of himself.

"You are not the only one who has suffered."

"What do you mean?"

"Yo también he sufrido."

Pause.

"Do you remember how you and Omar used to call me 'maricón,' 'mariconcito'?"

They may have continued talking for longer, but relatives were around, and everyone was pressed for time.

The rest of this story was elaborated in Edwin's tears.

Dos

You and papi have a rocky relationship. It survived your coming out, barely.

"No hables así, papi," you said when toxic homophobia fouled his unhinged macho plepla while you visited. "Que tengo amigos que son así" (Don't talk like that. I have friends like that). He was directing his vitriol at gay people. You were not letting this pass this time.

"¿Cómo así que tú 'tienes amigos así'? ¡Entonces tú eres como ellos!" (What do you mean that you "have friends like that"? [Beat pregnant with anticipation and punctuated by a glare directed at you.] Then you must be like them!)

And there you were: faggot son unmoved. No admission, no denial.

El que calla, concede. If you are silent, you concede.

Your silence did not concede to homophobic bluster. This was silence as defiance. In retrospect, badass. No wonder that, in response, Don Dario lost his shit.

But it was better that way. Doña Xiomara spared you talking about this whole issue. Edwin's marathon "cry-fest" at graduation and all the weeping they told you they did later had you rolling your eyes, as it turned attention away from Edwin's impending court date.

Papi spared himself, your mother, and you whatever fantasies of homophobic rejection from the Latino family that you had in your head before this anticlimactic "coming out" moment spiced with adobo. People wailed for the kids you would not have and all the lawyers and doctors lost in nonreproductive fornication, but they complied with your request for them to stop feeling sad for you.

Then you adopted the "shock therapy" of gay pride by visiting more often and shoving the loca down your family's throat.

That was some idea of healing. A la cañona.

People did not ogle tetas or culos on television that would not be followed by your commentary on how hot the men were. Your brothers talked "tits and ass"? ¡Mierda! ¡Qué bueno 'tá ese jevo! ¡Diablo, qué macho!

Your mother was initially scandalized but soon enough chuckled, finding humor in commentary that was not funny to others. Suddenly, Doña Xiomara and you had a surprising thing in common, as you salivated brazenly over men on television. Cool madre-hijo bonding! Men were beginning to show torsos on Univisión. The 1990s were a fun time.

Your queer-nation self now was too real for Edwin and Omar, and their reaction to your mariconadas was to get up, grab juice from the fridge, and go back out on the street. They continued to avoid you and made themselves scarce when you visited, but your father made it a point to show up after the week that followed the initial yelling and light wall banging. He was his usual self—restless, always on the move with something up his sleeve. Life with him had always been that way. He was the trustworthy paternal tíguere, but don't try to figure out what he is up to, because there is no coming back from that rabbit hole. He looked you in the face during that visit and began talking about having been "on business" in New York. Instead of being in Washington

Heights, he had been selling the electrical supplies he used to take into the city to store owners in Greenwich Village. You worked extra hard to keep your eyes from rolling.

"Y entonces vi a uno que iba en patines en la Quinta Avenida" (And then I saw one going on Fifth Avenue on rollerblades), he said, having no need to explain what he meant by "uno." You thought about all the words he could say but didn't. "Y pensé que a lo mejor un día ese sería mi hijo" (And then I thought that someday that might be my son).

His tone lost its cool, and that last sentence was delivered unevenly, as if his breath had a power outage; he was emotional. By this time, your jaw had dropped down to the basement. You did not know how to respond, and it took a while to set your jaw back in place. A few beats later, he asked, "¿Cuándo es la marcha?" (When is the march?)

¿La marcha de los unos?

"In a few weeks," you said.

"Quiero ir contigo" (I want to go with you).

Thirty years after you first came out, you have yet to attend gay pride together. Your relationship with Don Dario has had highs and lows. But the gay thing is embedded in the frame of your immigrant story and in the way you came to understand your embodiment in US society. A bridge of return to your family and to working-class Philadelphia, held in your father's loving wish to accompany you.

Quiero ir contigo.

Don Dario handled this like a champ, even though you rarely gave him credit. He did not know the man his oldest son had become. But he still loved you.

You had become a man, even though that word always felt to you like a pair of jeans too big to hang on your hips.

Paths were multiplying as you and your brothers grew, life trails moving you away from one another.[6] The coming out process crystallized a divergence of trajectories too thick for anyone to see or articulate, because so much of it exceeded gayness. You were on your way to the future of what Kusch calls "ser alguien": that of being a professional, academic, card-carrying member of the bourgeoisie—a being someone calibrated in blunt and subtle ways by your light skin, thus providing hints on how to revise and enrich Kusch's race-blind vision of Argentine urbanity.[7] Your black-presenting brother Edwin was on his way to jail and then deportation, eventually landing deeper in the Dominican working class. And your brother Omar, the youngest and lightest-skinned, was on his way to a lifelong battle with the impossible conditions of the inner-city working class in the Kensington neighborhood of North Philadelphia, cycles of addiction and recovery and problematic choices. You may all be black, as you remind yourself, but it was the one of you three who most presented as black who was caught in the quagmire of the criminal justice system, with the choice of jail or the military. Where is that "ser alguien" for your brothers, forbidden from becoming the "almost the same but not white" you became?[8]

Fast-forward to college graduation, the faces of your parents in what you tell yourself was their only occasion of pride in their children. Your brothers are nowhere in the frame. Don Dario and Doña Xiomara beaming in front of the camera—he wore a light-gray suit, and your mother wore a black-and-white dress you never saw her wear before, her makeup and full head of recently colored black hair on point, as it was every Saturday afternoon after her customary trip to the Korean hair salon. They face the camera; you are at the center—the smug, smiling younger you, holding up a glass of champagne, the embodiment of immigrant success. Phi Beta Kappa, magna cum laude; I mean, maybe you were not white, but you were surely on your way to honorary status.

Or, at least, the hint of pride and entitled innocence in your smile suggests that there was something about US history, the conjunctures of your moment, and the scaffolding of your camino that you had yet to grasp in your bones, even though it went on all around you. A few days earlier, before you spoke to the graduating class in the English Department, your mentor introduced you; spoke about your trajectory in the department, which he knew better than anyone; sang your praises. He must have mentioned that you were a kid from North Philadelphia and that the two of you had met in the context of a partnership between Penn English and Edison High School, which brought university students to interact and workshop writing with inner-city kids. You enjoyed participating in that program as a Penn student and considered it a way to "give back." Penn English saw it as partnership with "the community," something they seemed more at ease doing in North Philadelphia with Latinos than with their African American neighbors in West Philadelphia. He then talked and thanked your other supporters, which included a professor who became one of your gay parents.

Your speaking mentor informed everyone in the room that the gorgeous Italian suit you were wearing was a graduation gift.

You powered through prepared remarks, something about the strawberries being dipped in chocolate at the celebration, probably a ditty informed by your penchant for ribald, campy juxtapositions. Your models for gay were pure white camp, so where else would you look for humor? Dr. B was there, but you don't remember your parents at this celebration. The picture and the champagne were at another celebration during graduation week. Or maybe this was it? It must have been so special to have this platform in the English Department, of all places, for someone who could barely express himself in the language five years earlier. You had always said to Dr. B that you wanted to major in English, to speak it better than Americans. You wrote the first serious college essays for your mentor when you were fifteen, with the support of Dr. B, who helped you get into one of the professor's summer classes on poetry. You worked hard writing these two one-page pieces, and you were happy to get more than a single-spaced page of feedback from this man. Like Dr. B, he took you seriously, and he was Jewish. The first two white people to take you seriously.

A few days later, as you walked up the stairs in Bennett Hall at Penn, one of your college friends stopped to talk to you and said that he found the comment odd. You don't recall the exact words he used in that exchange. (Was Generation X using the phrase "fucked up"?) You don't remember your response, either, but you remember the feeling of vergüenza ajena—that kind of shame you feel on someone else's behalf. You probably tried to excuse your mentor, turning him into the "inappropriate uncle" who pulled crazy stuff out of his mouth, and whose verborrhea you defended the way Doña Xiomara made excuses for the tío who decreed, at a family function years later, that HIV-positive people should be shot.

Nothing is wrong with naming and expressing gratitude for our gifts in public, but something about the generosity of liberal whiteness runs into shaky (shady?) ground when pointing out that the only Latino in the room, and the person of color from the inner city who was the center of attention in that specific moment, was wearing a gift from white patrons. You had never faced racism, but that comment prompted a turn in how you were thinking about yourself, not as a creature residing in the specular veil layering the pupils of the other, but as living in the other's noblesse oblige. Elite Penn came to the rescue of the latinito and succeeded! How does it feel to be a problem wrapped as a gift?[9]

I stated earlier that "you had never faced racism," but that's incorrect. The combination of your light skin and immigrant gaze meant that throughout your time at Penn, you would not recognize racism even if it struck you with a baseball bat. Yes, you listened to your (mostly white) Penn classmates discuss race and racism, especially during the year of the "water buffalo" incident, when a Jewish student shouted to a group of black sorority sisters celebrating "Founders' Day" and hanging out outside his dorm: "Shut up, you water buffalo! If you're looking for a party, there's a zoo a mile from here."[10] In the aftermath of the national and local controversy sparked by this incident, some black female students who were targeted sat in front of you and others to process what had happened to them. You remember the sessions going on for weeks of meetings where the incident was the only topic of discussion. You beheld how women you loved became undone by what was going on, but you did not understand the source of their pain.

You listened; that was all you could do. You looked at suffering in its face and worked up empathy and silence to be supportive, but you had no clue what was happening to them. What is a water buffalo? You could not know pain like the kind these women were trying to process; you had not and would not be likely to encounter it directly, and you had yet to become aware of it.

I equivocate again. You brought to your Penn experience an immigrant's awareness of what is structurally rewarding about staying as far away from blackness as you can. That awareness acted in consort with your racial schemata to shield (or inoculate?) you from the racism that black-presenting people faced on campus every day—for a while. Distancing oneself from blackness as a prerequisite for success was part of the air you breathed; it informed your choices. Blackness was the (w)hole all around you, like the weather. Remember the precollege training program where you got to know black students at Temple, picked up their English, and then had your Jewish piano teacher point out to you that your accent and vocabulary had changed in one week? Did you want to continue to speak like that? You clearly had a good ear, but this could not stand. This piano teacher then came after you for inserting "Valley talk" in your speech. "Please speak in sentences that have a beginning and an end," she would say, exasperated by her discovery of this white girl in the Hispanic boy with the mustache sitting at the piano, playing Chopin.

Maybe you did not experience racism directly or in a way that was intelligible to you, but you learned the "Western canon." You used to style yourself after Caliban, learning the master's tongue so he could curse the hell out of Prospero, but is that where you get down? Or were you more like the servile Ariel, always ready to abide by the wishes of the old white man? You found the view of the colonized useful in Shakespeare, though your path proved that things were more complicated than they were in *The Tempest*. It was legitimate for you to get to know the Western canon, absorb it, and incorporate it into your writing and sensibility, but there was a limit to what that canon could (or should) look like. Your mentors were white, mostly Jewish, educated, and upper middle class—a striking detail of how you "learned to be white" but also drew upon elements of Jewish history, culture, and values to think about the status of outsiders in Western culture. You avoided taking courses with any of black faculty in English, though two of them became informal mentors, and you did not take courses with the two Chicana faculty who came through English and either left or were not renewed. A white mentor said that one of the Chicanas in the department would not be reappointed because she was not "up to snuff." She eventually left the academy. You attended a meeting of the Movimiento Estudiantil Chicano de Aztlán (Mecha). You got to know other students of color on campus only through a fellowship program, but you read no writers of color in your English major until your senior year, when Gloria Anzaldúa blew your mind. Her tripping on the racist mestizaje of José Vasconcelos as somehow progressive would later trouble you. Never mind that (1) Piri Thomas, James Baldwin, Malcolm X, Nicholasa Mohr, Jesús Colón, and Claude Brown were part of your literary bridge to the English language at Edison/Fareira High School; and (2) watching *Paris Is Burning* at sixteen (in the company of Dr. B, years before you would come out) was a revelation to the frightened Barbie inside.

The Holocaust became the preferred vehicle through which to articulate your adolescent fear regarding your own life, wedded most heavily in your mind's eye to your homosexuality. This helped, but it also obscured the deeper price exacted on your psyche in becoming somebody. I mean, you were reading Kafka and nursing the metaphor of the apple thrown and stuck in Gregor Samsa's stomach as if the apple lived in your own gut, rotting—as if its collecting maggots symbolized a putrefaction consuming you. You cried inconsolably and inexplicably down Walnut Street with Dr. B after watching *Europa Europa*, feeling as if the infection in the penis of the young Solomon Perel (caused by his attempt to manipulate and hide his circumcision as he hid his Jewishness to save his life) was a metaphor for the festering, infected wound of your truth. Despite his whiteness, if you did not share in his cut pecker, his plight and his agony brushed you close. Your initial reaction to *Paris Is Burning* in discussion with Dr. B eschewed any hint of identification with the queens in Jennie Livingston's documentary. The movie stayed with you, but you held them at a distance, their flesh continents away from your own. Perhaps here is where your mind's eye settles on the deletion of black queens and femmes in your own plight, first as a working-class barrio kid and then as an Ivy League college student. Unlike the black pioneras in San Juan Bosco, the *Paris* locas lived in a country separated from you by the magic of celluloid, residential segregation, blight, and elite education. Theirs might be additional corpses piled on your path, but their ends did not brush you—yet.

You have long thought that coming out delivered you closer to yourself, but there were small and consequential signs of your being educated in the protocols of whiteness, even as you began to live under the banner of gayness.[11]

Remember the light-skinned Puerto Rican guy who made possible your first stab at sucking cock, telling you the next day that he "needed space"? You were calling him from the public phone around the corner from his apartment after taking a bus ride there from North Philly, a day after your coming out to him delivered you your first taste of a penis and the texture of pubic hair. How about the Jewish bisexual guy who wanted you to meet his mother so she would practice her Spanish, but then decided to disinvite you to his family's Seder because you had been fucking for only six weeks, and he would not take a girl with whom he had been kicking it for that short while anyway? Remember how Latina-chancletas-crazy you became when he told you the night after you missed seeing each other that he had been fucking a woman? Oh, and Stephen, the white guy who dumped you over table manners—you fuck good, but you do not know how to handle your silverware, so let's blow a load, but no way you will meet mom and dad. And wait, the Uruguayan model (hot body and as loquacious and beloved by his fawning friends as he was unemployed) who spoke five languages but was so distressed by your Penn petulance that he called the whole thing off, explaining that he just couldn't deal with you having "an ego the size of Montana"?

You entered this "gay world" looking for a sense of self; this was largely a vanilla world in 1990s Rittenhouse Square in Center City or at Penn. You made no effort to gravitate toward black people, let alone people of color, unless they moved within these tony circles. Or unless you took the El to go visit Papi y Mami. You may visit with fantasies of messing with men (with meat that looked like your own) anonymously or "casually," as was the parlance then, or by watching the ghetto porn of the Latino Fan Club or the male orgasmic pyrotechnics of Kristen Bjorn porn videos. Like you are still wondering how Bjorn made his men just cum on queue without touching themselves, their flying man juice a signature of the times. You also had trysts with black and Latino men, but nobody stepped off the celluloid to convince you men like you were more than the fetish objects in Robert Mapplethorpe's gaze and introjected into your eyes as you watched and milked your own meat, staring as cultural theorist Kobena Mercer did to the black dong sliding out of the polyester business suit (hot!).[12]

Yet Dr. B had also introduced you to the documentary filmmaker Marlon Riggs, and the chronology is getting crossed here—a knot in time. This encounter, like your encounter with Anzaldúa in the English course with Eric Cheyfitz, changed you in ways you are still untangling. You can't remember if you saw *Tongues Untied* upon its release or if it became yet another cultural object she brought to your attention after you came out to Dr. B. If it showed at the Ritz theater in the early 1990s, you must have seen it with her: apart from embracing and making space for you when nobody else knew you were gay, Dr. B let the librarian kick into high gear and filled you up with books, films, articles, everything she could lay her hands on. She reminded you of James Baldwin, whom you read in high school, voraciously. You recall how emotional your response was to *Go Tell It on the Mountain*, even though you read it when you were still learning English, and how Dr. B emphasized that emotion in Baldwin's prose was barely beneath the surface. The expression in Spanish equivalent to "up his sleeve" is "a flor de piel." Emotions as flowers up your skin—that's a Baldwin you sensed but could not fully explain to Dr. B or to yourself. She reminded you of David Acosta, the Philadelphia-based Colombian gay activist and poet who came to your high school and with whom you must have workshopped some of those Spanish-language poems of yours that were best left in your journals. Or Frances Negrón-Muntaner, a North Philadelphia–based queer trailblazer whose film *Brincando el charco* you saw in the theater and on TV (before your mother bought her house on E Street and while the family lived on Sterner). Frances also came to Edison and spoke to you and other students at the library. Your gratitude at their remembered bodies in your mind's eye gives you goosebumps.

Dr. B was your self-appointed Jewish mom, who risked mystifying and alienating everyone, including her own family, by taking you under her wing and taking you everywhere she went after you met in fall 1989 (the year you started at Edison). You want to credit her for taking you to your first classical music store—Tower Records on South Street—after taking the Test of English as a Foreign Language (TOEFL), but that credit goes to your cousin Carlos Alberto. Dr. B just took you to the Tower Classical Annex all the time, and you discovered the Canadian pianist Glenn Gould in a cassette recording of three Beethoven sonatas, which would be your soundtrack for months, together with a recording of three of Bach's *Brandenburg Concertos*. Hearing the Brandenburgs still brings you back to those first years. Before meeting her, you had never owned a classical music LP. In Santo Domingo, you heard the last movement of Beethoven's Ninth (at the home of Carlos the pianist in Gazcue), but you never owned records, let alone played them at home. Dr. B changed that. She was the companion, cheerleader, and dogged proponent of how much more you could be, decades before you could know.

You showed up bright and early at the high school library, ready to discuss a serious intellectual question you had that morning while your father ranted at home about how the three of you needed to get up and meet your bright futures. Breakfasts with Dr. B were accompanied with bagels and the teas she prepared, before you dashed out to homeroom. The library was your hangout in the half of high school you finished at Edison. You did not interact with students outside of class. You did not even go to lunch in the cafeteria. This woman was her own brand of a '90s search engine. You just had to mention something in your conversations; she would research it and return with a packet of information. She dripped curiosity and dropped knowledge with a shocking shamelessness—the same ferocity she brought to defending you, pushing you, pushing for you, and not giving a rat's ass about the quizzical looks thrown your way at Philadelphia Orchestra concerts, Borders book-store, or the Ritz film theaters. Admittedly, the pairing of a middle-aged white woman and an adolescent Hispanic man going together everywhere looked... funny? Everyone in your extended family talked about it, but no-body dared ever bring it up to your parents, who probably wondered, "What the hell?" but gave you space to have this relationship and never asked ques-tions. To Papi and Mami, Dr. B was always "la señora" (the lady). Some people must have seen the cougar with the brown boy/foster child/boy toy.

Dr. B's deadpan gaze back in response was a perennial "fuck off."

It cost her dearly with her family, mentoring you. You were the last of three mentees, but perhaps the intensity and duration of the relationship was what made things sour between you and Dr. B's family. That's hard to know.

Alfredo put it best, as always. He was talking about your experience, as well as his own. He was taken out of a hostile childhood home by a neighborhood doña. He then became the mentee of an Uruguayan diplomat, who mentored and adopted him as his own son. Alfredo and Jorge's children all address one another as siblings.

Nuestras vidas fueron robadas. A nosotros nos adoptaron. Por eso so-brevivimos. (Our lives were stolen. We were adopted. That's the reason we survived.)

Theft and adoption as condition of possibility for your survival?

One of your colleagues warned you that your use of the word *theft* can lend itself to critique for intimating that having mentors rerouting one's life away from the expectations laden to everyone else's path in a biological family can (or should) be compared with the kidnapping and theft of the African enslaved body. That comparison would be inappropriate, but something about the structures of educational opportunity is connected to class- and race-inflected "interventions" in support of "talented" and "unique" children. Can we imagine Alfredo's mother (or your mother, for that matter) befriending, mentoring, and "adopting" the neighbors' children? Perhaps the "theft" in question is not the literal theft of the body but, rather, what appears once your *futurity* is unmoored from that of your immediate familial horizon. What happens when you can't turn back, or when turning back means admitting a link one spends years conditioning oneself to erase? Could grappling with the uncertainty of what any of this means be what Anzaldúa calls *desconocimiento*, yet another condition of possibility for survival and success: not only to leave, but to forget that which you left? How does turning to the "black behind the ear" stand for your bridge of words?

To nest what happened to you at this nexus is troubling and disturbing. How could your parents just let you go? Did they ask who these mentors were and what their intentions were? I mean, have a white woman show up and say, "Hey Mr. and Mrs. Decena, I'm taking your son to concerts, dinners, movies, theater," and have them say, "OK." Huh? If that ever happened to you with one of your sons, you would already know, by the time that woman walked through the front door, her credit score, right after having checked her criminal record, and you would insist on coming as a chaperone. But that's you—middle class, suburban, trained in the ways of white women and mentored by black mothers, ready to battle whomever, wherever, for your black sons. Did your immigrant mother ask questions, in inner-city Philadelphia, in 1989?

You think not. Not Doña Xiomara.

Your mother grasped and respected what Dr. B did for you, even though she could not know exactly what that was, even though this meant that you grew apart from her, becoming close with another mother and increasingly less able to cross the bridge back.

This is what you think. Doña Xiomara never said anything. She never asked anything. She just let it be. As the Spanish say, Doña Xiomara understood and acquiesced to what was best for you. Dejarlo estar.

Mami loves like this.

Let it be.

Tres

The 31 bus, operated by Coach USA on South Orange Avenue, offers riders an itinerary of contrasts, from upscale and aggressively gentrifying and policed downtown urbanity to the inner city and leafy suburbia. He discovered the bus soon after their first home purchase, eager to find a direct line connecting him to the New Jersey Transit train commute to work. Some of his colleagues in the area did not know about the bus route. They drove and did not share his need to use public transportation after leaving New York City. There was also a tinge of the studied avoidance and skepticism toward all things Newark, where the conjunction of black, working class, and poor were materially articulated in daily life, tension hanging in every interaction and decision.

He failed the driving test five times when he was eighteen. He talked about this as if it was a badge of honor or else argued that this was residual resistance from the renegade New Yorker: passing the test would be the acceptance that he had finally left the city for Jersey.

The bus commute caused friction with his husband, who tried the bus route to commute a few times but eventually stopped; it was too stressful. The husband teased and warned, often, that getting on the 31 was an "ethnographic experiment." The bus could carry the civil servant going to work, as well as the junkie or methamphetamine addict waiting to go for a hit on Broad Street, the throwback to the crack epidemic literally on cloud 31 *while* on the bus, or the high school student and hospital nurse. But that was not the issue. Rather, the problem was what he saw and overheard on that bus: people on their way to court hearings; comments about people stabbed at a park; and arguments between irritable, demoralized bus drivers and passengers. If the bus was a lottery, throw in some heat at the end of the day, with everyone exhausted, cranky, and famished, going home, and sparks flew one way or another. Sooner or later, something bad would happen on the 31.

However, a decade of riding the bus passed without major problems. Drama, entertainment, comedy, and apocalyptic preaching? Yes, but no tragedy. "Well, nothing yet," the husband continued. "But why maximize your chances of it happening by insisting on getting on it?" There had been moments of tension: a fight that almost derailed into a brawl but was stopped by police; an older black man getting indignant with someone else over coughing one morning; and, yes, arguing with the drivers, times when you were not sure whether they competed for the best curser or loudest mouth. Some arguments met with the roiling laughter of passengers. Other arguments got tempers heightened enough that the elders stepped in to calm everyone down. One time, the driver was pissed enough to stop the bus until someone convinced his opponent—a man running late for work and upset that the driver insisted on packing even more people into an already full bus—to stop talking back to the driver; one could sense bodies shifting, clothes and extremities morphing into feisty feathers rustling in irritation, but the man eventually calmed down, and the driver continued.

A decade of bus riding is a long time, and he witnessed "crazy" combined with decency and generosity; respect for elders, pregnant women, and children; resolutely queer-presenting and flamboyant riders whom no one bothered; and people donating change to help the needy complete their bus fare. Other things occurred, many of them insignificant, but these commutes helped him hold contact with some of Newark's black working people and with his own black working-class roots.

At first, he felt voyeuristic. After all, this was the most intense and sustained period of consistent interaction with working-class African Americans and other black folks (from Haiti, Nigeria, etc.) that he had had since arriving in the United States. Newark is also strongly Latino, but not on the side he traversed. The class dimension of this mattered, because he rarely interacted with other black people in Philadelphia or New York, especially after leaving home for college. Blackness was central to Philly and the Bronx, but his contact with other black folks in these areas was episodic: either people avoided black neighborhoods on his behalf (Dr. B drove through some parts of Germantown but refused to drive through others), or he avoided them. But that initial feeling of being a spectator dissipated; interaction continued, exchanging hellos with fellow travelers, or sitting side by side with people going about their lives. He could see himself either as the suburbanite "slumming" it to get to work or as another man of color commuting. Either view enmeshed blackness with material class distinctions. However, distinctions collapsed temporarily while everyone hopped in. Occasionally, one or two whites would get on the bus when it arrived at Dover Street from stops in South Orange or Livingston Mall. In recent years, he had noticed one or two working-class white parents getting on the bus to take their children to school in Newark.

On the night of the call, he stood with the rest of bus 31 humanity as the vehicle crawled up South Orange Avenue, past beyond the Rutgers/UMDNJ hospital and deep into the recesses of Newark's West Ward.[13] It had been one of those days when the cool morning fades into a humid afternoon after one's skin turns out sweat with the same clothes you had needed for warmth barely a moment ago. The scene was the usual late-evening cocktail of unpredictability, grumpiness, crying children who should have been home by now, annoying teens taking up more space than they should, and no room to think without everyone else hearing it. He had been trying to concentrate on a podcast while balancing himself as he stood.

"Mr. Decena, I'm calling you from the Temple University Hospital because you are your mother's power of attorney," the voice said. "Her heart stopped. What do you want us to do?"

The head nurse had called him earlier on the day of this bus ride to say that the dentist recommended a tooth extraction. He authorized it and then learned a few hours later that she would be kept at the hospital because she had an infection.

"I know this is sudden, Mr. Decena, but we need a decision."

He was sure the voice was not a Latina from the way she sounded, but she pronounced his last name correctly. That was rare. He fell silent for a few more beats, feeling the volume turning up on one of the bus conversations held by someone whose idea of entertainment was to speak as loudly as possible. He could not make out what the man was saying or where he was located, but he could hear teens chuckling.

He asked the doctor to explain. His mother, who had been at a nursing home for more than a year with dementia and bipolar disorder, was sent to intensive care after complications connected to a tooth extraction. The person on the phone said that Doña Xiomara had developed something involving mucus, and some of that muck got stuck in her air pipes, prompting her breathing and (soon enough) her heart to stop. One of her lungs collapsed. (The voice said something like that; she was calm, and her tone was even.)

She needed him to decide.

"Do all you can to bring her back," he said. "I'm heading over there." He reached the cord to signal the bus to stop and began to push his way out. Before he got off the bus, he called the husband and explained what was going on; he would stay overnight at the hospital and take the first train back the next day. This was a time he wished he could drive so that he could reach his mother in less than two hours. He called Don Dario in Philadelphia and Edwin in Santo Domingo. His brother Omar was out of the picture, but he called, thinking of leaving a message on the last phone number he had for Omar. The person who replied was not his brother.

He moved through the next hours as if he was observing himself and everyone else playing parts in a play. Someone (perhaps the same woman) called to say that they got a heartbeat, just when he was getting in the Uber; they were not sure of the consequences of her heart stopping for more than twenty minutes, but Doña Xiomara was back.

"Thank you for this," he said. "I'm coming, and so is my father. We'll be there soon."

The streetlights outside Philadelphia's 30th Street Station seemed eerily bright as he grabbed a taxi, and so did the lamps on Broad Street. It was close to 10 p.m. The temperature had dipped ten degrees, and he felt underdressed, his sweat caked into his skin without an extra layer of clothes. Don Dario arrived; perhaps he had been crying? The father's eyes looked puffy, but he worked hard at seeming tough. He asked for his father's blessing; they hugged clumsily and went in to see Doña Xiomara, hearing that they could be there only briefly. He had already told Edwin they would call him to bring him into this moment.

The nurse opened the door, and they walked into a corridor partitioned into rooms smaller than the smallest bathroom in his suburban home, with glass walls, each containing a patient. This was his first time in an intensive care unit (ICU); he expected it to be different, his fantasy distorted by years of television series on the life and death of patients attended by medical staff busy having romantics trysts with one another. The staff at this ICU congregated in a central section littered with monitoring equipment, computers, and a counter that ran as a large oval through the whole room.

The woman brought them to where Doña Xiomara was; it took at least one heartbeat and a contained gasp to make out where the equipment ended and his mother started. Tubes were connected to her trachea, the remaining paraphernalia buried in her chest. Her lower jaw, where the tooth had been extracted, looked banged up. She looked as if she had been severely beaten. Refusing to look at Don Dario out of fear of losing his composure, he noted the smileys asking someone to signal what kind of day they were having, who the attending nurse was, and so on. What kind of questions were those?

He leaned over and spoke to Doña Xiomara, whispering something about being there for her, as if rehearsing his lines. Then he turned away from her rapidly, not sure whether the coming eruption was vomit or tears. Don Dario stood facing his wife of forty-five years, the tíguere of the glorious family parties, at the top of his world, broken by the sight of his life companion, a woman turned into a small spider whose life was sustained by metal and plastic tentacles.

He called Edwin and explained. The young white woman who came to them identified herself as the attending doctor. She said she would tell the family more about what was going on when they stepped out of the ICU. He kept Edwin on the line while they listened to the doctor. Once she walked away, Edwin demanded to see Doña Xiomara. It had been at least five years since the last time she and Edwin had seen each other in person. Edwin held it together after his initial outburst—the one where his two years behind bars, combined with the hell of being the one in the family who was deported, hit everyone like a loud thud through FaceTime. Technology could not alleviate his anguish for his mother, to assuage what he felt for not being there with her, with his family.

Outside the ICU, the same young woman came back and sat with them. This time, she asked the family to make sure that it could make decisions. He and Don Dario called Edwin again to have him join them in listening and deciding together. They were three now—the father and two out of three sons—listening to this medical update. She said Doña Xiomara's heart had stopped for several minutes. The medical team had brought her back, as the family could see, but they were not sure what damage had resulted from the heart stopping. She needed testing, but she was in critical condition, even though there were no early signs of damage. She further explained that medical resuscitation was a forceful process, and that her team was concerned that Doña Xiomara's body would not support a second hard-hitting intervention like the one performed to get a heartbeat, should it go away again. Did she have a living will? What did the family want the team to do in case her heart stopped again?

Doña Xiomara had no living will.

He and Edwin proposed letting Doña Xiomara go if it came to a moment like the one she barely overcame. Don Dario was adamant, showing resolve as he fought back tears: "¡Esa es mi mujer! ¡Que hagan lo que tengan que hacer para que se quede!" (That's my wife! They should do whatever they can to keep her here!) The doctor said she would leave them to discuss the matter. Don Dario prevailed quickly. His sons recognized and respected his wishes.

Once the decision was made, he told Don Dario that he would stay at the hospital and head back to New Jersey on the first train out that morning, in case something else came up. It was close to 1 a.m. The sterile and chilly waiting rooms were no place to sleep, but he would have to make do.

As he came in and out of sleep, his mind simmered on the thought that Doña Xiomara was coming back to a body and a life she would not recognize. At least she still recognized him, Don Dario, and most other relatives who visited, and her mind was often lucid, though she talked about trips (to Duvergé) that had never happened, visits of relatives who brought her arepa (cornbread) to Oakwood, and exaggerated statements about how often Don Dario visited.

His initial reaction to Don Dario's decision was to tell himself that his father was not thinking of what was best for Doña Xiomara. She was a late victim of the Great Recession, laid off work two years after the worst of the layoffs began. For a minute, he thought her job would survive, but it didn't. She never found another job because Don Dario kept objecting to the opportunities that came up, including one that her oldest son secured for her to become an elderly white woman's home-care aide.

What an irony: Doña Xiomara had rejected one of the last chances she had to keep structure in her daily life. This rejection set in motion the processes that led to her needing a home attendant. His mother had overstructured her work life to make sure she did not have time to dwell on what was wrong with it, but once unemployed and isolated in her house, she grew depressed, deteriorated emotionally, and had a meltdown. He was poor with phone calls, and there was little they talked about, being that Doña Xiomara was generally shy and had a hard time sustaining conversation. But he remembers her calling and leaving messages that sounded like verbal telegrams—for example, "Querido Carlos: Llámame cuando puedas. Te quiero mucho, tu mamá" (Dear Carlos: Call me when you can. I love you very much. Your mother). Despite the bipolar disorder in his family, Doña Xiomara was stable most of her life. The family recounted a distant episode in her youth, a breakdown that had no sequels in more than three decades. Nobody was prepared for what unfolded on the day it stopped to matter to her whether they made coffee or not, when she began to refuse to step out of her own house, when she either refused to take baths or stayed in the bath for long stretches to convince everyone that she was bathing. It all changed the day she told her husband at 9 p.m. that Don Dario needed to take her to the police station. She had been watching too many of the commercials about owing money to the IRS, and it had gotten into her head that she had defrauded the government. After Don Dario called him crying, saying that he did not know what to do with her, they decided to have her committed. Her life was never the same.

His mother was the stabilizing force in the family (both immediate and extended). All family members had issues, but not Xiomara. Xiomara was steady as a rock: she married Dario, her anchor no matter how crazy he ever got, and irrespective of the fact that they spent their whole marriage hiding pennies from each other. He was her man and (from what her son could surmise) the only one she ever had.

Esa es su mujer (She was his woman). Is this a claim of patriarchal possession, or could it be loyalty? If Doña Xiomara were in the same position, she would do the exact same thing for him. She had never said it with words, but the son was certain of this.

Don Dario's decision: to bring her back so she could be put right back into Oakwood? The father didn't even live with her anymore, as he (the oldest) had to take her away from her husband once Doña Xiomara became incontinent, after years of calls to emergency to take her away after she had mental breakdowns, a stroke, and falls (from years of neglect and medication mismanagement).

The story was a mess all around, to the point where the son almost reached a breaking point as he weathered calls from relatives he knew and from those he wouldn't recognize walking down the street, working his guilt, pressuring him to abandon his life and priorities and head to Philadelphia to become a parent to his own parents. One aunt had the audacity to leave him a phone message reminding him that Xiomara and Dario, "los que te parieron" (the ones who birthed you), needed him to come to Philadelphia as "a resolver," to figure things out.

Guilt turned him into a child in front of the mirror, shedding tears for the mother who no longer held his arms from behind as he manipulated his extremities.[14] Her body was still here, and her heart continued to beat, but much of Doña Xiomara was gone.

Why are theorists of the psyche obsessed with childhood but neglectful of the mother, the aging parent, the single mom or dad, and the bodies that grow without parents, mirrors, homes, or land? How about theorizing the woman, the man, the abuela, the tía (holding the child and having chores and a job), who have to deal with that bundle of joy until Chucky comes out; whose body and mind age? Can we talk about the psychic state of middle age or the fact that dementia feels like death to the ones grappling with the devastation of disappeared memories, of elusive lucidity?

How to think about the remains, about what remains of the body?

His choices had torn him from them; they eventually put him in a position of being the one son able to accompany the parents, help them get their affairs in order, advocate for them, do research, figure out policies, and throw carefully administered "shit fits" at the right times and in front of the right people. Like the returning John Jones in W. E. B. Du Bois's "Of the Coming of John," who eventually comes to "notice . . . now the oppression that had not seemed oppression before," he could recognize the structures within which he made choices.[15] He also understood well enough the workings of white supremacy in institutions to know that nothing was more effective than learning to "bring it like a white woman."[16] Whenever he was angry at a show of inaction or ineptitude by people who should know better, he crafted his phrases with just the right combination of affective neutrality, professionalism, and passive aggression. This often worked, because any hint of the chancletas y rolos of Etelvina la vecina, the barrio mama whom he could also channel, would mean that his questions would be ignored.

He struggled to connect emotionally with his parents and brothers, unsure of when his own heart left his parents' home. Did the lock and key on his bedroom door inaugurate it all? When did he introject the theft of his life from theirs and make that part of his corporeal schemata?

He never left. He just could not recognize his heart in their company. Still, he had also introjected a fierce love for them, a love modeled by his parents every day of his life, from the moment he awoke and was pushed into the bathroom to brush his teeth until Doña Xiomara came to pray the Padre Nuestro as she put them to bed at night. This love was bigger than the crater he thought separated him from the family of his birth. A working-class black kid like him held on to a lesson or two about love as work, love as endless and boundless loyalty.

Her heartbeat came back. After getting up from the waiting room and making another short walk just to see whether he had missed another spot that was comfortable for sleep, he returned to the chair. Don Dario was not the perfect husband, but he fought for the life of his wife—for whatever of it there was left.

He remembers one visit with Doña Xiomara, when the nursing home was still new to her, and they sat down in the lounge where the elder residents met with their visitors. She sat in her wheelchair—a metallic contraption that had become part of her body since she broke her hip and began to walk with a permanent limp. They tried to catch up. He mentioned Alfredo's mother, a miracle of lucidity and sass at eighty-seven. Doña Xiomara may have asked him about one person or another, and he had called Edwin to make sure he had a chance to talk to her, as well. He must have run out of things to say or ask, and his ability to fill up space with words fell flat before his mother's customary brevity.

As they faced each other, Doña Xiomara suddenly looked pained. Her pale skin turned red, and she began to cry, inconsolably. Nothing could disarm him more than his mother's open expression of pain. He hugged her. Back then, he still subscribed to the theory of his aunts and uncles—that her mental breakdown resulted from having witnessed a traumatic scene propitiated by Don Dario. The most awful ending to the life of a woman who had done everything right, paying with the loss of her mind the price for becoming the submissive wife without the courage to dump Dario. Too telenovela, yes. He kept on dismissing that whole plotline in his head, but upon witnessing his mother's tears—maybe they were right? Was she finally crumbling, ready to spill out the secret of her mental demise?

"Mami, ¿tienes algo que decirme?" (Do you have something to say?) He had asked her this many times, praying for a breakthrough moment when Doña Xiomara would spill the truth of her life and help make sense of everything.

Again, she did not reply.

As her son hugged her, Doña Xiomara shook, almost convulsing, her body turning to a vibrating mass in his arms. He asked her again, holding on until the tide shifted and the crying receded. He pulled away from her and looked again at his mother's face; her eyes were puffy but dry, as if the moment that occurred seconds ago had not occurred at all.

"Mami, ¿qué fue eso?" (What was that?) he asked. She did not explain. She stared blankly. A smile, a few more words, or a gesture to reassure him that she was back. They parted. He consulted with the staff at Oakwood; this behavior was consistent with dementia.

Doña Xiomara's mood shifts had settled into disjointed affects and juxtaposed recollections, coursing through her like passing clouds, making a fuss or making her laugh and then moving along. The remains of her mind were her truth, and Don Dario wanted this woman back.

He left the hospital and realized he was within walking distance of the North Philadelphia regional rail train stop, in the thick of urban dilapidation and despair next door to the gentrified renewals of Temple University. While picking up dark roast coffee before getting on the train he checked in with himself: he was in one piece, and Mami was stable. He boarded the train taking him to the home and family he had created.

deracinate, *v.*

    transitive. To pluck or tear up by the roots; to uproot, eradicate, exterminate. *literal* and *figurative.*[17]

Religious praxis (e.g., consultation, ritual) in Santería/Lucumí cannot proceed without homage to the ancestors, followed by the request to the deity Eleggúa to allow passage. He is the guardian of the pathways, the first deity to bless the journey and receive sacrifice, and the holder of the key to access all divine energies. Whereas the previous chapter paid respect to the ancestors by identifying and describing the landscapes traversed by a queer child, this chapter has mapped the conditions for immigrant success, upward mobility, and incorporation into the "US academy." This tryptic "bridge of words" highlights the relentlessness of socialization and its effects on subject formation by deracination. Tearing, uprooting, and eradication shape the subject formations and relationalities mapped out here. Whereas heteronormative masculinity is central to one moment in the narrative, constructions of the bourgeois intellectual of color are central to the other. These surface formations come to be introjected and epidermalized by the subject, the bleach that toxifies but cannot destroy whatever it seeks to "whiten" and the "being somebody" that is needed to fill the hole. Other "tearings" are in progress, as well, as brothers and parents wrestle with conditions and decisions that define their trajectories, or the mental stability that transforms life and relationship. Chapters 1 and 2 also insist on the formative role of blackness and black people in lending apparent yet transitive stability and clarity to subject formation, even if the role of these referents is to become one's "shadow beast" (Anzaldúa) or, better yet, the "black (w)hole" (Hammonds).

I hold these writings before you not to ask you to put yourself on these paths. Rather, I ask you to walk with these voices and narrators as they face the contradictions, blind spots, complicities, and dishonesties that condition success, with one's back turned to the black, the queer, the poor, and the femme. Chapters 1 and 2 both dramatize the costs and rewards of keeping blackness and black people at bay. That "distancing" may exile one from oneself or keep oneself from seeing how much of a life is livened through the currents circulating through disparate nodes. This rasanblaj refuses to compartmentalize expressively the hot mess of a life. The next chapters stage, through narrative and theoretical means, how the path toward a faggotology supports thinking and living blackness differently, which means living differently altogether. Hugging another mother offered me the first glimpse of the infinite grace in Olodumare—that black (w)hole that guided me even when I turned my gaze away. Through the hand of Oshún, I faced it and touched it.

As Jacqui Alexander invokes it, mojuba is memory unlocked, expansive, and energizing. It sutures disparate moments into an expansive circuit; an encounter with one's shadow; countries in geography, in memory, and in living. This mojuba turns microscopic histories outward in the service of something more expansive than one life.

Experiencing the Evidence

THIS NODE IN OUR CIRCUIT MOVES READERS ACROSS NARRATED
ENCOUNTERS WITH THE INEFFABLE THAT SEAM THE SENSORIAL TO
THE INTUITIVE, TO THE EROTIC, AND TO THE EMPIRICAL. It claims a
knowing, a conocimiento, that recognizes our whole bodies as instruments
for an expanded apprehension of the world. This is the opaque wisdom of
the ancestras and transcestras, the joining of street, body-mind cunning of those
walking at the edges of what can be known. Rigoberta Menchú put it best: "Sigo
ocultando mi identidad como indígena. Sigo ocultando lo que yo considero que
nadie sabe, ni siquiera un antropólogo, ni un intelectual, por más que tenga
muchos libros, no saben distinguir todos nuestros secretos" (I continue to hide
my indigenous identity. I continue to hide that which I think nobody should
know, not even an anthropologist or an intellectual. Even if they have written
a lot of books, they still don't know how to tell apart our secrets).[1] As we build
structures that support faggotology, as an otherwise morphology for being and
knowing the divine, what I call "experiencing the evidence" is a key task before us.

"*Experiencing the evidence*" inverts phrasing used in a feminist theme and
recognizes our bodies' capacity to apprehend ruptures that reveal sedimented
histories in daily life.[2] Experiencing the evidence suggests that there is more to
the world than what positivistic empiricisms offer. A faggotology repurposes
the projects, technologies, and tools of the master's house to do something other

than his bidding. Like Caliban, we use the old man's language to curse at him as our words also allow a touch of the divine in the grooves of our freedom.

After the three anecdotes, this chapter offers a reflection on the relationship between intuition and knowledge. I then interrogate Joan Scott's critique of "the evidence of experience." Scott's argument challenges naïve positivism in historical writing and illustrates the racial projects of poststructuralism. Making feminism white is not Scott's intention, but it is part of how the essay gets mobilized in the spaces where I have swished my way into being a feminist queer black man. I am interested in anatomizing and mapping these projects as they construct and support the position of "critic" and "theorist," produced in and through rhetorical movement through the erotic body wor(l)ds of the black gay male literary artist Samuel Delany while disavowing the feminist theorist's locus of enunciation.[3] The chapter closes via return to the narrated world of Delany, the black gay male fabulist whose memoryscapes prompt what Scott objects to in historical writing. A return to the erotics of the visceral, the sensorial, and the evocative through Delany's notion of kinesthetic saturation propels a vision of the body as instrument for a more capacious apprehension of the world.

Greeting Oshún

The year is 2013. It is the beginning of a Transnational Black Feminist Retreat in Santo Domingo, bringing together academics and activists from the Dominican Republic, Haiti, and North America to interact, reflect, and learn from one another's work.

The inaugural ceremony takes place at the Ilé de Abbebe Oshún, a Yoruba worship house in Santo Domingo. After greeting us, the Cuban mother of the house talks to us about her house and the importance of Yoruba traditions in supporting everyday people and social justice workers in the Dominican Republic. Before we go in, we are instructed to cleanse at the foot of the tree that presides over the backyard. Some members of the retreat group self-identify as initiated or as familiar with these traditions. They face the tree, bend over, and cleanse with perfumed water, herbs, and flowers. Hands move in a choreography brushing through the head; butterflies hovering on necks, trunks, thighs, backs. Shaking bracelets against wrists, clicking away, something felt around the neck, in the lower back. Some hands shake with force, and we hear the snap of forces moving through the tips of fingers and nails. Tap. Tap clip. Tap.

I see repeat performances of this, somewhere between taking a bath, scrubbing bodies with clothes on, and dancing in front of strangers.

I feel nervous about doing something I have never done before, in front of strangers. Several scenes of knowledge I am supposed to have gather around me: the baseball bat I should know how to swing as a little Dominican kid; the dancing of merengue before my incredulous and judgmental cousins, aunts, and uncles; the proper way to carry the body of the man I am supposed to be before the neighbors calling out "maricón."[4]

While the others cleanse and free up toxins and damaging forces collecting in the surfaces of their bodies, my fear grows around the force of the gazes shaping me before their eyes—the gaze of these others as the multiplying mirrors of this funhouse under the tree. Turning Rita Hayworth into my public scene of *The Lady from Shanghai*, I am dressed up in its plátano edition, having a momentary meltdown over the strai(gh)t-jackets of masculine deportment that anchor and hold me to the man I am not but long to be.[5]

When my turn comes, I imitate what the others have done. My hands and fingers gather perfumed water and flower petals, birds released to execute their handiwork, building a nest and dancing around the flower whose nectar juices they enjoy.

First the head, then the torso, then the feet.

No te partas.

I am relieved by a rehearsed lack of conviction as droplets and scents bounce off my head, the same gutting of feeling I learned to display dancing, the fake insouciance to avoid the slide of dancing form into mariconería.

Once the cleansing concludes, we walk into the house.

Inside, we sit near what is identified as an altar for Oshún, the river orisha and ruling energy of this house. We begin a conversation about Yoruba traditions, their connection to the African diaspora, and the importance of spirituality in the work we are doing this week. One of the Cuban godchildren of the house, a former Jesuit and a high school teacher in Santo Domingo, talks to us at length about his experience, and he addresses questions about multiply/complex-gendered and multiply/complex-sexed individuals in these traditions. He is dressed in white.

Few questions are being asked. Or maybe many questions are being asked and I don't remember.

It's a blur.

The mother of the house explains that we will move into an individual greeting of Oshún. This is optional. Those who opt out of the greeting are welcome to go back into the yard and wait for everyone else to finish so we can have dinner and continue the discussion afterward.

Silence and conversation follow as people get up and make a line facing the corridor leading to the altar. Thinking I am one of several people who would opt out and find ourselves in the yard, I step out, walking back to the tree.

Nobody else comes out of the house.

I am alone.

I simmer in perplexity for a few beats until a slender woman dressed in white walks toward me. She speaks Spanish with an accent and identifies as a Russian immigrant goddaughter of the house. Her large green eyes look at me calmly. I notice that she stands closer to me than I am used to, as if we were friends, even though I don't think we have met.

"¿Pero es que usted no va a saludar a Oshún?" (Won't you say hello to Oshun?)

"No."

"¿Por qué no?"

I do not have an answer. "No sé." (I don't know.)

She stands there, searching for my trailing eyes. "¿Será por vergüenza?" (Could it be shame?)

I take in her suggestion. Vergüenza. Pero ¿vergüenza de qué? (shame of what?)

Then I am flooded with certainty: vergüenza is what I feel during the cleansing; vergüenza pushes me out of that house; vergüenza is about to deprive me of participating in this greeting. I knew not who Oshun was, but why not say "hi"?

"La primera vez que me dijeron que fuera a hablar con un árbol," she added, "pensé que era absurdo y ridículo. Pero fui y lo hice." (The first time someone told me to go talk to a tree, I thought that it was absurd, but I did it anyway.)

Would I let vergüenza, the clammy feel of the other's judging gaze on my actions, have its way with me?

I walked into the house. The ceremony had ended, but I still asked whether I could say hello to the Orisha. The iya, offering me a smile, guided me.

I was the boy at the altar, paying tribute to the goddess and, through it, dándome permiso de ser (giving myself license to be). For a change.

¡Yalodde Yeyé Kari!

Yellows and Greens

A few days after the retreat inauguration, one of the organizers mentioned to me that the godmother of the house was available for a registro. A registro is a reading, but that word in Spanish had me dive through paths of imaginary trenches, military searches, and bureaucratic offices where I paid someone to hustle my way to my birth certificate in Santo Domingo, or the gun searches that security officers carried out in my high school in Philadelphia. If spirits do this, too, which of the senses of registro was the right one?

Would I be interested in this?

Yes.

As I sat down on her couch and waited for madrina to prepare, I recalled my maternal grandmother, Rhina Celeste Báez Pimentel (ibaé). A woman of striking beauty and elegance throughout her life, Niní was the towering presence in my childhood, the lady whose hand I held as we walked from my house in barrio San Juan Bosco to my aunt's house in San Carlos. Our walks were rare but memorable: Niní's presence, grace, and beauty commanded everyone's notice, even though she spent most of her later years battling declining health and bipolar disorder.

As Niní's grandchildren, we were always around her. We watched behind or at the corner of doors as Niní read tarot cards to strangers, stealing a sip from a glass of water with a touch of lemon that she stashed in the fridge so the water would be cold, or trying to understand what she claimed she could see about people's future in the dry coffee stains of their cups. Or meeting and having private time with the older gentleman with the hat and courtly manner who visited her once or twice a week in San Carlos.

All these memories, and more, waved through me, triggered by the smell of rosewater the madrina put on as she walked by me preparing to do her reading.

We sat at her table. Someone was taking notes. Madrina prayed and manipulated cowry shells.

Oshún was asking for permission to speak to me.

I said yes.

I don't recall what else was said, but the world took on new colors beginning on the following day. I was overwhelmed; crying and feeling all my body tingle; my pores erupting at the sight of flowers, the sea, the world.

I had given permission to this force of the universe to speak to me directly. And she would not stop talking.

A part of me—a sober gaze removed from the intensity unfolding on the days following the registro—pointed out the absurdity of this sudden and unabashed submission to feeling.

But I was not turning away from this.

I thought I was going crazy or that I would have a yeyo (mental breakdown). In other words, either (1) I would be sent to a psychiatric ward; or (2) something consequential was happening. Coming from a family with a history of bipolar disorder, this was a question of consequence.

One of those mornings, inebriated with the glee that is making you roll your eyes, I went out walking extra early, and I was soon taken by the figure of a young man moving toward me. He was light-skinned and had a naturally athletic build, with narrow hips and the sculptured presence of a dancer. OK, so my description is turning purple, but that was what he looked like to me, even if "naturally athletic" sounds like shorthand in a Grindr ad. I was struck by his tight-fitting yellow shirt and bright grass-green jeans.

I pondered the combination of yellow and green for a few seconds, but then I cruised him, and he cruised me right back. I was not going to stand around and ogle at a twink (as Gustav von Aschenbach does with the Polish boy Tadzio in *Death in Venice*). Sorry, not in Santo Domingo. This was more Reinaldo Arenas than Thomas Mann. The cruising was blunt, direct—the way it had stopped being in New York City after gay men became engrossed by phones to cruise, our zeal for an impromptu fuck also gripped by informational capitalism. I kept walking and saw my Tadzio turn around and follow me to an open area with stone benches facing the Caribbean Sea. Maybe this was cliché, but it felt fresh that homoerotic contact did not always have to be mediated and surveilled by a phone or computer screen.

He walked toward me, sat nearby, and said hello. I said hello back.

What was he doing out this early? It could not have been later than 7:30 a.m. Upon closer inspection, he appeared to have been out all night. He said he had been thrown out of his parents' home; he was homeless and had no money.

I quickly added that I had no money, either. Then I kneeled again, perhaps thinking that starting to tie up my shoes was an adequate response to what could be a hustle for money; I found a piece of green stone jewelry and handed it to him. "Fantasía," as my mother would have called it—a green emerald stone in a child's play ring.

"Esto es para ti." (This is for you.)

Tadzio smiled and told me about his family. They were religious, and he did not live up to their expectations. As our conversation progressed, making clear that we were engaging in something different from talk before sex, I told the desirable stranger about loving himself and finding himself. I might even have said something about God not making mistakes.

We now realized my full transition from sugar daddy to cura. Tadzio asked why I said what I said to him. I responded directly: "Si nosotros los maricones no nos cuidamos y nos aconsejamos entre nosotros, nadie nos va a aconsejar" (If we faggots don't take care of each other and give each other advice, nobody else will). Or perhaps I said pájaro? I don't know what led me to think that I could use either of these words in conversation with this stranger. He did not use either word for himself. But I recall explicitly using one of these words. My comment brushed past him like the morning breeze.

He thanked me for the advice.

We both got up, and he asked whether I could give him my name to add me on Facebook. I told him I did not have an account.

That was true.

Holding Space

The final scene is another visit to the Ilé de Abbebe Oshún as inaugural activity in a one-week "Alternative Spring Break" titled "Witnessing Social Change" in the Dominican Republic in March 2014. This was the fourth time I facilitated these experiential learning trips, which exposed students to social justice causes and issues and were staged as exchanges with activists, organizers, and scholars in the Dominican Republic and Haiti. That year, we focused on spirituality.

Prior to the trip, we held an introductory meeting in New Brunswick. We discussed our focus on popular religious worship. We would not visit churches because we were interested in traditions not aligned with establishment Catholics or Evangelical Christians.[6] The delegation was made up of "1.5-generation" and second-generation students, all students of color and most Latinx. The group included one African American and two Haitian American students.

In preparation for our visit, the delegation went on a bus to buy flowers in Mercado Modelo, located behind what used to be a slave auction market in Avenida Mella in Santo Domingo.

Our bus—overflowing with sunflowers; white, red and pink roses; hibiscus; lobster claws; anthurium; bougainvillea; and other flowers—worked its way through rush-hour traffic.

Once we arrived and members of the Ile came out to greet us, we were instructed to deposit the flowers at a ditch carved around the tree in the backyard. There was a repository of seeds that would be later used for a cleansing before going into the house. One of my students, a US-born Puerto Rican woman with long curly hair, asked whether this was optional. I replied that students did not have to join in anything that felt uncomfortable to them. By this time, at least two or three of the students had not even come in beyond the entrance of the house. They stayed in the front of the house. I thought it best to continue with our plans, reminding students that they could step out of the proceedings.

Upon the conclusion of the cleansing prior to entering the house, one team member told me that a student was having a panic attack. I found the young Puerto Rican woman—the one who had asked whether participation in the ceremony was optional—in the street, crying and howling, while other students stared at her. One team member was able to work with her and the other students on processing their reactions to this house and to the day's activities. I asked a taxi driver to take them back to the delegation hostel.

When most of the students who stayed got back on the bus, I asked them to think carefully about the range of reactions among them and to think twice before passing judgment on their classmates. I wanted to avoid enabling a group reaction that could negatively impact the dynamics of the rest of the week.

Later, when I rode back in the taxi to check in on the students at the hostel, I found them playing dominoes and hanging out, as if nothing had happened. I sought the students who had been sent back, including the woman who puked. She said she was fine.

Kneading

The "scenes" that open this chapter describe relationalities with what cannot be fully known, though they can be sensed. To be sure, not all the intimacies are certain, clearly articulable for critical empirical analysis, or desirable. But that "something else" goads the senses, challenging us to fashion ways to account for the ineffable in the banal.

Bodies eccentric to normativity offer sites to trace capacities to experience the evidence. Their friction with the normal has life-or-death implications, and this combined urgency and ordinariness is instructive for a faggotology. What results from the banality, tediousness, and repetitiveness of such decision making? For the most part, ensuring one's consistency and success is necessary to get through the day. Over time, *getting through* produces the sedimentation of strategies for dealing with a social world that is antagonistic to one's subject form, lifeworld, and life-form.[7]

Getting through is lived and practiced while moving, in transit. This is locomotion as one swishes out to run the errand; risks the caress of the longing gaze held for too long on a stranger; or is arrested by the flash of one's kin "in the life" in a wink across the counter at the bodega, the retail store, or the barbershop. This barometer alerts the queer, the raro, the tortillera, and the loca that even in the age of gay marriage and homonormative visibility, "queer is not yet here."[8] We are not all safe, and even when we are, "the social" continues to be regulated in ways that are mostly nonresponsive to legal and policy reform. If we are lucky, public displays of faggotry will get something close to the title that the poet Essex Hemphill uses to describe his witnessing of black gay men having an argument with each other on a Washington, DC, bus: "Without Comment."[9] But the lisp and the swish, if freedom erupts through our scandalous bodies, will still deliver us the appellations Marlon Riggs captured so memorably in his *Tongues Untied*: "faggot," "punk."[10] They can still deliver us blows, violence, and death.

The ancestras thought this first; they thought of this capacity to sense map walk hostile worlds with faggotological implications. Gloria Anzaldúa characterized the capacity of the marginalized to see beyond the surface phenomena of normativity as *la facultad*. "Those who do not feel psychologically or physically safe in the world are more apt to develop this sense," Anzaldúa writes, explaining that la facultad is a skill required for the ostracized to survive.[11] "When we are up against the wall, when we have all sorts of oppressions coming at us, we are forced to develop this faculty so that we'll know when the next person is going to slap us or lock us away."[12] La facultad is a requirement for survival. However, there is a deeper dimension of it for Anzaldúa: "It is anything that breaks into one's everyday mode of perception, that causes a break in one's defenses and resistance, anything that takes one from one's habitual grounding, causes the depths to open up, causes a shift in perception. This shift in perception deepens the way we see concrete objects and people; the senses become so acute and piercing that we can see through things, view events in depth, a piercing that reaches the underworld."[13] Anzaldúa's description of la facultad draws attention to skills developed to get by a social that does not recognize the humanity of perverse queerness. Yet this is a capacity that can be developed by anyone whose familiar moorings are undone by displacement from "home" spaces, though Anzaldúa suggests that, for some of us, "home" is already a space of chronic peril.[14]

How do we account for that which cannot be known beyond the speculative? "How to consider the meaning of an experience not concrete evidence of which exists, and of which we can therefore claim no positive knowledge?" asks the cultural and literary critic Phillip Brian Harper.[15] *He* asks this question of sexuality and its imbrication in racial, class, gender and other formations; *I* ask this question of sex and the divine. In his essay "The Evidence of Felt Intuition: Minority Experience, Everyday Life, and Critical Speculative Knowledge," Harper explains that the multiply marginalized find themselves speculating on the import of the most routine social interactions. "Minority existence itself induces such speculative rumination," he writes, "because it continually renders even the most routine instances of social activity and personal interaction as possible cases of invidious social distinction or discriminatory treatment."[16] What Harper calls "speculative rumination" is a necessity for minoritized subjects, who have to lean on what he calls "the evidence of felt intuition"—knowledge that does not lend itself to positivistic empirical protocols but that nevertheless makes the difference between peril and safety, between life and death. Upon being approached by a man on a train, as Harper was in the vignette he offers in his essay, with an invitation to go play cards, the recipient of the offer must decide "on the fly" regarding the question being posed. Could it be just an invitation to play cards and nothing more? Could the body language of the stranger suggest that something else was in the offing? And what would that something else be? A quick tryst? Being baited and then victimized through robbery or a homophobic attack? How about the cross-racial dimension of the encounter and the white interlocutor's inability to allow the English spoken by Harper and the scholar's identification as a US-born black person to coexist without the suggestion that Harper "couldn't be black," that he must be foreign-born, and so on, just to validate Harper's attractiveness to his interlocutor? Harper points out that living and traversing the world as a minoritized person demands making decisions based on small pools of evidence. One must rely on knowledge that derives from how a situation "feels," how one reads the body language of one's interlocutor(s), and the potentiality for harm or pleasure (or neither) that derives from a given situation.

Some moments in the scenes that open this chapter appeal to the possibilities of a speculative knowledge. The initiated woman who mentioned being asked to talk to a tree also suggested that the tree responded to her. How might one discuss that in an academic setting? Soon after I opened my ears to Oshún, something or someone spoke to me with relentless force. The student who had the panic attack and the students who refused to enter the Yoruba house found their bodies implicated in reaction to ceremonies, in reaction to what was said or what they could feel. My claim is that conocimiento manifests not through the appeal to our minds but through its appeal to our bodies, to historicities that sediment in them and that we cannot articulate. Furthermore, we cannot articulate the "why" of our bodily responses because these historicities do not belong to us and are unintelligible to us, perhaps because they pass through our bodies to some of the things that might compel us irrespective of what our brains will (or will not) make of them. A faggotology can draw productively from traditions created and cultivated from the vantage point of the experience of having our bodies directly expose and negotiate the historicities of the banal.

I remember sitting in front of the divination priest charged with performing my *itá* ceremony after initiation—a ceremony in which each orisha "speaks" to the newly initiated priest through the cowry shells that have been ritually prepared. He looked me in the eye and said, "Esta religión fue hecha para ustedes" (This religion was made for people like you [plural]). This man met me that morning, and I assumed then that by making this comment, he was pointing to my gayness as a dimension of the person in front of him that he surmised through his divination, through comments by others, or by looking at me and seeing something index me as a homosexual. I was also a foreigner in that small farmhouse on the outskirts of Havana, but he did not mean that Santería was "made" for "tourists" like me. Or maybe he did? What might it mean to grow a spiritual tradition for people like me, from our fierce zeal to affirm the freak? We start with a rearticulation of projects of knowledge, inspired by the experiential archives that rely on the Cartesian divide. People living in and through the cracks in normativity must live through constant fear, must put their bodies on the line and learn by trial and error, and must also figure out ways to pass on that conocimiento to others.

Dawdling with Joan Scott

The joining of "experience" and "evidence" intentionally reminds me of Joan Scott's provocative and influential essay "The Evidence of Experience" (1991). It is considered a turning point in feminist writing for its insistence to "make the historian's mode of thinking an object of inquiry."[17] Scott recalls that the essay "embodied my growing impatience with my fellow social historians who assumed that experience was transparent . . . that there was no need to ask what counted as experience. . . . The point was to ask what kind of work they [historians] were doing, how they were establishing meaning, how some things and not others came to be included in the term."[18] Emerging out of a cohort of scholars associated with Princeton University's Institute for Advanced Study, this essay and Scott's *Gender and the Politics of History* (1988) accompany other career-making publications, such as Denise Riley's *Am I That Name? Feminism and the Category of Women in History* (1988) and Judith Butler's *Gender Trouble* (1990).[19]

Even though it is directed at the writing of social history, Scott routes her critique through literary memoir. She introduces her analysis of realist vision in narrative departing from a scene from Samuel Delany's autobiographical *The Motion of Light in Water*. Her examination of a bathhouse scene in Delany's epochal literary monument to the pre-AIDS gay male world of New York City is what Scott interprets, in her first take, as Delany's reliance on vision as transparency. "As I read it," she argues, "a metaphor of visibility as literal transparency is crucial to his project."[20] In light of Scott's leading question, about how one might write a history of the moment Delany narrates, this "transparent vision" is a central problem for the feminist theorist.

Scott elaborates her analysis of Delany and critique of foundationalist historians through a pairing of the "visual" and the "visceral," which appears twice in the essay and does not distinguish among the genres of writing she engages. The first time, this pairing illustrates a causal relationship in Delany's memoir: "Seeing is the origin of knowing. Writing is reproduction, transmission—the communication of knowledge gained through (visual, visceral) experience."[21] The second time, the pairing comes up in a phrasing in which the slippage is noted, in a parenthetical aside, as a problem for feminist historians. At this point, Judith Newton is the target of critique, illustrating Scott's analogical tumble between memoir and historical writing: "In [Newton's] work the relationship between thought and experience is represented as transparent (the visual metaphor combines with the visceral) and so is directly accessible."[22] Scott's slope of visual into visceral, and vice versa, has the effect of flattening (or folding) distinctions between the two affective registers—as if the connection of vision to the rest of the sensorium had no mediation through the other senses, or as if "gathering information" or "seeing oneself" were all one searched for in writing about the past. Furthermore, the punctuation in Scott is telling. The visual and visceral: in one moment, neighbors meet at the fence of a comma; in the other, the word *combines* allows an amalgamation of the two, as if they were two colors of paint thrown together.

Scott's critique in the first reading, directed at the "transparent vision" of historical foundationalism, neglects a consideration of what Delany is doing as *literature*. The theorist misses that creative writing works through sensory qualities. It might be descriptive, but it is evocative; it may dwell on what has been lived, but it is mediated by words and the workings of memory. It is constantive and performative. The truth being sought in Delany is not a positivistic historical one but, rather, one that documents as much as it transmits the exhilaration of uncovering the world he found in the bathhouses, with all their possibility for sex, relationality, and community. Perhaps what baffles is the excess that jumps off the page and that Scott's theorist interprets as an unmediated interpretation of vision with identification and experience. The philosopher J. L. Austin describes speech acts as having a twofold dimension: a constantive one that describes that to which the speech act points and a performative one that is what the speech act itself does as an utterance.[23] In Austinian terms, might Scott's theorist have missed the performative dimension of the constantive? Could it be that in describing the bathhouse and drawing conclusions from it about belonging, Delany mobilizes description to activate the senses of his readers to approximate the embodied eroticism and deep insight of that moment as a moment of knowledge? Could the "truth" of what Delany describes live not in the fidelity of the scene but, rather, in what it felt like to a young man like him? As our eyes glide through the words in his memoir, is Delany inviting us to move through and with his remembered body?

Scott's first take on Delany and foundationalist historians weaves together literature and historical analysis close to one another. Delany's writing may be "primary" archival material for historical analysis. However, Scott's take suggests that Delany's writing illustrates the pitfalls of foundationalist history. "The point of Delany's description, indeed of his entire book," she writes, "is to document the existence of those institutions in all their variety and multiplicity, to write about and to render historical what has hitherto been hidden from history."[24] Actually, there is way more going on in Delany, but Scott is interested only in the memoir to the degree that it supports the critic's disciplinary intervention.

What is at stake in Scott's essay is not the facticity of the historical as recounted by those who lived it but, rather, the frames used to render such experiences authoritative: "The evidence of experience then becomes evidence for the fact of difference, rather than a way of exploring how difference is established, how it operates, how and in what ways it constitutes subjects who see and act in the world."[25] A pivotal illustration that underscores Scott's case draws from the work of E. P. Thompson, the British activist historian perhaps best known for *The Making of the English Working Class* (1963).[26] "In Thompson's use of the term," Scott writes, "*experience* is the start of a process that culminates in the realization and articulation of social consciousness, in this case a common identity of class."[27] Shortly after this, Scott explains that the problem lies in that Thompson's treatment of experience as evidence obscures the interpretive dimension of historical writing:

> Thompson's own role in determining the salience of certain things and not
> others is never addressed. Although his author's voice intervenes powerfully
> with moral and ethical judgments about the situations he is recounting, the

presentation of experiences themselves is meant to secure their objective status. We forget that Thompson's history, like the accounts offered by political organizers in the nineteenth century of what mattered in workers' lives, is an interpretation, a selective ordering of information that through its use of originary categories and teleological accounts legitimizes a particular kind of politics (it becomes the only possible politics) and a particular way of doing history (as a reflection of what happened, the description of which is little influenced by the historian if, in this case, he has only the requisite moral vision that permits identification with the experiences of workers in the past).[28]

Here, Scott objects to a "God's view" writing praxis, a rhetorical sleight of hand that obscures the ordering, editing, and proffering of evidence to support interpretive views of a historical moment. This is what Denise Ferreira da Silva calls the "transparent I." That critique is valid, and it is one reason Scott's essay has been so pivotal for feminist theory and feminist history. However, Shari Stone-Mediatore points out that Scott's "strong poststructuralist position on experience highlights both the lessons and the limitations of an approach that reduces experience to an effect of discursive practices."[29] For more than two decades of living, teaching, and walking with this essay, I have sat uncomfortably with the theorist's rhetorical maneuvers. Although Scott's theorist critiques authors (e.g., historians such as Thompson) for their inability to engage the sites of their enunciation, this same critique can be leveled at her own effort. In other words, she critiques these texts and authors for not interrogating their own positionalities and for the way they organize, present, and rely on (or "essentialize") experience to bolster their arguments. However, Scott tells her readers little regarding the position from which she issues her defense of the theorist, and she does not interrogate these presuppositions. She advocates an antifoundationalist stance that is not self-reflexive of its site of enunciation but is clear about *not being implicated* in either black/gay male formations or working-class loci in its utterance. This, to my mind, is the work of a white feminist political stance, for Scott's positionality disappears in the performative work of constructing the theorist.

"White woman feminist political stance" indexes the complicity of some feminisms with white male privilege. This phrase situates rhetorical moves that produce authorial mastery through the disappearance of the locus of enunciation of the theorist/critic in each historical and political moment for specific ends in intellectual work. There were conditions shaping the discipline of history in which Scott constructed authority as a theorist. I appreciate that. However, her stance does identity work through its disavowal: the metaphorical bodies on the line are those of others to the transparent I of the theorist. The white feminist gaze (turned outward) scans through the life-worlds and life words of the black gay male memoirist. When she turns to her colleagues, she demands that they question and critique how they frame and interpret their findings, disavowing theirs as interpretations of evidence. This is fine and well, but the construction of Scott's authority and voice do not model what the feminist historian advocates. Instead, her body disappears.

Readers might object and argue that I seek recourse to the "personal," and that observation might have validity. Another objection (following the first line of thought) might be that Scott could not put her body on the line without losing legitimacy as a scholar. This second objection is a telling yet compelling reason to sustain the disembodied gaze. There is a rhetorical move to task others with performing self-reflexivity while not doing that yourself; this relies on complicity with the securing of the authority and legitimacy of the theorist, her transparent I. This disavowal of identity is the identity work of the white female theorist. Ernesto Martínez has critiqued Scott, highlighting the instrumental use to which artists of color have been put in her work, as well as in the work of other feminist theorists. "Knowledge claims, including the antirealist claims of queer theory," writes Martínez, "are based in traditions and practices that . . . take Europe, the West, and the unmarked categories of white existence as an unacknowledged starting point, dismissing as naïve or crude anything that departs from that familiar terrain. . . . The examples set by Butler, [Donna] Haraway, and Scott are illustrative, pointing to the propensity of certain theoretical projects to undermine the insights of writers of color, even as they proclaim a desire to think complexly alongside their work."[30] In other words, the identity work of whiteness, through the disavowal of its location, achieves for the white lady the unmarked legitimacy of the master.

I encountered the Scott essay when I began teaching in a women's and gender studies department, but the skepticism and challenge to "experience" that it advanced were familiar to me from my doctoral training at a time when academics (as well as emerging and established scholars of color) had begun to negotiate an emergent critique of experience. Scott's essay was part of my doctoral education. The essay was invested in dissing "identity politics" in New York City in the late 1990s while defending a hip version of it to support pushback against the white male critical assault on identity and epitaphs of the progressive left by self-appointed moirologists (e.g., Todd Gitlin). Mentors of mine were fighting with the older white "statesmen" on the left who were mourning that their unearned privileges no longer defined radicalism.

However, there was visible discomfort and aversion to positioning founded on identity. It was bizarre to be in classrooms where newly enfranchised and recently tenured feminists and queers held court for the dissing of identity. I sometimes still discover myself wearing a neoliberal white mask. Despite this push to diss identity, I could not forget my body. My mentors and classmates reminded me of the excited glee of the immigrant-kid-turned-Ivy-League-success-but-living-with-impostor-syndrome. He made it to Nueva York (but not as a drug dealer, as some of his people had). A radical white feminist mentor of mine once mused that I seemed too "perky" in graduate school because I did not have the jaded pose of most graduate students. This observation troubled me, because it cast as a problem a sunny disposition that drew from my working-class embrace of the privilege of attending graduate school in New York. She "rained on my parade," and I internalized a sense that there was something wrong with my joy.

Some of those discussions, in graduate seminars and public venues, cast *identity politics* as evidence of false consciousness and a capitulation to essentialism that was "problematic" for women-of-color feminisms. I was to avoid the *identity essentialisms* out there, though it would take a while for me to figure out what that meant, particularly given the value I placed on reflecting, jotting down, revisiting, listening, and taking in the city and communities that I straddled in daily life. I was trying to live in my body as a queer Latinx man in New York. Was I to become the disembodied "theorist" or "analyst," paying homage to women and queer-of-color feminisms while running away from the experiences that were central to those formations?

After I became an assistant professor, I heard a white female colleague extol the quality that Scott's essay had to "shake students out of their 'uncritical' position" toward their experiences. She discussed this at a faculty meeting, hinting that this was especially important for women of color walking into feminist classrooms for the first time. I suspected then that she was thinking about black women as they figured out our institution and their backgrounds while negotiating race and class position, race and class privilege and discrimination, and the racism of their white female peers and white feminist professors. Her argument was that Scott could be important in shaking students out of the sense that their personal experiences had a direct relationship to the "real" of social relations and that no critical reflection was needed. I have no quibble with this argument. Still, I have seen Scott's essay put to uses about which I am concerned. I am troubled by the disciplinary push to join the circle jerk of the transparent I, at moments when people like me grasp how we might pursue the "life of the mind" yet repeatedly hear that we must leave at the doors the bodies that are our sources of conocimiento.

The stance of Scott's theorist has been critiqued in feminist theory, as Linda Martin Alcoff (one of Scott's strongest interlocutors) points out:

> Let me return first to Scott's formulation of the task of theory. Convincingly, Scott notes the importance of recognizing the knower's stake in the production of knowledge, and she argues that we need to explore the relations between discourse, reality, and cognition. But the problem is that these questions cannot be effectively pursued given her account of experience as simply the end-point of explanation, and never an authoritative source for knowledge. What could it mean to say that we must examine "the situatedness of subjects to the knowledge they produce" other than to say that we must examine their identity and experience? But given Scott's account it is unclear how experience could stand as an explanatory variable in accounting for knowledge, since experience is only that which is constructed for the individual by macro systems of meanings.[31]

My take on Scott parallels what Alcoff describes: I am concerned with her focus on language. Is language enough? Scott asks us to pay attention to the linguistic mechanisms we mobilize to make experience intelligible. Still, what about that which stands outside, beyond, and more than systems of meanings and articulation? How can we write about that which we cannot see but can feel, sense, or intuit? How can we write about that which we cannot name?

Toward the end of "The Evidence of Experience," readers realize that they have spent much of the essay moving through a view of Delany that Scott appears not to condone. "The reading I offered of Delany at the beginning of this essay is an example of the kind of reading I want to avoid," she writes.[32] Returning to Delany's bathhouse scene through the literary critic Karen Swann, Scott sketches a view that is "closer to Delany's preoccupation with memory and the self in this autobiography."[33] Following this interpretive turn, Delany now "sees this event not as the discovery of truth . . . but as the substitution of one interpretation for another. Delany presents this substitution as a conversion experience, a clarifying moment, after which he sees (that is, understands) differently."[34] As she follows the trail of this interpretation, Scott echoes Swann in suggesting that Delany's appeal to the visible puts stress on its blurriness: "In this version of the story . . . political consciousness and power originate, not in a presumedly unmediated experience of presumedly real gay identities, but out of an apprehension of the moving, differencing properties of the representational medium—the motion of light in water."[35] Stone-Mediatore supports the view that Scott misreads Delany's take on experience. Because the memoirist underscores tensions in vision and narrative transparency, Stone-Mediatore submits that Delany does not naturalize experience: "Delany . . . agrees with poststructuralists that experience-oriented writing does not represent but, in fact, produces what it calls 'past experience' through creative discursive work; however, departing from poststructuralists, he also recognizes such writing to be rooted in lived experience—not because experience is self-evident but because the excesses and ambiguities of remembered experiences are indicative of existentially meaningful struggles, including conflicts between experience and discourse."[36] This turn at the end of Scott's essay is easy to miss, given how much time she devotes to an elaboration of the implications of her first take on Delany. Still, it makes space for a consideration of the theoretical work the memoirist himself does to illustrate how his apprehension of the lived and remembered world can be of value to different forms of inquiry.

Experiencing the Evidence of Being Chip

I sensed more than I understood, and I wanted to know more.[37]

> [The sense of] touch suggests that I touch something else and then process that information. But if we think about proprioception, where the body is constantly shifting its own sense of "being" where it is, as a whole, but also in parts, the "touch" sensation is more about the whole skin organ becoming aware of the air currents, air pressure and other subtle energies around it and on it. The sense of touch then becomes relational and, to whatever degree, phenomenological. . . . From my experience, as a performer in dance, my body has had the sense of enlargement, that it is now a part of a larger entity called the "stage" or "the theater." . . . Often we use auditory sensing to tell how big or how tall a space is, often with a subtle echolocation sense that bats have so much of. But I believe that the body senses space in other ways—through the skin and, in combination with sight, hearing, expanded proprioception, etc. Sometimes we even choose to use slightly higher anchor points offstage to make sure that the performance is acknowledging audiences in the upper seating, in balconies. . . . All of this comes to kinesthesia, which is like proprioception but is about the body's movements in space specifically (i.e., how one knows that the body IS moving in space and, to some degree, HOW it is moving in and through

space. Again, this sense is probably combinatory with proprioception, haptic, touch, audition, and also sight, but notably sight comes last in this hierarchy, for me.[38]

A return to Delany's word body helps close this chapter by elucidating the stakes of his intellectual and expressive project, which grasps the limitations of the visible and a distrust of truths held captive by normativity. Together with Scott's advice to interrogate the categories, grids of intelligibility, and historicity shaping the making of experience, I draw out the faggotological implications of "experiencing the evidence" by extrapolating from Delany's appeal to kinesthesia. I suggest that (in connection with la facultad, felt intuition, and other modalities of conocimiento) kinesthesia offers paths toward the broader agenda of this book that embrace fleshy and embodied knowing, consistent with queer-of-color praxis and Afro-Caribbean religiosity.

Kinesthesis is defined as "the sense of muscular effort that accompanies a voluntary motion of the body. Also, the sense or faculty by which such sensations are perceived."[39] I first encountered the word through a collaboration with my colleague Jeff Friedman, a professor, choreographer, and theorist of dance. We were teaching a Body Languages seminar. On our first day of class, the two of us and the students had begun to work with bodily movement as we sought to get the students to connect the verbal articulation and the expressive work of the body. As we moved (following Jeff's guidance), he told us that kinesthesia is our sixth sense. I find tremendous value in thinking of kinesthesis (following Friedman's suggestion), as well as the comment that opens this last section. The kinesthetic has important valence in Delany's engagement with lived experience, with the path of spirit and soul work described in the opening chronicles of this chapter, and in the faggotology this book performs and describes.

To begin, let's move through Delany's depiction of the scene at the bathhouse:

> Then I stepped across the dark hall, in which a tired attendant sat on a stool, to enter the upstairs dorm.
>
> It was lit only in blue, the distant bulbs appearing to have red centers.
>
> In the gym-sized room were sixteen rows of beds, four to a rank or sixty-four altogether. I couldn't see any of the beds themselves, though, because there were three times that many people (perhaps 125) in the room. Perhaps a dozen of them were standing. The rest were an undulating mass of naked, male bodies, spread wall to wall.
>
> My first response was a kind of heart-thudding astonishment, close to fear.

I have written of a space at certain libidinal saturation before. That was not what frightened me. Rather the saturation was not only kinesthetic but visible. You could see what was going on throughout the dorm.

The only time I'd come close to feeling the fear before was once, one night, when I had been approaching the trucks, and a sudden group of policemen, up half a block, had marched across the street, blowing their whistles.

It had been some kind of raid. What frightened was, oddly, not the raid itself, but rather the sheer number of men who suddenly began to appear, most of them running, here and there from between the vans.[40]

"Not only kinesthetic but visible."

Delany refers to (1) his movement through this space; (2) what he can see and surmise near and far; and (3) his reactions. Yet when he notes his fear, Delany leans on the notion that his "saturation was not only kinesthetic but visible." This moment went beyond the perception of the proximity of fellow travelers in perversion. "You could see what was going on throughout the dorm."

If vision offers no transparent or reliable correspondence to the real of experience, if it arrives last, as Friedman explains, then why does Scott center a visible that we understand we cannot trust? If the kinesthetic saturation to which the memoirist alludes is more pervasive on its own than it is in conjunction with visibility, if the moment of "heart-thudding astonishment" is provoked by this aggregation of kinesthetic and sensorial knowing, then why focus on the visible instead of kinesthesia?

Delany explains what provoked his reaction: "What the exodus from the trucks made graphically clear, what the orgy at the baths pictured with frightening range and intensity, was a fact that flew in the face of that whole fifties image [of homosexuality as a 'solitary perversion']."[41] Though the moments of encounter with authority might present confrontations with the finitude of sexual dissent in the historical moment Delany describes, his emphasis leans on the potential infinity of perversions. This might be what Scott describes as a change in Delany's individual interpretation of the historical transitions from the perception of homosexuality as an isolated perversion rather than an infinite collective. However, Delany's descriptions suggest awareness, intuitions, and inchoate socialities based on pools of knowledge unavailable through verbal articulations or through visibility. To lean on Friedman's comments to me regarding kinesthesia, "sight comes last in this hierarchy." Delany writes,

The myth said we, as isolated perverts, were only beings of desire, manifestations of the subject (yes, gone awry, turned from its true object, but, for all that, even more purely subjective).

But what this experience [the baths, the raids] said was that there was a population—not of individual homosexuals, some of whom now and then encountered, or that those encounters could be human and fulfilling in their way—not of hundreds, not of thousands, but rather of millions of gay men, and that history had, actively and already, created for us whole galleries of institutions, good and bad, to accommodate our sex.[42]

Delany pays attention to the "turn" in his thinking as it grasps the historical: what appears to be the perversion of radically atomized individuals turns out to be larger than one; it is part of the infinite many. This might be a change in interpretation of Delany's historical moment (as Swann suggests via Scott), but I hold on to Swann's view of it as a conversion experience, following which "he sees [i.e., understands] differently."

The conjunction of kinesthesia and the visible points to the limit of an enlarged sense of erotic sexual possibility. Delany "gets" the limits of vision. This hint of larger connectivity produces a visceral reaction in Delany's narrator, coupling fear with saturation—a saturation that can be a jarring, confounding, filling. A conocimiento is possible within that sudden and surprising sense of infinitude: a "sensing" that tingles, incites, and excites; that knows it cannot fully know. Whereas Delany's memoir is partly an exploration of the workings and traps of memory, *The Motion of Light in Water* is also a mapping (of what I am calling) to "experience the evidence" as a mechanism of knowledge transfer—a way for "faggots" who were to be recognizable to the faggots who are or who will be. In his ability to capture an expanded access to the sensorial through language unafraid of the erotic, Delany's narrator entreats readers to walk through narrative bodies to produce and incite leaps of the readers' imaginative, sensorial capacities to grasp the historical.

Delany discusses his (libidinal) saturation that "was not only kinesthetic but visible." I want to stay with the kinesthetic and close (by way of allusion) to the dancer, anthropologist, and practitioner-theorist Yvonne Daniel as she describes a Yoruba dance ritual in Havana in 1987. This moment in ritual dance is one of several that Daniel describes in her body ethnography of Cuban Yoruba in dialogue with Haitian Vodou and Bahian Brazilian Candomblé:

Within each set of chants [to the orichas], there was distinct tempo acceleration from slow to faster speeds. The organization of time within each set seemed to introduce and then reinforce a characteristic mood through a series of gestures that identified the elements associated with an oricha. . . . As the pace quickened, an intensification of both the quality of movement and the amalgam of mythic symbols in gesture and sung lyrics deepened the physical, mental, emotional, and spiritual atmosphere toward a composite experience. The kinesthetic accumulation, both within each individual dancer and among the similar energies of other community members in the shared space and at the same time, yielded a body experience for performing participants. What resulted was a set, a repeated cycle of hypnotic, rhythmic, melodic, and kinesthetic dynamics for the distinctive temperament of each oricha. Each oricha's section, while a musical and danced entity within itself, was part of an accumulating, larger event.[43]

Daniel describes a circuitry of sounds and movements to be heard and witnessed through ears and eyes attuned to the imagination, and as she ties her observations of "kinesthetic accumulation" and "body experience for performing participants" to the power that her images and words, she affords a sense of experience. That proximity of performing bodies to symbols and histories codified in lyrics and gestures cannot be described in ethnography, but it can be activated through allusion to the performative, writing that energizes circuits of codes. This performative work in Daniel brings us back to Delany's bathhouse with bodies eager to touch/fuck/smell/lick/feel, as our body-minds become greedy for that which pricks, that which opens pores desiring to mount/ravish/open; yes-no-yes-no-yes. There is a hunger to know more of what we can't know but must know because it is hot and makes us hot.

A faggotology points to the conjunction of conocimiento and desire as an enlarged sense of the queer infinite. It supports the view that queers may be exiled from traditional religions, but many of us find the goddess precisely in those places of kinesthetic saturation shunned by religious authorities, reading theory and eating ass or drinking cum and piss through a glory hole. Let us rethink the edifice of imagining who and what we are in the universe based on those moments when we experience closest contact with truths in pleasure of relation, as funked up as it might be.

Je demande qu'on me considère à partir de mon Désir. Je ne suis pas seulement ici-maintenant, enfermé dans la choséité. Je suis pour ailleurs et pour autre chose.

FRANTZ FANON, *PEAU NOIR, MASQUES BLANCS*

I ask that I be taken into consideration on the basis of my desire. I am not only here-now, locked in thinghood. I desire somewhere else and something else.

FRANTZ FANON, *BLACK SKINS, WHITE MASKS*

Dos Puentes, Tránsitos

PART II

Loving Stones

A Transnational Patakí

CHAPTER 3 DESCRIBED EXPERIENCING THE EVIDENCE AS AN EXPANSION OF OUR EPISTEMO-LOGICAL CAPACITIES, A KINESTHETIC SENSING THAT GRASPS ITS LIMITS AS OPENINGS. This chapter centers two voids to draw political and spiritual lessons from the edges of what can be known. The late Argentine philosopher María Lugones calls this "pilgrimage": "different levels of liberatory work in company forged through the practice of *tantear* [exploring someone's inclinations, as well as putting one's hand in front of oneself as one is walking in the dark] for meaning, for the limits of possibility; putting our hands to our ears to hear better, to hear the meaning in the enclosures and openings of our praxis."[1]

How do we touch the sacred (w)hole—the way it engulfs, the way it energizes, the way it touches, the way it brushes? Afro-Caribbean traditions and liberation theologies (especially womanist and mujerista) afford us access to modalities of being and of practicing the spiritual that help us reimagine how to live the sacred. "Our knowledge is conjectural because to know it is not to copy or reflect reality but rather

The Divine knits together the quotidian in a way that compels attunement to its vagaries, making this the very process through which we come to know its existence. It is, therefore, the same process through which we come to know ourselves.

M. JACQUI ALEXANDER, *PEDAGOGIES OF CROSSING*

to interpret in a creative way those relations, structures, and processes that are elements of what is called reality."[2] We desire Fanon's "somewhere else and something else." Still, M. Jacqui Alexander reminds us that "the central understanding within an epistemology of the Sacred . . . is that living matter . . . links us to each other, making that which is individual simultaneously collective."[3] We perform the tanteo in relation: in Afro-Caribbean and other Afro-Atlantic traditions there is no "book" you consult, no privatizing of the spiritual path. Transfers of knowledge require accompaniment, mentorship, and the labor of elders in alerting one to the nuances of form, work, and how to engage spirit. Furthermore, accessing that "living matter" of sacred praxis—the glue that sediments collectivities—demands building and sustaining community and coalition.

The following analysis, which centers an examination of otases (ritual stones), describes processes, exchanges, collectivities, and contradictions held by sacred objects. What objects are these, and what do we learn from a circuitry that includes their absence? What remains as they retreat from immediate view? Music teachers and composers say that silences are an active part of a score and its performance. The more insightful of them, in fact, would underscore that we play and listen to silence *as* sound. The travel narratives that follow demand that we attend to the implications of the absences of sacred stones and (to a lesser extent) passports to intelligibility and mobility, putting pressure on the faggotological by underscoring the enmeshment of the human in the circuitry of sacred objects. These silences demand grappling with complicated dynamics of inequality, privilege, power, and legibility. Following the two anecdotes in this chapter, I consider sacred stones and ritual work in relations of exchange. Through a dialogue between Karl Marx and his contemporary Black Atlantic interlocutors J. Lorand Matory and M. Jacqui Alexander, I argue that the absence of ritual artifacts stress, hold, and valorize the intentionalities and entangled relations of exchange that energize them. Anatomizing this messiness gets at how Santería and other Afro-Atlantic traditions hold and negotiate the contradictions of the sacred in black diasporic life.

Pataki

Since I began traveling to Havana for research and religious tourism, my madrina hosted misas espirituales with a "long-range" medium.[4] Admittedly, this characterization has a problematic racial valence, as if moving through the "spiritscapes" of one's ancestors were an excursion into the African wild on the National Geographic channel. These events confirmed and deepened misas that were carried out in Santo Domingo while introducing me to an extended religious family. Their main objective was to identify and cultivate a relationship with egun in my cuadro spiritual—an assemblage of energies and presences that are connected to me; some of them could be deceased relatives, historical figures, archetypal figures without specific names, slave spirits, and so on. The misas were also meant to help cultivate my relationship with my main muerto, understood to be an ancestor entrusted to care for, protect, support, critique, and guide me.[5]

I developed a special fondness for this long-range medium. She led events that held up to twelve people in small rooms for two to five hours of divination, singing, praying, and possession by her guiding muerto—a ribald male slave who entered her body to give advice, crack jokes, drink, dance, smoke tobacco, ask questions, and bless the audience. The medium's body demonstrated who was present through her movement, contortions, and change in gait and posture. This muerto could drink up to two bottles of rum, go through all the tobacco, and channel messages to those present, treat those assembled to wave after wave of raucous and bawdy commentary, make one person cry, and make another laugh.

While the medium and I sat together catching up as everyone else prepared the adjoining room, she shared that one of her personal rituals at the end of each year was to wash and clean the otases and their receptacles. Her eyes, which until then held mine, traveled elsewhere from the conversation we were having. As her expression turned wistful, she declared, "Uno llega a encariñarse mucho con sus piedritas" (You come to feel a lot of affection for your little stones).

I kept a mental note of that marginalia because of the emotions, devotion, and love it communicated. Loving your stones was not something given to me; it was something to be cultivated. *Cariño*—a word that brings together "care" with "affection" and "caress"—suggests an embodied and warm expression of love; you give cariño when you caress a beloved object. This in an intimate practice of the divine. Given the expectation of "handling" one's orishas and ancestors in daily life, practitioners inhabit their bodies differently and develop new orientations for their touch, handling otases with water, tobacco, rum, cocoa butter, animal blood, and more. Tactility becomes part of a sensorial, embodied archive recruited to pray, sing, and dance. Touching the stones, imbibing sentience to what appears to be inert matter: finger the ineffable.

There was an insistence on forms, process, and work during my two-year-long path to initiation, as well as during and after the celebrations, ceremonies, rituals, cleansings, and offerings carried out by me or on my behalf in New

Jersey, Havana, and Santo Domingo. "¡En esta religión se trabaja!" (One works a lot in this religion!) My iya made this affirmation several times. The largest illustration of the work done within religious families was the initiation, which involved priests, cooks, musicians, and other religious workers for seven days. The assemblage of habits, dietary restrictions, relationalities, and other elements implicated in one's movement from outsider to initiated priest was solidified through consecration of the otases themselves.

Because priests are initiated into the worship of their head santo, stones consecrated to this deity are important in a person's daily life. While adjusting to the rigors of the first three months of initiation—a period during which I was not to handle them at all—I also consulted my elders regarding how to befriend the stones. I thought that traveling with them would be a way to befriend them.

Several months after the conclusion of my initiation and almost halfway through my year of iyaworaje, I traveled with the otases to an academic workshop in Santa Cruz, California. I looked forward to exploring what sense of the divine I could find in attention to the piedritas. In between workshop sessions, I returned to my room and (despite being unsure what to do) devoted time to the otases. Because conference attendees were staying at a hotel near a beach in Santa Cruz, on several mornings the sounds of seals, sea lions, and seagulls and the quality of the light that came into my beachfront room suggested that perhaps I would get there some day.

Before flying to the West Coast for this workshop, my New York State identification (ID) card expired, so I took my US passport. A colleague volunteered to drive us back to San Francisco Airport in a rental car, though we first went with colleagues that morning to a "bourgie brunch." We left our bags in the back seat and our luggage in the trunk, had brunch, and returned to find that someone had broken into our vehicle.

Our backpacks and computers were stolen.

My passport and otases were gone.

I had forty-five minutes to board my plane and return to New Jersey. The colleagues at the brunch took me to the airport while my driver reported what had happened to the San Francisco police. Despite having lost my passport, I still had my expired ID card. Airport security let me through because, as they explained, my ID was still within the three-month grace period of its expiration date. I spent most of the five-hour flight accessing computer applications and changing passwords to prevent whoever had gotten hold of the computer from accessing whatever was in there.

The loss of the stones was a source of deeper panic.

I had lost the otases; the uglier side of my childhood Catholicism suggested I was being punished for something. I dismissed the idea immediately, again on the plane, and again after returning to New Jersey. I could have not done anything wrong, but I turned to my elder for answers. In our first conversations, she noted that these situations come up for people with more frequency than most will admit; we would need time to pass and for me to let things settle before having new stones consecrated.

I thought: "The otases will come back."

Things started shifting in my religious family. My relationship with madrina had turned distant. Conversations with practitioners in Havana and the United States, and consultation with the literatures, revealed that asymmetries over resources and the tensions they spawned were an ingredient of the transnational experience of initiation and religious tourism for people like me.[6] At the end of my initiation, I realized that I had never felt as happy and loved as during those seven days. Returning to the United States and living through the rest of my initiation year away from this community made me increasingly uncomfortable with my interpretation of what had taken place in Havana. How does one hold on to happiness and love experienced transnationally while also keeping one's eyes open to the material conditions subtending those feelings? Many people labored in my initiation as process, so how could I account for these webs of work, leisure, pleasure, spirituality, and inequality? I recall the supermarket-style botánica in Havana and my walks with my iya in and out of this and a few other botánicas, entrepreneurial operations to do spiritual work in a setting in which spirit and commerce are *copresent* and intertwined in a diffractive relationship. Such is the blurring Aisha Beliso-De Jesús explains regarding *copresence*—"microintensities of erupting power": "They are active spiritual and religious subjectivities intimately tied to practitioners' forms of movement, travel, and sensual bodily registers."[7] Hear the grating, the sonic frottage, of spirit in commerce, commerce in spirit, spirit-commerce-spirit— what Beliso-De Jesús theorizes as shifting our thinking of connectivity away from the "trans" in transnationalism to the "trance" of copresence.[8]

In some of our exchanges after I lost my otases, madrina discussed ceremonial measures needed for replacement stones. My head spun at the thought of the financial implications of what needed to be done, given the size of the derecho for the initiation. My husband pressed me to consider what it would mean to invest more funds in replacement otases after all the family had paid to cover the initiation.

And there was another problem: I lost my passport in mid-May, two weeks before traveling to the Dominican Republic and one week before attending a conference in Puerto Rico. When I returned to New Jersey, I filed a passport application and tendered the one original document I had to prove my US citizenship and identity: my certificate of naturalization. After dropping the passport application in the mail, I went with copies of all the documents (including a scan of the missing passport) to the Department of Motor Vehicles (DMV) near me to see if they would issue a new ID card. The whole thing sounded outlandish as I spoke it to the befuddled officer. I had rehearsed what I would say with Alfredo first, being that he has a better sense than I do of how to communicate with state officers. Still, this was too baroque. She responded with a flat "no" to allowing me to go in for a new ID, because I had no original official documents to prove my identity. I went to another DMV office and explained what happened; I was turned away again.

After conversations with friends about traveling with an expired state ID, I decided not to risk being a Dominican-born US citizen with an expired state ID in Puerto Rico. Who would believe this story? Could I even tell it in less than thirty seconds? Technically, I could travel to Puerto Rico with the expired New York State ID, but did I want to risk having to explain myself there?

Confronted with this lack of documentation and with the cancellation of upcoming travel, several smaller quotidian exercises in proffering proof of identity and citizenship became more obvious than they would have been otherwise. I had problems with one of my bank cards but had to wait for a passport to arrive before I could prove who I was at the bank; I also had to prove to my university that the computer had been lost to theft, after filing a report that must still be sitting in someone's files or on someone's desk, collecting dust.

I exchanged texts with my fellow traveler in misadventure; she shared photocopies of the report documents she had obtained from the San Francisco Police Department. My new passport and naturalization certificates arrived. Two days before travel, my colleague texted to let me know that the San Francisco State University police had found our bags. The laptops were gone, as expected.

It took a month to bring the otases back; they traveled back to my home altar.

THIS NARRATIVE THEMATIZES TWO absences related to religious versus secular intelligibility. The fact that they take place experientially and narratively within the one frame allows me to consider the mediations that make them possible, as well as what they reveal in each other.

CHAPTER FOUR

In the unfolding of events, the operations of the divine happen backstage. My first impulse was to rush and blame myself for what happened, or else think that I did something wrong. However, this narrative contains lessons to be extrapolated but not fully known. In ways analogous to a pataki or a Christian parable, the story being told contains moral lessons, but these lessons demand a movement away from Manichaeism and a mapping of the larger forces at play. We may not be fully aware of the overall picture in a social situation, but that incompleteness is part of the lesson from the void: the awareness that what is operating is more than one can comprehend, and certainly much more than one's will.

I want to set up the interpretations that follow as individual lines in an analysis that results in something close to what Fernando Ortíz called *contrapunteo*. This suggests a return to aspects of the narrative to demonstrate the utility of holding the perspectives together, to hear one in the other. The first of the two perspectives is that of a Marxist analysis of relations of exchange. Although dimensions of Marxist analysis could be of use, given the growth of religious and other tourisms, that perspective is incomplete. The second section in the chapter draws on Matory and Alexander to recalibrate my initial ruminations on religious labor, artifacts, exchange, and the fetish of the commodity. My choice of a contrapunteo analysis is deliberate because it underscores the utility of the foundational work of the Cuban thinker Fernando Ortíz in its appeal to impurity, negotiation, and diffraction as features of faggotology. Listeners of counterpoint music will recall that, in this musical writing, the central challenge to players and listeners is to render clear to the ear and with integrity the voices as they interact with one another. This integrity in relation, this "hearing" of interacting voices alone and together, is what we are after in what follows.

i

Skeptical of reason and rationality, conocimiento questions conventional knowledge's current categories, classifications, and contents.

GLORIA E. ANZALDÚA, *LIGHT IN THE DARK*

Over the years, I have observed that serious readers of oracles mobilize refrains and stories from combinations of numbers or signs to allow their audience to interpret *as they live*, or walk, the path of the signs captured by an adage or pataki. Mediums in traditions such as espiritismo and tarot cards also work in this way—speaking of present, past, and future at the same time and tasking the recipient of the message to find the connection between what is being said and the recipient's life. Conocimiento is born out of listening and engaging a corpus over time, dwelling in insights and questions. Unanswered queries remain, and tentative answers arrive but are not guaranteed. Conocimiento also obtains from relationships, including relationships with one's elders, mentors, guiding spirits, and others. As Anzaldúa puts it, "Llevas la presencia de éste conocimiento contigo" (You carry the presence of conocimiento with you).[9] Presence is to be carried, not found: truth is not a wildlife and our quest is not a safari. Most people visit a medium to solve urgent personal problems. These "readings" also turn on confirming what one intuits or knows. The meeting point of individual experience and oracles may be uncertain, but the truth of parables and patakís is not. Furthermore, conocimiento operates as a presence one decides to acknowledge or not acknowledge. You carry it with you—a copresence, or another muerto.

When first thinking about the opening of this chapter, I recruited Marx's commodity fetishism to account for the messiness of discussing Santería/Lucumí and its economies of exchange while grappling with the insertion of practitioners into leisure economies. Santería was once a maligned and persecuted alternative to official Christianity and Catholicism. Now it has become an object of Cuban postrevolutionary pride and a possibility of commercialization in neoliberal service/leisure economies.[10] Other Afro-diasporic traditions (e.g., Brazilian Candomblé and Capoeira) have met analogous fates.[11]

A perspective shaped by this way of taking up commodity fetishism would, inevitably, grapple with the contradictory nature of the conjuncture: the marketplace of world religions and the commoditization of religious travel are not the same as the religions themselves and their cosmological visions of bodies, sacred objects, and exchange. This conundrum is apparent in Marx's initial conceptualization of the fetishism of the commodity in *Capital*:

> The commodity *reflects* the *social* characteristics of men's own labour *as objective* characteristics of the products of labour themselves, as the socionatural properties of these things. Hence it also *reflects* the social relation of the producers to the sum total of labour as a *social relation between objects, a relation which exists apart from and outside the producers.* Through this *substitution*, the products of labour become commodities, sensuous things which are at the same time supra-sensible or social.... The commodity-form ... is nothing but the definitive social relation between

men themselves which assumes here, for them, the fantastic form of a relation between things. In order, therefore, to find an analogy we must take flight into the misty realm of religion. There the products of the human brain appear as autonomous figures endowed with a life of their own, which enter into relations both with each other and with the human race. So it is in the world of commodities with the products of men's hands. I call this the fetishism which attaches itself to the products of labour as soon as they are produced as commodities, and is therefore inseparable from the production of commodities.[12]

Marx draws attention to the separation and co-implication of spheres of relationality. The first part of this statement sketches out a distinction between "social" characteristics *as* "objective" characteristics—social relations as they pertain to producers and objects. These spheres of relationality are "outside" one another. The word of choice to characterize these spheres as they face one another is "reflect," as accounted for in the first two sentences of the translation. By the third sentence, Marx portrays the movement between spheres as a "substitution" of one for the other. This substitution is a movement between spheres of relationality.

Marx's separation of spheres stresses the autonomy of each, even though the separation is far from neat. To elaborate on the distinction, he appeals to a startling "analogy": the way (in religion) "products of the human brain" enjoy an autonomous life, interacting with one another and with "the human race." He then sutures the analogy through the word *fetishism*. Commodities become autonomous figures that develop their relationship with one another and the "human race" that produced them. *Substitution* does not mean that one sphere *replaces* another. Instead, two separate domains of exchange enter a stage of play within and outside of themselves. Marx holds a space for autonomy and interdependence in this passage.

The analogy of commodity formation with the "misty" world of religion, which Marx uses to explain the interdependent yet autonomous operations of fields of exchange, presents a challenge, being that Marx suggests that the "autonomous figures endowed with a life of their own" in religion are "products of the human brain." At first glance, this establishes Marx's thinking squarely within positivist, Enlightenment reason. This view of the matter subjects the "autonomy" of these figures to the interior of the operations of the mind, keeping out of view the possibility that such figures exist and operate independently from and in relation to human perception. An alternative to this limitation suggests that there is more to these figures than what human minds can comprehend. Given Marx's sense of these as animations characteristic of somewhere other than the Europe of his time, a teleology of progress in collusion with European colonialist and civilizational discourse is central.

ii

As Matory asserts, racial play with the fetish is central to how Marx articulated "progressive" critiques of European capitalism through deployments of tropes to distinguish Europe from Africa: "As articulated by Hegel, Marx, and Freud, the anti-African trope of the fetish was central to a sequence of European social revolutions intent on conferring upon the European bourgeoisie and proletariat rights once limited to the European aristocracy, and doing so at the symbolic and material expense of Africans."[13] Furthermore, Matory suggests that part of what is at stake for a Jewish man such as Marx (and for Freud, the other thinker on the fetish at the center of Matory's examination) is the development of theories that secure their own legitimacy and standing in the societies of their time: "The theories of social-evolutionary and racial difference that structured ... Marx's social-evolutionist historical material-ism ... were not just about the non-European Other. They were also about why the narrator of this history deserved to be regarded as superior to that Other and not inferior to a range of fellow European populations."[14] In other words, what was being negotiated in and through figurations of the fetish and figurations of Africa was the teleology of civilizational progress and freedom that helped white "ethnics" sediment a racial coalition.

Are otases—as sacred objects resulting from exchange, ritual preparation, sacrifice, and so on—commodities shaped in and through the fetishism Marx describes? Otases are not commodities (in the way Marx uses the term *commodities*), especially when we account for Marx's emphasis on the separation of spheres, replacement, and transposition of relationships between humans for relationships between things.

As sacred objects, otases can be defined in a way that is consistent with the conceptualization of the fetish offered by Matory. "A thing is most likely to be called a fetish," he writes, "when it mediates the relationship between parties with very different or even opposite perspectives on their social relationship, perspectives that are also expressed in opposite perspectives on the thing it-self."[15] Matory explains that Afro-Atlantic religions are open to "globalizing merchant capitalism, money and profit" and that they lean on "hierarchical imagery of royalty and slavery, with the conviction that such relationships are alive with intimacy and personal efficacy"; thereby, Afro-Atlantic religions emphasize exchange as life-giving and relation affirming.[16] Seen through an Afro-Atlantic lens, otases are meaningfully exchanged objects: "Each divinity or person is a set of relationships materialized through commerce, ritual gifting, and souvenirs of long-term debt. Like communities, gods are assemblages animated and kept alive through such repeated exchanges."[17]

Questions related to economic resources, derechos, etc., are the source of intense (albeit muffled) debate within religious communities. Throughout my initiation and beyond, disagreements over the costs of ceremonies and suspicion of bad faith generated intense disagreements among the practitioners and elders with whom I have interacted. But much of this is consistent with Beliso-De Jesús's suggestion that "practitioners describe having to 'pay debt' to different copresences, often with African-inspired terms of barter and bargaining."[18] Relationships structured around the payment of debt—in tributes or as means of obtaining ritual permission to exchange resources—suggest continuous interaction, a "walking together" that requires reciprocity, a circuitry livened through exchange. One might posit, for example, that the contracting (or subcontracting) of priests not aligned with a specific house to play specialized roles in a ceremony could be construed as an instrumentalization of expertise; such a view would be consistent with the notion endorsed by my elders that derechos support the livelihood of religious workers who are not otherwise employed.[19] Nevertheless, these services tend to be secured within bonds of exchange and trust, pointing to socialities that are densely enlivened through exchange.

Nevertheless, economic exchange created ambiguous situations. Questions surfaced regarding the assignment of derechos; the locution is *marcar derecho* (to assign derecho through consultation with an oracle). On occasion, others and I discussed derecho as if it was something one haggled over with a practitioner, and some practitioners were infamous for marking high derechos. This turn oversimplified the complexities of ritual, rendering it analogous to fruit one purchases in a market or a taxi ride; in other words, ritual as service and derecho as price: something one negotiates in informal economic networks depending on the practitioner's reputation, their assessment of your position and economic privilege, your proximity to those best poised to negotiate reasonable derechos, and so on. If this openness and embrace of commerce was part of what made traditions such as Santería thrive, what exactly was my problem?

When faced with questions of money and spirit, I defaulted to my childhood view of Catholic priests. My friends who were raised Christian were also concerned about the role of money in all of this. Didn't I see that as problematic? I recalled learning that pursuing the priesthood also meant that I would not have had to concern myself about finances because the church would take care of my material needs. Or, at least, that was what the adults around me said about life as a priest or nun. I was also aware of the collection of tithes, and I understood that payment was made to cover religious ceremonies. Maybe the overarching material structure was not visible, but resources were moving and being exchanged. If this is the case, and if it is also the case that some religious leaders in more "traditional" denominations make profit through televangelism, why the surprise, concern, and outrage experienced around derechos and Santería practitioners? One way to cast what I saw was that practitioners and priests usually spoke directly about the costs of ceremony and religious labor. Still, outrage is the best way to describe the affects that littered commentary on early versions of this chapter, especially from anguished former practitioners who approached me after the talks.

The more involved I became in initiation activities, the more the words of elders resonated as they described the ensembles in ceremony (e.g., cooks, consecrated priests, cleaners) *as workers* whose labor would be recognized through the derecho. Exchange mobilizes and glues together the pueblo we needed to make santo. Apart from recognition of their contributions, there was a redistributive ethos to these operations: financial and other resources coming out of ritual (including animal meat) supplemented a family's finances or, in some cases, diets. Relations of exchange do not subvert or transgress hierarchies of economic advantage. However, ceremonies required the specialized knowledge and consecration contributed by certain priests. Contracting someone to play a role in each moment in one's journey was insufficient; you need to ensure that the priest is happy with the arrangement to ensure the proper flow of energy so all rituals come out with blessings and benefits from the participants' ashé. *Desenvolvimiento* is a locution, literally translated as "development" but meant in a positive sense, as growth in one's access to economic and other resources and blessings. Desenvolvimiento should result from ceremony to the person who is the object of focus *as well as to all involved*. Untoward energy brought into ritual could result in a complicated process for the young priest; one's elders were charged with ensuring that the process conforms to established protocols and that derechos conform to expectations so that everything will go as planned. In other words, leading elders were charged with carrying out care and emotional labor for the success of the initiation as a whole, not only to contract and assure proper form.

That redistributive ethos addressed, in small measure, the stark inequalities between my material conditions and those of the mostly black-presenting Cubans and black Dominicans with whom I collaborated. The pooling of meager resources available to those who collaborated in my ceremonies (and who received derechos in some cases) supported other initiations and consecrations, joint rituals, and so on. Being that the orisha who rules my path "no va a la cabeza" (does not go to the head), the consecration of that deity was required so that they would "supervise" my initiation ceremony a few days later. This three-day ceremony required a sizable derecho, but I received this deity together with three Cuban women. Perhaps the pooling of material resources, the repurposing of funds, or the mobilization of the multiplicity of uses of money was pushing beyond what could be apprehended through a narrowly focused materialist analysis.

Notions of redistribution sometimes provided comfort, but negotiating inequalities through restructuring measures that compensate and recognize religious labor-cum-labor leaves untouched the entrenched hierarchies that obtained in my initiation. I still got on the plane and left Havana after becoming a new priest and adding initiation to class and geopolitical advantages I already enjoyed. The priests and priestesses who collaborated in my initiation were part of this network and perhaps also part of other networks etched on a religious entrepreneurship like that of the long-range medium, though they dealt with a differentiated set of demands, restrictions, and capacity for (im)mobility.

A deeper problem with a materialist analysis of the traveling otases and much of my involvement in Santería reflected the fact that Black Atlantic traditions developed as mechanisms for coping, reinventing, and healing from a system that made enslaved black bodies into commodities. Matory describes it accordingly:

> The making of gods is at once production and exchange. And this exchange is no more extraneous to capitalism than are slavery and the formation of corporations. Throughout its known history, the making of Afro-Atlantic gods has depended on cash-ridden translocal exchange and has served to generate material profit for insiders through the deft management of trade in goods produced expressly for exchange and often produced far away. In the Afro-Atlantic religions, the making of a god is also a self-conscious immobilization of commodities and their conversion into permanent nodes of social relationship—namely, a fully spirit-stocked senior priest and the score of vessel-altars through which he or she and the community of followers are managed.[20]

An important dimension of the limitations of materialist analysis had to do with the splitting, in "substitution" (as explained by Marx), of the intentionality of the worker. The severing of hands from the human labor in the commodity form also aligned with an "enlightened" view that stripped social actors of a connection, through intentionality, to everything we do in the world.

My view on intentionality as unimportant to meaning making, a product of my antifoundationalist training, had come increasingly under pressure in my path to initiation, as it was consistent with commodity fetishism but incompatible with Afro-Atlantic cosmovisions reworking the principles through which we use the "master's tools." My elders have always insisted that in Santería/Lucumí, "todo tiene un por qué" (there is a "why" to everything). Practitioners are tasked with observing and seeking explanation for matters of form and ritual, even when they appear most banal. But their task is also to remain humbled that one cannot know it all. In addition, there was an emphasis on the intentionality of action, which is in large part what prompted care and a delicate balance when it came to negotiating derechos and ensuring that one attended to everyone's financial and emotional needs during rituals. Walking the path as a priest and eventually facilitating and accompanying others demanded an increased awareness and engagement with these nuances, part of the care and emotional labor I would perform for younger priests, my elders, and my piedritas.

As Matory explains, the making of Afro-Atlantic traditions builds from exchange practices that precede the advent of capitalism. The coexistence of production and exchange and the insistence on the transformation of things into nodal points of relationships to be sustained over one's life in these religions include making profit.

iii

A response to concerns stemming from an initial materialist analysis of relations of exchange might be formulated through the work of a Marxist feminist critic engaged in Afro-Caribbean traditions. Alexander, as she considers the remaking of the body in Santería/Lucumí, writes this:

> Of what significance, then, is the body in the making of experience if it cannot merely be summoned instrumentally to serve or explain the axes of violence that stem from the crises of capitalism's various plantations or from its attendant modes of financial timekeeping? Clearly the focus on spiritual work necessitates a different existential positioning in which to know the

body is to know it as medium for the Divine, living a purpose that exceeds the imperatives of these plantations. . . . Far from being merely superficial, these markings on the flesh—these inscriptions—are processes, ceremonial rituals through which practitioners become habituated to the spiritual and this habituation implies that requirements are *transposed* onto the body. One of these requirements is to remember their source and purpose. In this matrix the body thus becomes a site of memory, not a commodity for sale, even as it is simultaneously insinuated within a nexus of power.[21]

First, in Alexander's account, the cosmovision shaping Santería/Lucumí and other Caribbean traditions builds from a refusal to experience the body "instrumentally," as the transfer point of relations of exchange that yield monetary profit from labor in plantation economies. To the degree that the exploitation of chattel exacted the productivity of captive populations on a time clock, maximizing gain for landowners on the shortest duration, plantation economies thrived on the potential of bodies not only for a plunder of human productivity, but also for the extraction of life energy as unpaid labor. Body energy became yet another natural resource to extract for its exchange value in metropolitan markets. This extraction of life depended on a procedural movement that prompted the radical alienation of workers from their work but, crucially, also from the *memory* of labor itself. Whereas plantations were driven by the impulse to extract maximum labor power from enslaved bodies for as little investment as possible, Afro-Atlantic traditions offer radical alternatives in viewing the human body as irreducible to instrumentality. The working bodies matter. Intentionalities matter, and energies are to be not extracted but, rather, cultivated so they continue generating sparkle and life.

Alexander asks us to suspend our investment in an instrumental view of the human body. We are not to use it in the service of or as an illustration of "the crises of capitalism's various plantations." Our quest, she explains, takes us to an existential positioning as an epistemological foundation: "To know the body is to know it as a medium for the Divine." The body, in Alexander's revisioning, is a bridge of divine energy, our bridge to the divine in its most banal manifestations. The distinction between *instrument* and *medium* underscores how indebted Alexander's analysis is to "bridge" thinking in the radical vein of queer-women-of-color traditions in which she has participated. To *mediate* is to broker forces, to dispose of the body to be something other than a "thing" that can be used or dropped according to the vagaries of the marketplace. Could this be the deeper meaning of the work of the "long-range medium" with whom I worked in Havana? She did not lead a "tour" into the spirit world for the entertainment of her audience; instead, she was a bridge builder who opened vistas to allow us to see, hear, and feel the copresences, the sites of spirit. Wasn't she entreating me, with her remark, to feel and touch love/work/care expressed in the habitual sentience of that which I assumed would be inanimate?

In the section from which the earlier quote was extracted, Alexander discusses ritual markings made on the flesh of initiates and practitioners of Afro-Caribbean religions. The next sentences describe the markings as "habituations" (both "formation of habit" and "creating space to inhabit") of the initiate's body to "the spiritual." The head of the initiated priest, rendered sibling to the otases in sacrifice, is also the opening to the settlement of orisha energy in the body, a process analogous to the way the energies settle in the stones that populate one's altar. The term *habituation* emphasizes the intentional repetition of quotidian procedures—habits—that sediment over time. That sedimentation takes place through the memorialization as repetition and the access to our kinetic sense, thus allowing habituations to be implicated in (though not subsumed by) the mechanized motions of the body. This ritual inscription, place making, and "settling" in the body performs an operation different from what happens in commodity formation in Marx, where pairings of relations "substitute" for each other. Alexander instead argues that ritual inscriptions "demand that their requirements [be] *transposed* onto the body" (emphasis added). Habituation seeks not mindless repetition but, rather, a transfer of habit and what Alexander names "requirements" for it to achieve a "transposition" into the body. The preservation of these traditions does not get fully realized unless *habituation* comes to mean repetition and requirement. Instead of movement and the assertion of autonomy and interrelatedness between spheres, Alexander's sights are set on the transposition of requirements as bodily placemaking and habit formation, a kinesthetic activation of muscle memory of the soul. An observation of how one comes to *encariñarse* (feel affection/love) for one's stones—this marginalia, this little leftover phrase, laced over with an explanation of how she washed and cared for her otases in preparation for the new year—draws attention to the performative dimension of the habituation being transposed by the medium to the new priest. She was not just describing something she does with her otases. Her description goaded me and beguiled my desire to open my heart to the divine through quotidian care.

The verb *transpose* has several meanings in English, all of which support the theoretical benefit of dwelling on Alexander's usage:

Transpose, *v.*

1 *trans.* To change (one thing) *to* or *into* another; to transform.

2 To change (a writing or book) *into* another language, style of composition, or mode of expression; to translate; to transfer; to adapt.

3 To change the purport, application, or use of; to apply or use otherwise; to give a different direction to; in bad sense, to corrupt, pervert; to misapply, abuse.

4 To remove from one place or time to another; to transfer, shift . . . ; to transplant; to convey, conduct.

5 To alter the order of (a set or series of things), or the position of (a thing) in a series; to put each of (two or more things) in the place of the other or others, to interchange; *esp.* to alter the order of letters in a word or of words in a sentence.

6 To discompose, disturb the mental composure of.

7 *Music.* To alter the key of; to put into a different key (in composition, arrangement, or performance).[22]

These meanings share an emphasis on movements of matter that produce change. The degree, severity, and acceptability of shifts may be in question, but a shift is in the offing. Alexander's choice of *transpose* is felicitous in its elasticity, as befits embodied sedimentation. Unlike what settles on a page, Alexander describes ritual and the transmission of knowledge about where ritual comes from and about what habituations help hold place in the body as space and as site for historical congealment. For populations for whom colonial modalities of knowledge transmission (such as writing) do not fully capture what needs to be communicated, the bodies of individual practitioners become the instruments through which conocimientos move from elder to initiate: Solimar Otero's "archives of conjure." Alexander underscores that one of the requirements of habituation is to "remember their source and purpose," further clarifying what distinguishes Afro-Atlantic "transposition" from the "substitution" of relations that shapes the commodity form in Marx. "Transposition" results in the body as "a site of memory, not a commodity for sale, even as it is simultaneously insinuated within a nexus of power." With that last phrase, Alexander reveals this recalibration of embodied divinity not to feign naïveté or to claim purity from relations of exchange, for it is not separate but, rather, insinuated at meeting points where power is operative.

Matory's view of Afro-Atlantic religions comes together with Alexander's vision. Matory urges his readers to disabuse themselves of the notion that the divine and the commercial exist in separate spheres. His observation is supported by evidence that the making of these traditions is entwined with the establishment of elastic relationalities to be cultivated over the long term; across distances; and where the pursuit of profit, the creation and sustenance of hierarchy, and the fostering of relations of exchange are central. But there is telling contrast between the focus of the two authors. For Matory, the circuits of exchange condense the power of the senior priest and in the launching of altars of which these priests and their followers will be stewards. Alexander's view of the matter, without denying what Matory offers, rests more centrally in her orientation as a black feminist and a priestess. In her view, the body of the priest becomes the site where these powers are "transposed," but these sacred bodies become archives of histories that they are meant to re-member.

Returning to the otases, habituation traveled through the initiation and throughout what were supposed to be my ongoing and quotidian engagements with them. The sacred stones were caught and charged through a "nexus of power" that included the work of elders and monetary exchanges. However, Alexander's analysis points to a model of exchange that reconfigures the body and the otases as more than commodities. One might view them as "nodes of relationship" to be managed à la Matory, and this assessment is supported by how crucial mentorship is to evolving as stewards of the assemblages that become one's altars. But there is something to be said about how crucial one's way of carrying oneself in the world becomes engulfed in a new religious sensibility, an expansive circuit of the sacred. In other words, though the altar matters, this is an important yet relatively localized expression of how one's overall outlook on life—and one's behavior—are expected to shift post-initiation. Santería/Lucumí becomes much more than the blown rum or the lit candle because insights drawn from the path are meant to infuse and energize the totality of one's outlook, and they reconnect one's present with those who have come before and connect one's life to the accompaniment of the orishas and the ancestors. Furthermore, sacrifice in ritual results in the consecration of stones, as well as the head of the young priest; thus, through sacrifice your head develops a filial relationship to the otases.

My arrival at a realization that there had to be more to interpreting the anecdote of the traveling stones than could be accounted for in a materialist analysis of the fetishism of the commodity prompted me to look further into what is erased by Marxist analyses. Alexander, a Marxist critic, discerns that transposition preserves and transfers traditions to the degree that the "whys" and "hows" are communicated. *Transposition* (in Alexander's usage) proposes not an easy transfer or replicable movement from elder to younger practitioner but, rather, an adaptation and reconfiguration—the birth of a relationship (if you will)—that preserves within view the histories held and condensed in objects, processes, exchanges, relations, and bodies. This movement shifts the directionality of commodity fetishism because it refuses to divorce intentionality and history from sacralization. Transposition allows for the formulation of a religious subject in and through tethering the meanings and energies that live in religious objects, gestures, and markings. The key attachment is directed not at stones qua stones but, rather, at the relationships, intentionalities, and histories discharged in them.

THE SECOND "VOID" in the earlier narrative concerns the disappearance of my US passport, along with the expiration of my New York State ID. The disappearance of the passport challenged my legibility and legitimacy as a subject before the law, which one could be tempted to contrast with religious subject formation. Nevertheless, I want to stress the materiality of relations, exchanges, and possibilities for mobility revealed by this absence. Although no equivalence is being sought between religious and state objects, thinking of them together reveals productive convergences.

The process of applying for a passport—a document issued and owned by the state (even though the bearer pays for it)—requires culling together several layers of state-sanctioned archival evidence. As I transitioned from a US permanent resident (green card holder) to a US citizen, I recall having had to renew my Dominican passport for any prospect of travel before passing the citizenship test. My Dominican birth certificate was another document that needed to be current to be acceptable, and its validity depended on the fees one paid to the state and on it being translated and notarized (which I paid for). Once I passed the citizenship exam and attended the ceremony where my Certificate of Citizenship was granted, that certificate became the one mechanism available to certify my identity—like a new birth certificate. As it was clear when I lost the passport and sent in the official certificate I received, I had no other way to prove who I was. And even though dual citizenship is acceptable in the eyes of the Dominican state, I could neither produce renewed Dominican identity documents nor use them to replace my US passport.

The absence of the passport signaled a temporary lack of mobility that is steeped in the privilege of having one's subjecthood rendered viable in state archives, as well as being a subject of surveillance and state control. Though my situation felt urgent to me, it was only a minor (and temporary) inconvenience relative to the millions of undocumented people in the United States and relative to many others who negotiate restrictions in mobility. Despite the specific location and grounding of my "glitch" (if you will allow the word), I discovered that the expired ID had a grace period and that I could travel. Access to banks and other daily errands and international mobility were restored once the identifications were restored.

Still, aspects of my mobility were shaped by ethnic, national, and geopolitical histories thrown into relief by the absence of official documents. I had heard continually about the issues Dominicans faced when entering the United States through the San Juan and Miami airports. Some warnings were cast in relation to (1) the populations assumed to play the role of state brokers (Cubans and Puerto Ricans); and (2) their presumed "antipathy" or skepticism toward the legitimacy of Dominican travelers claiming to have visas, green cards, or US citizenship. Therefore, it was reasonable for me to cancel attending a conference held in San Juan while bearing an expired New York State ID. The San Francisco airport officers might have given me the benefit of the doubt because I might not have fit a profile that prompted suspicion. However, I could not take that risk as a Dominican in Puerto Rico or Miami.

The absence of the passport and otases brings into focus a few convergences related to a faggotology. Both artifacts reside in distinct and strictly enforced circuits of exchange: The otases require vetting and preparation by an elder and a community, as well as a derecho. In contrast, the passport requires submitting an application, state documents, money, acceptable pictures, and so on. In other words, the artifacts point to complexities of process and protocol that make them distinct from other objects—as ones that will reside in the altar of a priest or as "proof" of identity for travel and other more mundane transactions—and protocols for legibility and legitimacy. Amitava Kumar writes, "If it can be allowed that the passport is a kind of book, then the immigration officer, holding a passport in his hand, is also a reader."[23] What if the book is missing? What lies beyond the finitude of the archive—the proffering of proof that confers legibility? A combination of names that we can link to a picture and perform quotidian operations of mobility? Furthermore, one might twist the question asked of the passport back to the otases: if they stand in for the condensation and consecration of intentionalities, blessings, and divinity, what are the protocols for the legibility of these energy discharges in these communities? Who reads? How do they read? Throughout this chapter, I have "gathered everything" to mark and apprehend descriptively and analytically the scaffoldings and enmeshments of inequality, exchange, and impurity sketched by the circuitry of traveling otases as artifacts indexical of intimacies and relations deeper than what meets the eye. Instead of sitting comfortably in the high moral ground framed around expectations of horizontality in transnational exchange, my faggotological impulse is to highlight the copresences, impurities, and messiness of the financial, emotional, psychic, and spiritual entanglements produced by my quest for the black (w)hole. Ours is a peregrinaje for an enlarged sense of the divine in the hot mess of "trance-national" religious life.

¡Santo!

Repurposed Flesh and the Suspension of the Mirror in Santería Initiation

THIS CHAPTER MODELS THE REPURPOSING OF SUBJECT FORMS THROUGH AN APPEAL TO THE TACTILE AND THE KINESTHETIC.[1] *Repurposing* is an adaptation of excess in a quest for alternatives to the tyranny of normativity. The narratives in the chapter have in common intimations that there is more to us than that which resides in the "positive real." Dwelling in being out of tune is still dwelling in sound; dwelling in the blur is still dwelling in sight. There is an elsewhere that is not yet here—the one José Esteban Muñoz wrote about—an elsewhere of freedoms won by disposing otherwise of what we learn about who we must be for what we must become.[2] This brings us closer to a *faggotological rasanblaj* turning lacras into black and queer and ratchet affirmative sentience for jotería locas sucias of the world.

In the first section of what follows, I describe and perform codes in a circuit to map relations and ideations of a subject in Afro-Caribbean religion through a crónica of selected moments in my path to initiation as a Santería priest, inclusive of evocative glimpses of the sensations in the initiation ceremonies. This

Repurpose, v.

transitive. To convert or adapt for a different purpose or for use in a different way.

OXFORD ENGLISH DICTIONARY

chapter also moves through another moment of initiation, a remembered and anterior moment to "fieldwork" in which race, masculinity, and sexuality were implicated in ideations of the imago. Those sensations, those moments of training and learning through imitation of what remained elusive to the eyes of a child, also demand something less beholden to positive truth than a crónica. For this part of the work before us, I am offering an autobiographically inflected short story (cuento) as an expressive vehicle and condensation of that moment of subject formation.

The cuento and the crónica are laid side by side.

This juxtaposition posits neither teleological resolution of one subject formation for another nor a comparison/contrast between a "naturalized" subject and a "constructed" religious embodiment. The banality of normativity resides in its apparent ability to resolve the subject, even if transitively, to make it legible as such, through the disappearing "naturalization" of the codes that sediment on the body. Nevertheless, this side-by-side layout will allow a narrative mapping of the visual and sensorial economies at play in both initiations while giving us the opportunity to later consider the role that the erotic plays in suturing a transitive yo (I). Transit and erotic play should alert us to how implicated the gaze, touch, and animated circuitry of relations with others are in self-making, pushing toward ineffable horizons where one's embodiment joins either as (1) receptible of unseen yet felt spiritual forces; or (2) idealized codes of normative deportment concretized as fantastical and regulatory ideations. What stands in as the ineffable might appear most normative even if it resides in the fantastical: the realm of what you know yet cannot see; what you learn to conform to; expectations never spelled out yet compulsorily applied to your arms and legs, your gait, and the swing of your hips as you walk or dance. Yet the black (w)hole, which itself also lives in what one's eyes cannot meet or see, in that which you sense but never fully establish, alerts us to the possibility of play and rupture in projects of freedom—an invaluable realization and resource for queer-of-color lives and futures.

As in chapter 4, I ask you to read "diffractively"—to hear these narratives in each other. How does hearing them side by side support discerning how they grate into each other? How do words relevant in one narrative move through your mind's ear as you work through the other narrative?

I mobilize the "flesh" throughout what follows in a way that is consistent with the paradigm-shifting distinction laid out by the critic Hortense Spillers in her essay "Mama's Baby, Papa's Maybe: An American Grammar Book."[3] Spillers sets out to map the conditions of possibility for being in what she calls "the socio-political order of the New World" for African and indigenous peoples marked by a "*theft of the body*—a willful and violent . . . severing of the captive body from its motive and will, its active desire."[4] The resulting "particular space" is one at which "interlocking detail" (the coming together of multiple dimensions of individual life, particularly gender and race as Spillers centers black women in her frame) faces the "disruption" prompted by "externally imposed meanings and uses," which the author lays out in detail:

> 1) The captive body becomes the source of an irresistible, destructive sensuality; 2) at the same time—in stunning contradiction—the captive body reduces to a thing, becoming *being for* the captor; 3) in this absence *from* a subject position, the captured sexualities provide a physical and biological expression of "otherness"; 4) as a category of "otherness," the captive body translates into a potential for pornotroping and embodies sheer physical powerlessness that slides into a more general "powerlessness," resonating through various centers of human and social meaning.[5]

In the face of these impositions, Spillers presents the distinction between the "body" and the "flesh" in colonial regimes of representation, "American grammars." The difference between "body" and "flesh" is between captivity and what exceeds its hold. "In that sense," Spillers explains, "before the 'body' there is the 'flesh,' that zero degree of social conceptualization that does not escape concealment under the brush of discourse, or the reflexes of iconography."[6] The "flesh" precedes, follows, and exceeds the will of the captors and their technologies: it is "primary" and unruly form that must be regulated and adjusted—subjected—to achieve legibility. The literary critic Michelle Stephens elaborates on Spillers's concept: "For those in this subject position, before the 'body' there is the 'flesh,'" that is, another sense of the body that is a remainder of the body concealed and covered over in discourse. The skinned body that remains left behind by both physical captivity and cultural capture is what Spillers means by the 'flesh.'"[7] Following Spillers and Stephens, colonially inflected regimes of representation present as a skin, as a sheath that sutures the body form to the eye of the master—or, perhaps, we might consider these regimes of representation as regimes of captivity, capturing as they name. Strai(gh)tjackets.

I am interested in lacing together Spillers's notion of a body "severed" from its own will and desire while its flesh and its longings exceed and remain beyond the markings of discourse. These tunings of banal normativity might condition us to hear definition, clarity, and agreeable sound and everything other than that as noise, but what obtains from listening to noise as sound, to appreciate its properties and what it tells us about dwelling in instability, in what remains, in what exceeds? How do our ears adjust to finding the swing groove that lives in noise?

To be concrete, these two narratives present bodies as surfaces on which elaborations develop and sediment through ritual, adornment, codified gestures, body moves that slip into the banal, and so on. But turning embodiment into a negotiation of the imago through two sites—the gaze of the other and the mirror—points to the benefit of a renewed inquiry into the workings of the mirror and the gaze as important, but not the only, existing mechanisms of mediation in primary bodily structuration. In this way, I follow what Stephens calls for when she remarks that Frantz Fanon added a layer to the modes of black self-consciousness (double consciousness) articulated by W. E. B. Du Bois a half-century before him, what she calls a "triple or 'third-person consciousness,' which he described as 'a slow composition of my *self* as a body in the middle of a spatial and temporal world.' This is where Fanon's more radical interventions in thinking about the skin begin, as the site of a black body that is more, experiences more, signifies more, than the gaze can see. This 'corporeal schema' is that of the subject-as-body, the bodily ego, the body-without-an-image that knows itself instead through 'residual sensations and perceptions primarily of a tactile, vestibular, kinesthetic, and visual character.'"[8] Stephens's observation in Fanon underlines his insight regarding the expressive and ontological excess represented by black bodies, bodies aware of being caught before the white gaze but also grasping for their life capacities beyond and in excess of capture. To establish what he calls a "historical racial-schema" under a "corporeal schema," Fanon quotes from Jean Lhermitte's *L'image de notre corps* (1939) to explain that the schema he describes contains not these elements but, rather, those provided "by the other, the white man, who had woven me out of a thousand details, anecdotes, stories."[9] Yet the "corporeal schema" remains, and what follows maps out how we might trace these elements kinesthetically, working in excess and living within what remains beyond the gaze. I rely on metaphors of sound, smell, and touch as I lace the analysis to an insistence in the transitivity of the gaze and in the usefulness of thinking the sensorium expansively as we search for what can be recognized and activated elsewhere.

The juxtaposition of gender training and religious initiation illustrate economies of the gaze and of the mirror as mechanisms for subjectivation under coloniality. "Mirrors" articulates the ideation on the body of a boy, the collaborative training of becoming a man, and a suturing of male subject forms to an ensemble of performative codes associated with normative masculinity. "Looking for Santo" explores the suspension of the mirror in Afro-Caribbean religious initiation or "rebirth." What happens when the imago of the "santo" who settles in your head is that of something you are not supposed to see, something you will not see, and yet becomes the presence that others acknowledge and engage when they face you? What happens when strangers call out "¡Santo!" not to address you but, rather, to address the force of the universe that you carry and ask for their blessing through your words? Our narrative jumps allow for surprise meeting points between these bodily structurations. An analysis that holds space for diffractive relay should alert us to opportunities for expressive critique of black queer subject formations, a transition and opening from the mirror and the gaze to the broader imaginative possibilities through the sensorium.

MIRRORS

Mirrors flattered, sometimes, but Pepe Aguilar knew better than to be swayed by what they gave back.

They were not his friends.

Pepe was a chubby kid, and that tormented him, but the episode was a dance lesson from his cousin, the first girl who became his friend. Her skin was light, and she was already taller than most kids their age. He was the older cousin by several months.

"Move your hips side to side," she instructed.

Pepe looked and imitated her in front of the mirror, in her parents' bedroom, which was literally that: the room that held a bed of gargantuan proportions. Fortunately for the cousins, there was a nook in one corner where they could stand a short distance from the full-body mirror. Matilde moved and Pepe observed, though he did not get the difference between their swaying hips.

He tried again.

"Not like that. Men don't move their hips like that," she decreed.

But men move them, no?

"They do, but not so far," she said as she placed her hands on his left hip. She stood behind him. "Go too far to the side and people will think you are a woman."

Mujer.

LOOKING FOR SANTO

Before wanting to be a writer, an artist, a scholar, anything, the aleyo wanted to be a saint. This desire hid somewhere between childhood and adolescence, when his increasing intolerance for Catholic dogma had him sitting down, criticizing the curas during recess at school in the 1980s. Just like Martín Lutero, he thought. But his was the broken heart of the former monaguillo, the altar boy who held on to the path of priesthood as a possibility despite several confrontations about it with his father. Dad liked the education that the curas provided at Colegio Don Bosco, but he abhorred the idea of his oldest male child becoming one of them.

The aleyo's fear of the proto-queer yo must have been hovering in this desire for a life of spirit permanently exiled from his flesh. That was fear of his body, a fear that hovered over everything he did, as if he bore his own microclimate wherever he went and adults were observing. But what of the eyes drawn to the imagery of an athletic (if wounded) Christ at the cross, the buzzing of doñas rezando el Rosario at the Legión de María meetings he attended? What about the waves of open pores in his skin, like earth greedy for water, as he smelled the incense burning during special masses? What about the irrepressible wish to cry in mass when people are asked to give each other "peace," the way Christ would have done it?

Mujercita, as Pepe's mother called him when he cried after a scolding. Don't cry, mujercita.

Little woman. Here was Matilde demonstrating how a sway of the hips landed him in womanhood. How could moving your hips get you there?

Matilde went to the bathroom, and Pepe stayed in front of himself. He touched his hips where her hands had been and put pressure on them, as if pushing a mill to extract juice from sugarcane. Right, left. Right, left. His aunt had told him never to look at his feet. "No matter what," she said, "you look at her. Smile. Dancing is fun. No seas pariguayo." He looked at himself and held his own eyes through the glass, but the memory of his aunt dancing tickled his feet.

Matilde was back, her hair rolled into a ponytail, looking at him, moving her head sideways.

"Not like that." He had continued to sway while distracted. Matilde's critique brought him back to his own image.

How about this? He then recalled the lesson imparted minutes before. He was stiff, nervous.

"Look at yourself."

Pepe looked. He was shorter, thicker, and darker than Matilde. This was not fun.

"Look at yourself," she repeated. "The image will tell you." Matilde stood behind Pepe again and grabbed his hips to demonstrate how far to go. Her head

Immigrating to the United States at fifteen gave him an opportunity to start over and practice in his life the acts of forgetting characteristic of incoming Dominican governments: borrón y cuenta nueva. Scratch the account balance; let's start over. His balances? No amiguitos to remember the sissy boy that he was, the mousy walk down the street to the colmado, the studied avoidance of the eyes of the neighborhood tígueres and cueros who did know something about the aleyo that he could not know, the feathers he recognized later in life. How could a yo be formed as if walking on eggshells, ever so aware that each step produced a crack in comments, the snide laughter that pinched his walk, the evolving obsessions calibrating every movement?

Borrón y cuenta nueva in Philadelphia afforded him English, a new language where one *needed* to pronounce the *s*, releasing the sibilant he had edited from his speech in Dominican working-class Spanish, where proper pronunciation made class antagonisms metamorphose into accusations of effeminacy. Permission to pronounce the *s* was permission to be free through the sibilant.

sssssssssssssssssssssssssssssssssssssssssssssssssss

Time and an elite education afforded him access to the ser alguien, the being someone of neoliberal homonormativity. But the achievement of stability and access to the charmed circles of the academy prompted him to find his way back to those desires for what lived beyond bent forward, almost on top of his, with pedagogical intent. She was so thin that the rest of her got lost behind him, but Pepe could feel the wiry girl who should have grown breasts by now. It was that head that touched the top of his, those hands that touched him the way she swayed the broom when she danced on her own, singing all those full-throated salsas of lost loves, the Juan Gabriel songs sung by every maid in Santo Domingo, the bachatas of un-hinged men betrayed by women defying their possessive love. Pepe was a spider, a centipede turned upside down, the extra arms doing as they pleased. Matilde guided those wild extremities with her touch, her body pressed against his back.

She loved him.

The dancing lessons continued because Matilde wanted a credible partner at the birthday parties they attended. Having Pepe also helped Matilde, whose life was a sprint marathon to adulthood through a long obstacle course of male hands bent on grabbing her nalgas. Pepe's touch inoculated her.

But Pepe's own touch did not protect him from the person he saw when he crossed a mirror, so he began to search for his own image whenever he walked from his home to Matilde's house.

Mami, that's a mirror, right? He asked her once as they walked by the store.

She stopped with him and got close to the store diorama. Unlike him, his mother's full head and shoulders appeared when she came

the social institutions that rendered him legible and legitimate.

This is when a childhood desire for saint-hood returned as a quest for santo, a proj-ect prompted by encountering Santería in transit between Santo Domingo and Havana. In March 2014, the aleyo was in Havana for his first time, taking a morning walk through El Vedado, going to his iya's house already dressed as an iyawo, even though he was formally initi-ated later that year, on another trip. The familiarity of the streets, the lightness of the morning air in March, and this neigh-boring capital he was meeting for the first time felt a bit like déjà vu to him.

I've been here before.

As he walked, noticing that a few others in the street were dressed in white like him or carrying visible signs of religi-osity, he also noticed that a few people gestured toward him. The signs ranged: a few people nodded; some hugged their elbows and pointed their upper torsos in his direction; and one young man faced him directly before crossing the street, stood and stopped, wrapped his right fist in his left hand, and bowed at a slight angle. The jevo could not have been older than twenty-two, with a shaved head and a face the aleyo could get lost in.

He smiled as the young man stood and greeted, said something, hugged his elbows again and put his right fist in his left hand as an additional salute, and continued walking.

close to the display window. She looked at him and nodded. "Some people use them to make you think there is more space." Pepe's mother went on to explain that mirrors like that reflected the original space back to itself, doubling it. "You think there is more space."

From where Pepe stood, the mirror reflected the seat at the far end of the display. It was as if you could walk into another room with that chair. Pepe wondered what it would be like to sit at the rocking chair of the other side and see his world from it.

Upon arrival at family functions, Pepe's mother ordered him to go say hello to everyone.

Pepe's father was dead, but the man's memory hung heavy at family gatherings, as his uncles and aunts remembered what a dancer he was. Dancing lessons with Matilde came in handy as the son tried to live up to the standard of the father. Or at least make sure that it was clear that Doña Tatica's son did not father a pariguayo. Pepe later learned that the word came from "party watcher," the Dominicanization of what happened to men while the US Marines danced with women at the bases during the first invasion in the twentieth century. Before Pepe ever knew this, he thought the word meant that boys like him would birth a guayo. Parir guayo. What was wrong with giving birth to a grater, he asked himself often in front of the mirror in his mother's bedroom. Maybe the pain makes you dance weird? The circles of smiling, talking adults

He arrived minutes later at his madrina's house, recounted the trajectory—editing out the erotic slide in his reception of the young habanero's greeting.

"Están saludando al santo," she explained. They are saying hello to the saint. She then modeled the greeting and his response to it, which should be to bless the greeter.

Bendición. Bendiciones.

Cierra los ojos. Close your eyes.

[Loud knocks on wood]

¿Quién es? Who is it?

¡Yo! It is I!

¿Qué busca? What are you here for?

¡Santo!

The hands

the water

the herbs

his clothes being torn

his hair being cut

the blades shaving him.

He had pledged to keep his eyes closed for the duration of the ceremony. What he looked for lived in these movements, smells, handlings, elaborations on his body by strangers, elaborations he would feel but not see, the hands and fingers, ants moving up and down. The aleyo had no idea how many. Birds, bees all over his body. "Tener fe es como boyar," sickened him, but he knew better than to show an attitude and earn a lecture delivered during breakfast the next morning.

His uncles and aunts told the same stories and laughed at the same jokes, peppering their banter with opinions about the children. Once, after witnessing the beating of a cousin for starting a fight with his sister over pizza leftovers, he heard criticism hurled at the boy's mother for spoiling her child. Never mind that mom requested the belt and began to beat the crap out of her son in front of everyone as her husband sat silently through the round of negative talk without saying fu or fa. When the seven belt lashes had been duly applied, and the unhappy pizza scraps fighter wailed an octave or more above the pitch of *El baile del perrito*, someone reminisced about how effective it used to be to have children kneel, a guayo supporting each knee, in the sun for a good while. Ay, Doña Tatica. How much they missed her!

That was how Pepe's aunts and uncles felt, but Pepe was comforted by the thought of his grandmother being dead. He had no clue of how any of his cousins felt, and he never dared to ask, but facing Doña Tatica meant standing in front of someone with an X-ray to his insides. She was short, stocky, and broad-faced like his father, except that her eyes had the dull finish of bullets. Having raised nine children on her own must have done something to those eyes, he thought. She was a titan at discipline and an authoritarian matriarch, having beaten one of

said Alfredo Labour. "Así es que te tienes que entregar." (To have faith is to float in water. You must give yourself to the experience.) Entregarse: the English "surrender" is power-laden in the wrong way. To give yourself: you are the gift to the gods.

The iyawo remembered learning to float with his father at the beach. He released his body to the water, resting his back and looking at the sky while dad held him slightly: left hand holding his back close to the surface of the water, while dad's right hands guided his legs.

Papá would not let him sink.

Tener fe es como boyar, and his task was to trust what he could not see. As if a movie set moved around him. They bathed him in fragrant water that was too cold.

Becoming an iyawo required preparations and a wardrobe for seven days of ceremony. He might be released after day three or four, but the gods instead decreed that he would sit the full cycle. But the most important ensemble was composed by their iya in collaboration with the iyawo's oyibona and a tailor in Santo Domingo. They were taken to the woman's house for measurements; they saw the complete ensemble and tried it on in Havana, and they wore it during the Día del medio, when other practitioners would come in, offer derechos in Cuban pesos, CUC (Cuban convertible pesos), or US dollars, and ask for a blessing from the orisha just consecrated to the iyawo's head. A woman wore their own dress for el Día del medio as an end to their own her sons with a stick the day he turned forty just because she could. Pepe held his breath when he knew she observed him, waiting for the criticism she would deliver at the end of the ten eternal seconds she devoted to Pepe when he and his mother first came to the door.

Don't walk like an old man. Lift your feet.

Don't speak through your nose.

Don't use your hands so much, niño.

Doña Tatica delivered her don'ts to her grandson so punctually that after a few rounds of this, Pepe began to count the seconds until she said something, from the time she first really looked at him. She stared his way often at family gatherings back in the day, but Pepe was one of the quieter grandchildren, so her eyes generally slid past him. Furthermore, she scolded Pepe directly, and he was grateful to be spared the presence of witnesses other than his mother, who generally sat next to him and to Doña Tatica. He knew his mother did not like the critiques of her son, either, especially because of the casual way Doña Tatica let her and the other women in the family know that a mother of nine knew better than any of them how to raise children.

When her death came, a heart attack provoked by the imprisonment of one of her exemplary children for drug trafficking, Pepe's mother cried for days. No dancing for a while. A relief.

Sitting in front of the mirror in his mother's bedroom, Pepe figured out how

initiation year—so they accompanied the iyawo at the throne. Accompanying one another for a few days, the two priests could see each other in full formal dress before, during, and after the formal ceremony. They would not see themselves.

They came to the Día del medio to wish them health and to salute the santo in the iyawo.

One of the well-wishers was a professional English-language instructor who spoke the language with a slight British accent. He looked at the iyawo and, visibly moved, raised a US dollar bill to the saint and wished out loud that this initiation would harbor better days for relations between the United States and Cuba.

They receive the ceremonial greetings. They eat from white plates, spoons, cups dedicated to them and laid at the foot of the mat. They spend all the seven days sleeping and hanging out at the estera, near the throne. Madrina said to be careful of what you say at the throne because the orishas listen in and might comment right back during your long divination sessions to close the week of ceremony. It delighted him to think that the gods gossiped about him, but yes, some themes touched at the throne in discussions came up again during the divination readings. Going to the bathroom requires assistance from the oyibona. All mirrors are put away.

They see a gown, but they will not see themselves in the gown. There is a to make a genuine sad face. He was too little when his dad died, so he couldn't conjure up sadness related to that. Tweaking his mouth one way or the other, he voted for keeping his eyes angled toward the floor.

That worked, he thought, congratulating himself with the flirt of a smile. But a boy shouldn't smile at faking grief after his grandmother's death.

Don't sway your hips too far.

Don't.

Don't.

He looked again, tried to smile again. He couldn't.

Pepe stared at his own eyes, finding the opaqueness of her grandmother in them. Everyone said Pepe had her eyes. Could she be peering from inside of the ones he saw now, wearing on their sleeve the disappointment of the vieja, judging him? Did she live on the other side of the mirror?

"Look at you," Matilde noted. "Ready."

prohibition against seeing oneself in the mirror for the first three months, maybe for the whole year. A small ceremony is conducted toward the end of initiation just to allow the iyawo to look at their own image for professional purposes, but viewing oneself is forbidden during the year of initiation. Part of it is discipline, part of it is to let time settle their asentamiento so they will eventually take note of changes in bodily morphology, to see the role of initiation in transforming how they present.

Back at the Miami airport, in front of the officer, dressed in white, nuevo iyawocito.

"¿Usted viene de Cuba?" Colombian accent.

"Si, señor. Vengo de hacer santo."

"Eso veo. Bonito el santo," he remarks, matter-of-factly, detached. "Lo veo," says the officer while looking behind the iyawo. "Vaya bien."

I see that. Nice saint. I see it. Be well.

The narratives above do not hold a linear temporal relationship with each other. They do not "translate" into each other, either. In both cases, we see subjectivation as process and collaboration. Analysis, then, is one opportunity to map these circuitries while leaving the expressive sections open for the reader to intervene in, engage with, and contest the project. The goal is to foster a faggotological practice where performative excess is useful surplus value for feminist queer of color bodies seen as too loud or too much.

First, the narratives pluralize the sites, gazes, and mirrors operating in the formation of the yo, calling attention to a cooperative process, a tenuous accomplishment, and a transitive operation. They condense operations that exceed what is narrated. The emphasis is on an analysis of the mechanisms and relationalities activated in the scenes as they are *in progress*, signaled through evocative language about the senses: sight but also touch, hearing. The hip that might slide beyond the boundaries of what I call an "andrographic" performative, or an "imagined form of masculinity" tethered to legitimacy and power under patriarchy.[10] The hailing of a santo borne by a body that holds it yet does not see it. Both narratives allude to the sensorium as the generalized field of perception that affords access not to the certainty of the *ser* but to transit in location, its *estar*.

Second, in both narratives the presence and guidance of black women is central to the making of bodily ideations, but this is a regulatory matrix in which the intervention of women is not strictly maternal. These narratives hold on to mother figures in one way or another (Pepe's mother and grandmother; the madrina/iya) while illustrating in other ways how women outside of the nuclear family (the cousin; the priestesses at initiation) participate in the making and marking of bodies and subjects. The narratives highlight how central the role of women is to the making and remaking of legible embodiments and how women's physical labor, their erotic subjectivities in formation and negotiation, and their access to bodies in formation through touch actively construct, instruct, and discipline bodies in relation to viable dispositions for projects of social or religious legitimation. That these are mostly black women is also crucial to the narratives to the degree that their bodies are burdened to discipline (the grandmother) or guide (the iya) in different moments and projects of masculine and saintly becoming.

Third, the narratives implicate sensorial dispositions with the erotic. Touch, in particular, becomes a crucial sense invoked in both narratives. Pepe Aguilar is guided by his cousin's direction up to a point at which they become one new creature, a centipede, together in front of the mirror. The iyawo's closed eyes suspended vision to experience the guiding touch of strangers at initiation. Yet in both scenarios we can discern that the erotic can also be a source of danger and disruption: the whole exercise in teaching Pepe Aguilar to dance is not only about proper dance steps, but also about how to dance *like a man* and avert the possibility of signaling something else, an aversion instructed through the touch of the cousin; Matilde's own position as a woman and her erotic subjectivity are implicated in the stakes of her effort to make her cousin into a "credible partner" who can "inoculate" her against the potential predations of older men.[11] The religious and the erotic/sexual commingle in the iyawo's reception of a greeting by the young habanero, hinting at the liminality of religious and erotic/sexual economies in contemporary Havana—a disruptive elsewhere to normativity that the anthropologist Jafari Allen has theorized as "transcendent erotics."[12] A dimension of this disruptive play implicates vision and touch in each other: Pepe and Matilde touch each other; the iyawo hears and senses, invoking metaphors of birds and ants to describe sensations in a scene they can feel but not witness.

Cannibalizing the Mirror

The narratives trace codes, gestures, training, and negotiations that socialize bodies. They point to the visual realm and its centrality in mediating legibility. "Mirrors" draws attention to a moment of subject constitution in motion, as Pepe is being instructed in how to move his hips while dancing. The moment of dance offers insights about calibrating his body, as well as the price exacted for "sliding" into hip movements associated with womanhood, the immanence of "failure" in producing (and stabilizing) andrographic performatives. At the same time, the narrative suggests that Pepe's cousin has something to gain from making him into a "credible dance partner." Proper dance shields him from ridicule, but it also shields Matilde from vulnerability to unwanted advances. One might suggest that the scene in front of the mirror is formative for both of these young people, though it is so in ways that are distinct and that lean heavily on the body work of the hips and ass—making clear that playing with one's body, and even hips and ass play as narrated in the cuento, is serious business.[13] Furthermore, gendering slides through the body surfaces of both characters if we consider that Pepe's slide into womanhood feminizes him in a way that brings him closer to the vulnerability to unwanted touch from which Matilde seeks protection. What these young people are negotiating is not "gendering" in general but the potential risk of *femininity as vulnerability* in bodily morphologies for all bodies. In other words, being read as femme/woman/sissy is the liability, and Matilde asks Pepe to mobilize his kinesthetic sense to "get" the proper distance in movement that will hang *hombría* on his hips.

At the same time, "Mirrors" stitches movement to mirror, resulting in the learning of a code one can never articulate precisely, a transfer of knowledge that happens through imitation and the incorporation of one's complete body and disposition into the frame. Matilde and Pepe understand that if the lesson is successful, the young man will incorporate a memory and sense of the "right" angle of his hip movement into his dancing in general, therefore achieving an incorporation of this new habit into how he moves. Although the story at the end suggests the "what" of what Pepe "channels" is the gaze of his dead grandmother, this figure and others observing, disciplining, and training the young man instill in him body codes to move through the world. Beyond suggesting the making of andrographic performatives as collaboration, the cuento illustrates that Pepe learns to see what he cannot see but aim for in his own body—a knowledge that he can carry forward in collaborating in the evaluation of his own and other young men's masculinities. This is part of the social work of the relative stabilization of andrographic performatives, even if they may be subject of debate and even if the possibility of failure is ever-present.

One might also return to this Caribbean cuento for how it can help us elaborate on Fanon's insights regarding the conjunction of schemas—what Stephens describes as "triple consciousness"—in the making of racialized masculinities in motion. A dimension of the story involves Pepe's avoidance of being cast as a "pariguayo," an allusion to the Dominicanization of the phrase "party watcher," allegedly used to describe Dominican men as they watched US Marines dance with local women at their military bases during the first US occupation of the country. Although Pepe playfully misreads the word to mean "parir guayo" (to birth a grater) and even recalls how his elders invoke the grater to discuss the strict disciplinary strategies of the grandmother, "pariguayo" refers to an undesirable heteronormative masculinity, one that basically "has no game" with women. A "pariguayo" is also a man who is considered socially inept. In Dominican working-class street culture, men are legible and legitimate to the degree that they are astute interlocutors or "players" in daily life.[14] The fact that we are talking about men considered viable in contexts of already existing class and racial subordination is hinted at, though not explicitly thematized, in the story. But one can appreciate the pressures Pepe feels and that the story hints at through thematizing Pepe's concern with his own image and the manipulation of his own body. At the same time, there is a distance between the languages of the body and the body's interiority—an aspect of the narrative articulated in the discussion distinguishing Pepe's tears in the aftermath of his grandmother's death from his "real" feelings about Doña Tatica. The education as socialization of Pepe Aguilar unfolds through his awareness of the distance between the truths of how he feels and what he presents to others, how he performs code.

"Mirrors" allows us to sense what brews, moves, and remains in the efforts of Pepe Aguilar to learn the proper codes of masculinity. Fanon's "racial schema," in this case, operates in relationship to class inflection: producing an "able" working-class black heterosexual Dominican man involves avoiding the slide into the feminine, as well as the slide into the space of the "pariguayo" as nullified heterosexuality, a masculinity "without game." The acquisition and incorporation of those codes works in tandem with other parts of the young man's emerging map of bodily deportment. This twinning of acquisition of one's racial and class schema with other dimensions of bodily deportment demands Pepe's reckoning with the distance between the energies moving through his form and grids of intelligibility that the cuento traces through the dancing class, as well as through his encounters with relatives at family gatherings.

"Looking for Santo" operates in a more fragmented way than does "Mirrors," as it draws on memoir, autoethnography, and a third-person narrative voice to unpack the movement from the Catholic child's quest for "sainthood" to a search for "Santo." At the beginning, this impulse toward sainthood addresses and moves away from the suspicion emerging around his inchoate though feared queerness. While the child understands becoming a "santo" as an achievement drawn from the successful pursuit of ascetic life, the abandonment of Catholic dogma is juxtaposed to the opportunity/excuse afforded by migration, the "borrón y cuenta nueva" of leaving Santo Domingo for Philadelphia. The remembered child views sainthood as linked to as well as divorced from his desire, and there are signs from his own rearing that the aleyo interprets religious life as concretizing a permanent exile from his own body.

Religious initiation into Santería provides a scripted dramaturgy of the transition of aleyo to the iyawo, or the bride of the orisha. This transition marks the shift from a loose to a serious commitment to the religion, captured in the moment when one knocks at the door and says that one "wants santo." Initiation effects a borrón y cuenta nueva; after all, it is a religious rebirth, a return to an infantile stage as primary stage of body restructuration, a new morphology that takes on femininity as openness to spirit. Nevertheless, the "santo" elaborated in the body of the new priest begins to be shaped in the image, qualities, and attributes of one's head orisha. Those qualities might include associations with Christian notions of "sainthood," yet these qualities range widely and can be inclusive of cunning and skillful dealing with adverse conditions. What is most crucial in the differentiation between Christian sainthood and Santería's vision of the santo is that the body of the priest is understood to carry the orisha, a force of the universe understood to achieve a "reconnection" with the body in initiation. Going forward, the charge of the priest is to sustain and strengthen that connection. Unlike the "borrón y cuenta nueva" of the Dominican national state, which sustains elite power complicity in corruption through an refusal of accountability from president to president and government to government, "hacer santo" is a rebirth as facing, as grappling, and connecting to historical lines seen and unseen.

Unlike the cuento, where the narrative resource of the mirror is front and center to the making of the subject, "Looking for Santo" chronicles transformations in embodiment that take place without direct access to the mirror. Looking at oneself in the mirror is forbidden throughout the first months of initiation. Preparation for initiation entails training oneself to the discipline and emphasis on proper form from the elders. The change in bodily morphology takes place through dress, ritual cleansing, and training in an ensemble of new performatives. Although the aleyo connects this process to his reminiscence of learning to float in water under the guidance and direction of his father, religious initiation in this case does not involve biological kin but ignites hierarchy, obligation, and kinship built in and through initiation itself, as your age and place in the religion is tied chronologically to the moment of initiation. Even one's bodily disposition in ritual possession is calibrated to be consonant with a given deity, to the point that possessions hinting at the movement of forces not recognizable as of that deity will prompt inquiries to ensure that the person has been initiated correctly.

The narrative of "Looking for Santo" brings together Santo Domingo, Philadelphia, New York City, and Havana in the experience of the aleyo/iyawo. These sites stand in as geographical markers as well as nodes in a circuit. We might guess that most habaneros greeting the aleyo dressed in white might simply understand him to be another "iyawocito" in Havana, but moments of border crossing such as the return to the United States highlight the confluence of geopolitics with religious tourism and specific routes for movement. For example, the immigration officer of Colombian background might have read the returning US citizen as a religious tourist, without dwelling too much on the specificities of their being a Dominican-born returnee. By contrast, the Cuban immigration officers who greeted me on my first trip to Havana—a trip that I took dressed in white—could not make sense of my insistence on being of Dominican background despite the US passport I waved in front of them. They might catch the nuance of my presence, yet the overdetermination of the circumstances might make me read as just another gringo.

So what or whom do we greet when we say ¡Santo!? We are not before the Althusserian subject hailed and turning to the call of the cop, the subject made in the moment of responding to the call of state power.[15] Indeed, the relationship being established between interlocutors expresses a reversed power differential: the person issuing the call does not exercise authority but, instead, asks for the power of the deity to be activated through the blessing. In other words, there are at least three nodes to this exchange: (1) the person calling; (2) the iyawo; and (3) the orisha. The call and the blessing move through a circuit.

Furthermore, the call does not make a subject of the iyawo; instead, it energizes the divinity that has settled in that head. One is being asked to respond to the call through the blessing, channeling the force being asked to provide it.

How do we think of the body of the religious subject, a body vested with carrying the power of a deity? What kind of subjects are being made here? Initiation is a densely social process, carried out to offer practitioners resources they need to get through a world in which they cannot carry themselves explicitly as bearers of divine force. What's on offer is not a modality of freedom that returns primal form to something outside of subjection. Instead, religious initiation establishes the link between an individual priest and their head deity as the starting point for the project of broader bridge work to one's ancestors, to everyone who has ever been initiated to a given orisha, and to future generations. "Looking for Santo" also articulates what I call a queer morphology of the social: the iyawo becomes a sibling to everyone who is a member of their house, but they also become a sibling to everyone else who has been initiated to a particular head orisha. In addition, the process of recognition and greeting of the orisha, apart from articulating and activating the circuitry of the blessing, suggests the coincidence and coexistence of Santería mappings with other mappings of the social. The stranger who greets you does not know from looking at you what your head orisha is, yet that person expresses religiosity and respect through the greeting. The expansiveness of the Santería vision of kinship as articulated through the call to bless is nothing short of extraordinary in its porousness: we can be the stranger's kin in ways indexed but not fully recognizable to them or to us, but we do not need to know the stranger to give (or receive) the blessing.

Finally, the coursing and sliding of the erotic through the divine offers us a sense of the life of the spirit that is deeply connected with what we seek through fleshy engagement, a recognition of rachet life that has import for queers of all colors and the root route for our quest for faggotology. Omi Tinsley discusses this in connection with her consideration of the theoretical import of the lwa Ezili in Haitian Vodou and in black feminist praxis and critique. As she explains, "Ezili is the name given to a pantheon of lwa, who represent divine forces of love, sexuality, prosperity, pleasure, maternity, creativity, and fertility."[16] She elaborates this in relation to the role of the lwa in Haiti:

> If Ezili is water, then you know she contains all kinds of trash. . . . The trash that circulates in Ezili is not only a concrete collection of detritus but, literally and metaphorically . . . a (hi)story of remains. . . . But the waters, the Ezili, become a history of remains that at once archives their past and

predicts their future. In serving as a waste receptacle they collect unclaimed cadavers, (literally) broken homes, household waste, shit, blood, and, why not, unwanted dildos—which, like all the Ezili and unlike most official histories, tell stories of women's, masisi's, madivin's, and poor people's lives. And, in serving as drinking water, they witness that it is possible for the remnants of the past to poison you, yes—but, if properly filtered, that same water can become the key to survival.[17]

Tinsley's consideration of Ezili is linked to her encounter with the lwa in the aftermath of research activities conducted in response to media representations of the 2010 earthquake that shook Haiti. Nevertheless, the way that Tinsley links the "mirrors" of Ezili—the ability of water to collect, contain, and hold space for what is desirable and what is repellent, to be turned from poisonous to life-affirming—underlines the importance of the lwa as a resource and archive for her project. What is crucial to the discussion here in Tinsley's observations of Ezili is the capaciousness of the metaphorical reach of Ezili as Tinsley interprets the lwa, a tapping of valences that afford space for the femme and queer. The traces and movements of the embodied sensorium throughout "Looking for Santo"—in particular, the cruise as call to santo with the young man; the feeling of initiation as being in a dark room—should do much more than alert (and maybe jolt?) the reader to the linkages of perverse desire to divinity. They should support an understanding of these proximities as crucial to what queers of color and others look for and long for in the life of spirit, or perhaps alert us all to the fact that fucking is also soul work. Delighting in the stench of the unbridled freak that can erupt in us, dwelling in our humanity at its most grating, perverse, and open—or, as L. H. Stallings puts it so resonantly, "funking the erotic"—is what is on offer.[18]

Thinking with the history of water as a history of a vast reservoir of what stays, what goes, and what remains, los desechos, also gives us an opportunity to better grasp diffraction relay between the two narratives I have laid out before you. Water can operate as a mirror, as it does for Narcissus, but the image that it gives back to the gazer is tenuous, unstable, excessive, and sensitive to vibrations, currents, and other events that interrupt it. Pepe Aguilar stands in front of the mirror seeking an education that affords him a conocimiento of proper codes of masculine normativity, but that is also a transitive accomplishment pooled from what he learns through his mother and other women in his life—some, such as his cousin Matilde, even going to the lengths of doing a hand-over-hand with him to sway into manhood. The suspension of the mirror effected through the mandate to "close your eyes" in Santería initiation does not cancel the gaze; instead, what is realized and materialized are capacities to sense beyond the positive real, and to understand the bodies of priests as bearers of divine force, a force recognizable and legible to those who grasp the code. In the process of signaling recognition and engaging in the circuitry, they ask not for capture or to be called out by the power of the cop; they ask for a blessing. But one set of realizations does not cancel out another. I have asked you to listen between these narratives partly because they suggest that there are many mirrors through which to refract and that the significations and formations of subjects operate over one another closer to waves as they move through water than images captured in a photograph. There is no gun here to crack all and resolve this house of mirrors into one femme fatale, as Orson Welles's protagonist does at the end of *The Lady from Shanghai*. The mirrors, in their delirious multitude, stand and stay. What I have sought to capture goes beyond the suggestion that there is more to subject formation than one mirror stage. It seeks to illustrate the shapes and structures of gazing to underline that there are several sites to hold space for what remains, what exceeds, and what overwhelms. This is the surplus with which we work and werk; what Delany gestures toward as the evanescent multitude of queers who escape the hold of the raid.

Perhaps the sounds of freedom reside not so much in the longing and realization of pure and unbridled access to one's flesh as in our collective ability to tap, feel, swing, hear, and energize otherwise sensibilities, spaces of spark and flight and sexy. Or perhaps the great space of radical possibility resides in the irresolution of the blur, the jump without end, the dwelling on the irreconcilable juxtaposition that becomes music on its own, a music to which we move not through a model but, rather, through a feeling of countless hands on your head, body fluids feeding one's nascent aché, and the swing of hips near you, prompting you to groove, to move. Tanteando.

Lips smoking what could tranquilize, restore
ghosting, silent gestures. Yellow lines, green
ink folded over, opened as a Christ
-mas gift: A new you, with complicated
hands embracing my cold feet (which you swore
to keep warm). Forever? what a story,
my telenovela, red-carpet star.

OCTAVIO GONZÁLEZ, "EUCHARIST"

Trances

PART III

Indecent Conocimientos

A Suite Rasanblaj in Funny Keys

THIS PART OF THE BOOK PERFORMS FAGGOTOLOGY THROUGH NAR-
RATIVES OF BODIES AT THEIR LIMIT, PSYCHIC/SPIRITUAL CROSSINGS
IN RITUAL TRANCE POSSESSION, OR "STRANGER INTIMACIES."[1] Its title
indexes the conceptual labor of the Tejana/Chicana activist-scholar Gloria
Anzaldúa and of the Argentine theologian Marcella Althaus-Reid. These ancestors come together to insist that different senses of the world and openings
to intimacy are available through a broad conceptualization of the erotic that
cultivates vulnerability, bodies as rich and vast geographies of contact, and a
sense of duration not detained by the temporalities of penetrative sex and
orgasm. This chapter also builds on the philosophical dimensions of Audre
Lorde's vision of the erotic, elaborated by Jafari Allen as including and going
"well beyond associations with sexual identity."[2] I echo and work through
the way Lyndon Gill analyzes Lorde to provide a vision of an ever expanding
and insatiable erotic. "Sexuality and spirituality alone, even when held close
enough together to begin to approximate a new vision of eros that might get
us there, comes up short of a solution," he writes. "We are nearly there, but
eros wants more."[3]

The previous chapters have laid a foundation for the work before us. I have
mapped the journey through an homage to the ancestors and the queer child,

a charting of paths to immigrant and scholarly becoming, the opening to the senses that calls into question the transparent "I" of academic feminist reason, a meditation on relations of exchange and what the silence of sacred objects tells us, and the diffractive relay between becoming a man and the becoming of santo. As nodes in the circuit that is this word *body*, the chapters are re-memberings and re-genreings modeling intellectual work as expressive and artistic labor, holding space for black Latinx queers who are too much. The writings in this suite practice faggotology as an apparatus of self-care, pleasure, sustenance, and soul work for all sucias.[4] The critic Farah Jasmine Griffin (in her rich meditation on the cultural meanings of the singer-musician Billie Holiday) underscores an aspect of Holiday's musicianship that challenged her accompanists and partners: her penchant for singing in G-flat, which the musician and composer Salim Washington calls "one of the hardest keys in which to play."[5] G-flat is considered hard for musicians who learned to read music but not for those (like Holiday) who learned to play by ear. Griffin explains that Holiday's often sudden and surprising shifts to this key confused and challenged her partners, but "this is the beauty of much of Billie Holiday's music: it's in the anticipation. She never goes where we expect her to go. When she shifts to G-flat, we sit in hushed anticipation."[6] In an exchange with the pianist Jimmy Rowles, Holiday taunted her accompanist by stating that she had "picked [him] another hardy." When Rowles responded that the key was "kind of rough," Holiday retorted, "Yeah, that's what I mean; me and my old funny keys."[7] I hold on to the anticipatory undecidability of G-flat—the rough, funny key of this rasanblaj suite—to task you to think of what comes in sound, as sound in time.

How do we enter touch; worship; fuck; and enjoy bodies of dispossession, alienation, captivity—bodies whose blackness is a "tumultuous derangement," an otherwise expression of how we freak through the human?[8] I pursue answers to this question through archival sources at the threshold of literary chronicle, memoir, short story, and autobiography—desechos, detritus fused together to map the circuits of bodies and intimacies. I start from the premise that mystical and sexual rapture are connected and related experiences of our bodies as they meet other bodies, energetic forces, and spirit.[9] What follows focuses on the collective work and contact of fleshy bodies in the pursuit of rapture without end, which makes "indecent conocimientos" a project sibling to "brown jouissance" (Amber Jamilla Musser). As Musser explains, "To emphasize the Other in theorizing jouissance, then, is to think with the pornotrope and emphasize the simultaneous projections of racialization and gendering that occur through its particular modes of objectification. Brown jouissance emphasizes the social relations at work in enfleshment and suggests that the pornotropic network of projection and objectification can coexist with Thingness and its opacity."[10] My choice of narrators grounds what they map as "individual" experiences. But these perform a gathering of everything, refracting collectivities through but not reducible to the one.

The notion of the compatibility of spiritual rapture and being horny, of having an orgasm or dwelling in the tryst without release or penetration, enjoying oneself as a bottom or as a woman, or enjoying oneself fucking with and without condoms in a dark room or in a park might still be a matter of scandalized blushing in some circles in queer(!) and religious studies. But ethnographic work has shown that many gay men become integrated into religious communities by engaging creatively with dogma and adapting it as needed to suit their lives. "Sex is one of the central axes around which [gay men's] spiritual practices and spiritual experiences are organized," writes Peter Savastano.[11] Other writings have recently illustrated an openness to think of spirit with more junctures of gay men's sex, including nonmonogamy, erotically constructed kinship, circuit parties, and BDSM, among other formulations of entangled embodied, enfleshed community.[12]

In what follows, I chart an *erotics of intimacy* where the *erotic* is inclusive of genitality but does not capitulate to one's genitals, to penetrative sex acts, or to linear temporalities of the orgasm. Rather, this erotic conceives of unexpected sites of pleasure in the body. This makes what follows consistent with the work of a cohort of sex- and freak-affirmative black and Latinx feminists, including Jennifer Nash, Mireille Miller-Young, L. H. Stallings, Laura E. Pérez, Juana María Rodríguez, Lyndon K. Gill, and Jillian Hernández.[13] I intend to model something useful for present and future efforts to develop a faggotology of black-, sex-, and freak-affirmative mystical theorizing.

Pursuing "indecent conocimientos" demands thinking outside of heteronormative and homonormative moral horizons, from an elsewhere to the "charmed circle" of respectable sexualities and acceptable corporealities— spaces that (I contend) give us an unusual glimpse of the historicity of cultural norms and possibilities for a praxis of reorienting desire.[14] In a related context, Ernesto J. Martínez explains that there is a problem with the erasure of queer subjects at the site of the fractures they populate—in their cracks: "The fractured locus, or what María Lugones and Gloria Anzaldúa have also called 'the wound,' is a psychosocial, already politicized and 'peopled' location, where sense is contradictory, where multiple worlds of sense are clashing, and where such contradictions are the ground upon which radical knowledge might be gained."[15] These cracks and border zones, beyond allowing us to grasp the challenges to our epistemological frames, reveal distinct dimensions of historical knowledge and experience that would otherwise be unavailable. From the "cuarto de santo" to the room where the misa espiritual is held, to the tambor, to the dungeon, to the ritual for which you kneel and keep your eyes closed for hours, to the circuit party, to the park, and to the dark or back room.

The convergence of queer theory and theology comes through in Althaus-Reid's critique of Latin American liberation theology. "Indecent Theology," she writes (in reference to the title and concept put forward in her 2001 book), "is a theology which problematizes and undresses the mythical layers of multiple oppression in Latin America. . . . An Indecent Theology will question the traditional Latin American field of decency and order as it permeates and supports the multiple . . . structures of life."[16] Althaus-Reid sees liberation theology being extended into a sexual theology for the enrichment of its political imagination to address the challenges facing the poor and the downtrodden. In *The Queer God*, Althaus-Reid explains that she uses "the concept of 'indecency' because the axis of decency/indecency is constitutive of the regulation of the order of society in my own country, Argentina, and especially for women."[17] When first introducing *Indecent Theology*, the author draws on the image of female lemon vendors in Buenos Aires, asking readers to notice how "they sweeten the air with parsley and lemons, but can you smell the odours of their sex?"[18] The appeal of the image registers racial and class differences at a visceral level: Althaus-Reid invites her readers to smell fragrances in the market in their full expressive range, from the lemons to the sex of the women selling them. Thus, her reader is tasked with grasping how easy it is to ignore the sensorially disruptive material conditions that not only produce indigenous women as poor but also further marginalize them through discourses of "decency." One might also specify that the regulation of fragrance, as either a refusal to smell sweaty privates or a misrecognition of that smell through its confusion with lemons, is tantamount to an erasure of the poor women's humanity.

At first glance, a skeptical reader of Althaus-Reid's exhortation might wince at the classed and racialized dimensions of the "invitation" to a whiff of the intimates of market women. What kind of queer feminist asks you to think and smell lemons and market women's pussy? Yet scholarship on indigenous market women, as described in the anthropologist Mary Weismantel's work on Andean women, for instance, suggests that upper-class criollos and whites in Ecuador, Bolivia, and Argentina mobilize odor as part of a larger racialized assemblage to cast indigenous women as undesirable and below the threshold of the human. Weismantel discusses how themes such as "bad hygiene, noxious smells, nonwhite bodies, and women's genitals" come together in the way an economically privileged Bolivian woman speaks about one of her Aymara maids: "I have an extremely well-developed sense of smell and was absolutely disgusted by the mortal odor of this maid." Weismantel points out that in the comment by her interlocutor, "racial fear and loathing cause one woman to experience revulsion toward another."[19] In asking us to "smell the odours of their sex," could Althaus-Reid be asking us to do something that she grasps in her gut as difficult and revolting? In "Introduction: On the Visceral," Sharon P. Holland, Marcia Ochoa, and Kyla Wazana Tompkins discuss a "blurring" that is effected by their conceptualization of the "visceral"—of "the theoretical pressure that the visceral conjures as the line between subject and object—the line between my shit and your shit."[20] The pursuit encouraged by Althaus-Reid, then, could be cast along the lines of thought articulated by Holland and her colleagues: "We are speaking, in some senses, of affect: more than that, we are speaking about relational maps that obscure the distinction between self and other, subject and object, persons, things, and animals."[21] In informal conversations with colleagues familiar with the class, racial, ethnic, and regional dynamics inflecting Althaus-Reid's comment, we also discussed the matter in connection with the work of her compatriot, Rodolfo Kusch, whose thinking touches on questions of *hedor* (stench) and indigeneity.[22] I learned that the layers of clothes worn by market women point to (1) the conditions of travel to the plazas where they sell produce; (2) their need to wear layers in anticipation of subtle and drastic changes in temperature; and (3) their lack of access to bathrooms while in the plazas.[23] As troubling as it is to cross this imaginative threshold through smell, could the problem be not of smell itself but, rather, of our knowledge of its contents? In other words, could the disruptions effected present themselves not as ontological disruptions but as epistemological and sensorial disruptions? What are we willing to know? What will we imagine? Are we willing to receive the other, to take in their smell in this more expansive view of what is possible in relationality?

Althaus-Reid leans on the obscene, the visceral, and the disreputable to challenge theology. In contrast, Anzaldúa's theoretical work centered on a loosely esoteric view of "conocimiento" to center intuition and embodied vulnerability. Mirella Vallone points out that in Anzaldúa's later writing there is "an 'invocation' for vulnerability as a necessary feeling for constructing spiritual/political communities to struggle for personal growth and social justice."[24] Vallone characterizes this turn toward metaphorical and somatic vulnerability in the later Anzaldúa as key to the Chicana thinker's path to conocimiento. Although *conocimiento* might be translated as either "knowledge" or "wisdom," Anzaldúa's conceptualization is capacious. "Tu camino de conocimiento," she writes, "requires that you encounter your shadow side and confront what you've programmed yourself (and have been programmed by your cultures) to avoid (desconocer), to confront the traits and habits distorting how you see reality and inhibiting the full use of your facultades."[25] Anzaldúa's view of conocimiento presents it as a path toward accessing and disrupting one's normative habituations, which preclude a more holistic view of reality, as well as one's spiritual gifts. For this discussion, the most useful moment in the passage is Anzaldúa's positioning of the English "to avoid" next to "desconocer" in parenthesis; this suggests that the English might be a translation for the Spanish or vice versa, though the polyvalence of the words do not allow for such an assumption. The verb *avoid* means "to keep away from, keep from, keep off" in its current usage, whereas *desconocer* has more to do with the pursuit of knowledge.[26] According to the *Real Academia de la Lengua Española*, the following are meanings of *desconocimiento*: "1. Not to remember an idea one had about something, to have forgotten it; 2. not to know; 3. when said about a person: to deny that something is yours; 4. to act like something does not have to do with you, or to ignore it; 5. to not see the adequate correspondence between an act and the idea that one has of an idea or of someone; 6. to recognize a noticeable change one sees in someone or in something."[27] Given these meanings (related yet distinct) of words sitting next to each other, Anzaldúa asks us to do something other than "translate" one word into another. She invites us to consider the diffractive relay available in semantic fields in two languages, as the two words sit side by side.

Instead of interpreting Anzaldúa's "to avoid (desconocer)" as an error in translation, I hold on to what she brings together by having these words neighbor each other. "To avoid" might require turning away, and that turning might be an abdication of responsibility for the recognition of that which faces you. An act of denial or willful ignorance, "to avoid (desconocer)" could be refusal to look at one's shadow, inability to grasp more than what immediately meets the eye, and focus on the fragrance of lemons at the exclusion of the smell of the women who pick them up in the fields and bring them to the market. Inspiring my effort is the work of Deborah Vargas, which identifies sites of disobedience to the homo- and heteronormative imperatives of neoliberal capitalism as *lo sucio*: "*Sucias* are surplus subjectivities who perform disobediently within hetero- and homonormative racial projects of citizenship formations, projects that seek to rid their sanitized worlds of filth and grime."[28] What might it mean, then, to face, move, and take in through smell that which we have been taught to "avoid (desconocer)"?

The first movement of the suite addresses the political dimensions of trance possession and transnational exchange, both in the case of an early moment in my path to initiation as it is linked to the extractive and violent ethos of tourist economies. The suite then moves into a short story, "Adagio," to present an expressive approach to intimacy, sex, and the mystical among gay men of color. Set in the late 1990s, this cuento is but one of many imaginable possibilities of stranger intimacy, and its inclusion provides an expressive calibration to the overall chapter. Tapping what Vargas calls *archisme*—"a way of acknowledging hearsay, murmurs, and silent gestures . . . as a base of knowledge production"[29]—I turn to a third-person narrative voice in the third movement, a crónica of growing into gayness in Philadelphia and New York of the 1990s and early 2000s. My aim is to allow for space between what is personal experience and what captures the experience of other men of my generation, to suggest not so much "representative" narratives but to guide the way we ask questions about the historical contours of important shifts in the erotic lives of gay men in the age of AIDS. "Closing Movement Open" elaborates the implication of these example narratives for the practice of "indecent conocimientos" in faggotology.

¡No te montes!

That Sunday morning in March 2013, at the closing ceremony of the Transnational Black Feminist Retreat that he attended, he ripped his old clothes and tossed them in the river before putting on what he wore for the tambor to Oshun and Anaisa. During the tambor, as he danced with the woman he had started to call "madrina" and with other attendants, he was another tourist saying goodbye to the Dominican Republic after a week of intense discussions. Out of the corner of his eye he noticed a friend watching him dance. She had commented to him earlier that he seemed more at peace with himself, more whole. He continued to dance as she came toward him and motioned to whisper something in his ear: "No te montes."

He kept dancing, inhibited by the unsolicited advice. He did not get possessed, but something in that warning rattled him. After all, here he was beginning to discover a bridge back to his body through dance, through the sound of drums, after so much of his life had been lived in exile from bodily movement.

Yet here he was, finding a path to that movement, to that body, and someone said, "No te montes." Do not get mounted. Derived from the verb *montar* (to mount) or its self-reflexive locution *montarse*, the comment means "to let oneself be mounted by" and "to mount." Doesn't the attraction to Santería derive from the possibility of having your body become a vessel for spirit? Isn't montarse about letting go of the straitjacket of hombría, losing oneself completely and "abandoning with abandon" as a mystical power bottom?

How can he mix up so much here—gender dissent, getting fucked, and hosting spirit?

This is our knot.

At this early stage of the game, he could not see how power and discipline were implicated in his access to trance possession as a tourist. His notion of "freedom" at the river on that Sunday morning did not consider that black women would labor and guide if he became possessed. "No te montes," which he heard as being asked to hold back from the intensification of his experience, was a protective warning for him and for others in the space. Perhaps it mattered that one less uninitiated person stay out of a trance possession for what that could mean for the overall dynamics of the party. His mystical fix would ultimately be black women's labor.

He remembers being possessed in the thick of his first misa spiritual: not the details, only the sensations, intensity of the emotions, and work required to bring him back. That was one of the first times he heard the expression *pasar muerto*. Translated as "channeling spirit" or, literally, "letting the dead pass," the phrase indicates a moving energy that intensifies emotions; an urge to cry; or the naming of unfamiliar names, memories, unexpected body movements. How do prayer and song move the group to that space of vulnerability—a kind of striptease of the soul, a point where being a mariconcito is the best way to be because that is the most open, the body most capacious of feeling?

In meditation, you observe the workings of your mind, acknowledging what is moving through you, and turn your attention to your breath. In the misa espiritual, you are instead guided into the space of the emotion, the hurt, the revisited horror or beauty, the desire to touch, the longing to greet a dearly beloved or the loved ones who have left. There is a message there, and your job is to receive it by letting what is passing move through your body, not by turning away from it. You don't control the message as it moves through you; rather it is in the collective work with your body-vessel that you learn what transpired.

Furthermore, trance possession holds a complicated relationship with tourist economies in which religious tourists participate. A brief cinematic moment of "possession interruptus" could help better discern problems he missed as an accidental religious tourist. In Laurent Cantet's film *Vers le sud/ Heading South* (2005), set in the 1970s Haiti of "Baby Doc" Duvalier, tourist

Brenda (played by Karen Young) is going out with the young Legba (Ménothy Cesar), a man she met and had sex with during an earlier trip to Haiti, when he was a fifteen-year-old boy. She and her husband had fed him and "adopted him" before she violently took him sexually: "I couldn't stop screaming."[30] Brenda was forty-five when she first seduced the young man, filling her pussy with young black dick, leading her to the first orgasm in her life, as she tearfully recounts for the camera—as if pity for her barren life justifies her predation of a child. Recently divorced, Brenda returns to Haiti looking to rekindle the flames lit by the adolescent, who is eighteen when they see each other again. Legba invites Brenda to the dance floor during a party; their initial joint dancing is modulated into a musical interlude led by the percussion. As Brenda separates from Legba, she dances on her own, apparently taken by the sound of the accelerating drums, now without the accordion and the acoustic banjo that open the musical piece. We get indications that what is happening is more than dancing, as the camera cuts to shots of the smiling hotel staff and one of the children hovering and staring at Brenda. We see Legba's profile as he examines what is happening, with interspersed cuts to the back of the leader of the combo (himself dancing), as well as shots of the tourists and locals congregated around the dancing white woman. Brenda's blonde hair waves and moves in an increasingly frantic manner. Without changing his steady expression, Legba leaves his companion and walks over to whisper something in the director's ear. After hearing Legba's request, the director stops the drumming, and a disconcerted Brenda is back in Legba's arms, dancing to a calmer rhythm now that the accordion and the banjo are back.[31]

The scene in *Vers le sud* replayed in his mind after the comment at the tambor. Legba's interruption of Brenda's access to possession through a change in musical language contrasted with the friend's warning not to allow himself to be mounted. Legba's name indexes a Vodun deity who opens the path for the connection between humans and the spirit world. Legba interrupts Brenda's access in this moment in the narrative when he asks for a stop and change in the music. The friend asked him not to allow himself to be mounted, the whispering voice counseling his body to avoid going over a limit he could not know himself. Or maybe this was a limit he had to consider and think further about before crossing. Still, this scene also dramatizes the asymmetries of power and access being worked out in both situations, even as the moments pointed to possibilities of something else hovering at the edge of the touristic gaze, something not as easily subjected to access by all bodies, something else making contact. Had he become Brenda, the depleted first-world subject eager for contact and sensation, willing to be violent to fulfill her desire? Had he become voraciously intense and aggressive bottom pushing to the limit, irrespective of who had to work to satisfy those needs to scream and experience bodily excess and shattering, whose bodies he would tax with dealing with the consequences of his experience?

His training toward initiation involved talk, guidance, and disposition toward the process. The more he participated in misas espirituales, the more he became aware of the skills involved in mediumship and aware of how much care, discipline, devotion, and work were involved. His homework was to watch and learn, but ritual was collective labor.

"Para prepararte bien, tienes que boyar" (To prepare yourself well, you need to practice floating in water), the husband said.

Floating in water. Practice.

He practiced floating in water as often as he could, but talk of "boyar" brought back the memory of how his dad first guided him through the breathing and muscular relaxation required to achieve proper form in the waters of Andrés beach, all of that while being guided by the gentle touch of a parent who found few occasions and excuses to express physical connection. The moment comes to his mind's eye, a conjunction of the old albums his mother collected, with all those pictures fading in a glow of light pink, with the recollection of the handsome man his father was, telling him to breathe and look up at the blue sky. There it was, in his line of sight: the father and the sky. His father: his sky.

A flash of recognition came to him while watching the swimming scene in Barry Jenkins's *Moonlight* in which young Chiron is instructed by his mentor, the local drug dealer Juan. They are black; Juan is Cuban. Juan is teaching the young man growing up in downtown Miami how to float in water. "Let your head rest in my hand," Juan says to Chiron as the boy hesitantly lies back in the salty waters, as if he is about to be baptized. "I promise you. I got you. Relax. I'm not gonna let you go. Hey, man: I got you."[32] His floating lessons with dad must have been analogous to this, the young boy entrusting his head to the guiding hand of a parent who loved him, who would never let him go, even after the boy became a man whom dad no longer recognized. He was baptized in the loving hand of the father. Like the critic Ashon Crawley, he saw that "*Moonlight* reminds me that black life is about a life touched and held, and that there is joy therein, that the touch I have sought and still seek is one that many of us desire, and that such desire is worthy of its pursuit."[33] But in that floating scene, as well as in the rest of the movie, he agrees with the critic Jared Sexton's assessment: Chiron "demonstrates in the enigma of his own living that the question—who is you?—remains strictly unanswerable insofar as it is a claim to self-knowledge."[34] As Chiron dwelled in an immanence of being unresolved in diegesis, he was held by Juan, and together they were enough.

Boyar was not easy, but he thought he grasped what the husband meant when he brought up the metaphor. Meaning "to float," the word *boyar* suggested a specific deployment of the body, a disciplined relaxation meant to calibrate and strike a balance of the body in the water. Achieving equilibrium involves both the weight of the body and the degree to which its tightening will precipitate sinking and (potentially) drowning. The only way to experience the benefit and relaxation that the practice would provide occurred once his body figured out how best to "be" in the water. In other words, an access to release did not eschew disciplined practice. Analogous to what Musser explains for brown jouissance, boyar does not result in definitions of who he is. "It reveals," she writes, "a sensuality or mode of being and relating that prioritizes openness, vulnerability, and a willingness to ingest without necessarily choosing what one is taking in. This is not the desire born of subjectivity in which subject wishes to possess object, but an embodied hunger that takes joy pain in this gesture of radical openness toward otherness."[35]

Walking with the ancestors and the orishas also involved figuring out a disciplined way to let go, guided by experienced elders and mentors, as well as by his spirit guides. Entrusting his head in their hands. Boyando. As he moved through, he learned by watching other people how their bodies could serve as hosts for other energies. Access to that degree of ability to instrumentalize one's body came with time and practice. "No te montes," then, was also a caution regarding his responsibility to his body and others' bodies. In evacuating his self so prematurely for other energies to move through him, he was in fact violating his learning process.

Adagio

Peach left. At the station, our eyes crossed paths again, for the last time. The train took him from me, his light gone and my lungs straining to work without air.

How would I walk back? The heat engulfed me. Someone had dipped my legs into wet concrete and let it dry in their embrace. I heard the train lose itself in a whisper. People walked and ran past me, disappearing.

Minutes trickled by and my eyes took note of a cold coffee, legs that moved, and a couple book bags.

I sat at a nearby bench.

HE CAME TO MY DOOR after we exchanged words on the phone.

I opened the door and scanned his sandals, the dark jeans, the fleshy pouch hidden in his light sports jacket. I did this quickly, I thought; when our eyes met, his pair had surveyed my sweats, pouch, dark face, and flat nose.

"You sure you look like what's on the ad?" We asked this in unison.

We laughed.

"What's up?" I said as we walked up the stairs.

Horny.

"Me, too."

There was no trace of a smile on his lips. I didn't smile, either.

"Come in."

Yep.

"You look like what you said." I stood facing him after closing the front door of my apartment.

"Truth in advertising"—my motto.

I looked at his lips as they stretched to a grin; then I discovered his teeth. We stood a few feet apart.

One, two, three, four beats. One of us inched closer. Don't remember who. One, two, three, four.

I asked him to keep smiling and I touched the left corner of his lips with my index finger, attentive to the new words his skin gave, crawling through the line where his lips met.

"You into kissing?"

He nodded and took off his cap. My tongue retraced the imaginary line my finger had drawn and then met his tongue. We lingered at that first meeting, tasting each other. I took in the salt of his sweat when we kissed, adrift in a sea of toothpaste and mouthwash. He had showered before getting here.

His nude body was a desert, and I touched him with the tip of all my fingers while looking into his eyes for a response. At first, he seemed perplexed by this test of his capacity to feel. The obvious places I would visit with my mouth, but he kept his eyes open while my hands caressed the small of his back, crossed the inside of his arms or began to rub his belly. With so many unstable people calling the hookup line or advertising online, he probably thought I could be a psychopath. He couldn't simply surrender to my touch. Not yet.

But as my hands glided across his thighs, and as I asked myself whether the hairlessness was natural or hygienic, I noticed with joy the incompleteness of his efforts to sculpt. His arms were too thin for his trunk, and his belly was more noticeable than it appeared when I first saw him.

I touched. Upon recruiting my mouth to engage Peach's chest, the cool brush of his hand surprised me. I had been so busy touching him that I forgot myself. His fingers walked down my back, cold with the memory of having touched something refrigerated.

It was fun—that first fuck—and we exchanged phone numbers. There was work, sex with one or two other people, books to read, music to listen to, and the prompt arrival of another nasty Philadelphia summer. Peach called one of those nights, and we met again.

Those first times, in the middle of whatever chit-chat topic we coughed up as background music to the opening of doors and the falling of clothes, I took mental notes on his scent.

One morning, as I had breakfast, his sweetness assaulted my nose. I noticed it, understanding that it had some relation to Peach, but I was unclear as to what and where it came from. I had not seen him in days, and there he was, lodged in my nose.

We talked little, clear that these encounters were strictly sexual. But we still talked, and I learned that he was in town on business and that a date was assigned for his departure, to a new work site. He made a passing comment about loving the scent of peach.

That's not right.

That couldn't have been unsolicited. I must have asked him about the scent.

As an anthropologist, I needed data. What was that scent? My memory betrays me again. Maybe it *was* unsolicited; one night he visited, and I told him to help himself to whatever he found in the fridge.

May I have a yogurt?

"Weren't you thirsty?"

Yes, but I love peach.

"That's pretty tropical of you."

"Not tropical enough," he countered, with the sly hint of a dimple gracing his chin. "Mango, yes, but not peach."

I walked to the square and back home the next morning, gladdened by the pressure I felt in my right forearm, which he had grabbed with force the night before. I sat reading and stopped at the end of every few pages to caress my forearm and to attempt (uselessly) to remember when and for what reason I could still feel his hand on it. They say people can feel a lost leg or arm, but my pleasure was in the pain of knowing I was growing one.

I smiled, eating a yogurt, feeling the acidic edge of the peach fold into the creamy whiteness.

I breathed in and got up.

In the kitchen, in the bathroom, in my pillow—Peach was everywhere, flooding me.

He called a few nights later.

"Come over."

The apartment set up by the company was as comfortable as a hotel room—furnished, on a high rise with a view of the city skyline and within walking distance of everything he could need.

"They treat you well," I said.

I sat at the square. People passing by on their way home were wearing formal clothes. Joggers. Dogs and their owners walking each other. To remember him: the texture of his sweat; the feel, smell, and taste of his cum in my mouth; his moans when I buried my face in his ass.

My breath returned.

Mahal, the only word in Tagalog I knew, crashed into our conversation one day, at Peach's apartment. He wasn't much of a talker, or maybe fucking didn't leave much room to be chatterboxes. My goal in those encounters, then, centered on getting a healthy dose of dick, and everything indicated that the feeling was mutual. There was little to talk about between rounds of sex.

Peach's departure date was set.

"Do you know where you are going next?"

Boston. Paperwork came in yesterday.

"You didn't even get to hang a picture here."

That's the job, mahal.

"Mahal?"

Dear. That's what it means.

[Pause]

"Boston is not that far."

It's not walking distance.

"Right."

For that night, summer gave us a break. I walked back to the apartment, taking in the coolness.

A week passed. Neither of us called.

I called. The phone went to voicemail.

I hung up.

I called again. And again.

Stop. I had to stop.

Two days later, he called.

Hello.

"What's up?"

At home. Tired from work. You?

"The usual."

A few inane sentences later, Peach said we might get together later in the week.

That went directly into my gut.

But you are well, he said. Or he asked. He let the end of the sentence meander, unsure whether he wanted to know or assure the two of us that all was well.

"Yes. Well," I said, right before a full beat passed between the end of his question and my answer.

Good. Call you later in the week.

"Bye."

Bye, mahal.

He didn't call. I didn't mind. I had plenty to do and could always tap my buddies for company. Maybe that's what he was up to.

I never asked and never learned what his work was. I was glad Peach did not ask me more than one or two banal questions about my day. I had already dumped too many guys for asking questions. Why do you need to know where I work or why I look black but speak with an accent? Can you wrap up my dick in that information, like whipped cream, and then suck it? I didn't get this need to "interview" before fucking. What a relief that all Peach did, other than say "What's up?" and muse about the weather, was take off his clothes. My life had become my favorite porn film—his body posed the questions, and my grunts were the answer.

Weeks passed, or so I thought.

He began calling again. Some calls were clearly for sex, but he then began to call for nothing. He liked going to museums, something I abhorred.

I'm meeting some friends later in the week, he said. Dinner and a movie. Maybe just a movie. Want to come?

"Yes."

It was a date, I guess, concocted after I knew deeply how most of him tasted. We got courtship backward.

What did I know? I knew that his mouth often tasted of peppermint at first but that beneath that his breath contained a mixture of sweetness and acidity. I knew that his tongue often got sore from kissing, that he stuck it in my mouth as if he wanted to give it to me and that the best time to kiss him (to give into the urgency of his passion) was when he fucked me. I knew that he liked burying himself in me several times per session and that when this happened I felt like a chicken who survived a feather plucking and a hot shower. With him, my ass was the most beautiful, hottest thing on earth. I learned to hold back and witness Peach enjoy himself. This I knew.

I met him and Sally, a work friend, for dinner. Others invited didn't show. Like him, Sally was Filipina. Unlike Peach, she had decided to stay in Philadelphia.

"Liked your friend," I said when we were alone.

She liked you, too.

"Excited about the new rotation?"

I am.

"Good for you."

Don't you think it's just good?

"Yes."

So why not say just "good"?

"It's just an expression." We paused at a corner to wait for our turn to cross the street. "You are right, it's just 'good.' I'm happy . . ." I stopped and turned to him: "for you."

Peach wasn't looking at me.

A worm moved slowly down my stomach as he undressed. I sat on a side of the bed that gave me a surprising angle on his face and body. Maybe it was the lighting, which he had reduced to a small lamp. But I sat observing him. This must be what happens to people who have patience for visual art. There was a glow to those legs, that belly, those arms, and that face so keen in looking anywhere but at me. I was fascinated.

Are you just going to sit there? he asked, looking at me directly for the first time.

"Oh, no," I said. I undressed quickly.

In one scene in a Marquis de Sade book, a woman participates in orgies. Fuckers come and go, but the climax of the story arrives when one of those men wants to kiss her and she refuses. The kiss, she says, is the one thing she won't give.

As Peach's ass sank into my face again, I couldn't help but think of this story someone told me. Here I was, sticking my tongue out into the part of Peach's body that gave me closest access to his insides. I liked fucking him, kissing him, but sticking my mouth in him was about tasting him, beyond the peach flavor that lived in his skin, beyond the mint that traveled in his breath. This, I said to myself, this is my kiss.

Peach appreciated the fervor I brought to this activity. The piggy in me, he joked once. This time, I felt the back of his thighs as I kissed, licked, and bit him mildly. I felt his back again, heard approving sounds from above, and then felt drops of water on my belly. At first, I thought he had climaxed, and I used my right hand to verify.

This was too watery.

The moans modulated into spastic sounds. Waves of pores swept through him while his hands grabbed inside his butt cheeks, opening himself for me. A few more seconds passed, and I felt his hands leave his cheeks while his legs adjusted from a crouch to a kneel to keep his hips balanced. Peach wanted to ensure that I did not stop.

In the dim light, I looked at Peach's hole. They say assholes open like flowers. This flower came alive when I spoke to it. I ran my tongue around it once, twice, again and again, until I lost count.

More groans, though I suspected they were not just groans. Peach had left his dick alone this whole time, but he began to stroke himself. More drops, and then Peach's moans modulated into hiccups.

I stopped. I hugged him.

Neither of us came that night. The next morning, the sunlight shining in his apartment awoke me. I opened my eyes and looked around. Peach had a rosary hugging a lamp, with family pictures: two boys, an older man and a woman smiling, and a black Labrador retriever. A thick CD binder was open on his kitchen counter, but otherwise the whole place was immaculate, as if someone cleaned it daily.

The picture could have been taken in California or Toronto, both places where Peach had spent part of his childhood. The brothers appeared to be between ten and twelve.

I turned to see whether he was awake. He wore a sleep mask.

I flipped through Peach's CD collection. Sade, Opera's Greatest Hits, Salt-N-Pepa, Vivaldi. He had wide-ranging tastes, or maybe his friends wanted him to widen his tastes.

No, this was Peach. I once heard him grooving to a Salt-N-Pepa song, humming it to himself. I was surprised by Sade. I kept flipping—Brandenburg Concertos, Kenny G, Cecilia Bartoli. I wondered when he played these CDs, how they came to his life, what ambiance they created in this place. Kenny G on Saturday mornings while making coffee; the "Folie!" scene from *La Traviata* while cooking dinner.

Stop.

I closed the binder.

I HAD WORK TO DO, lunch to pack for the next day, and a TV show or two to fall asleep to. I got up.

Time to go home.

Looking for Essex

With all due respect to Essex Hemphill, what he thinks as he fucks is not his question.[36] He grew up a member of a generation of gay men who knew that a death sentence could slip through the pinhole of a condom. It was the "plague" that decimated his elders of "the AIDS generation." He did not share in that direct collective trauma, but death "reared its rear" everywhere.[37] He knew of the stigma precipitated by HIV seroconversion—the moment in time when the tryst with the theater director ended—a sizzling and sustained bit of habitual post-lunch (dessert?) action interrupted by the condom that broke, when his other mouth hungered for meat. Another time one of them got tired of "wrapping it" and decided without asking that flesh on flesh was hotter, followed by the postorgasmic manic dance of the fuckee, between outrage and delight. Other times one came inside the mouth of the other—that oops that was not much of an oops. Also the times they powered through sense-full push-pull and then met the broken condom with an "Oh, well."

His friend Henry, in college, taught him something important about their moment. A mathematician, Henry kept precise, fastidious records of sexual encounters: dates, locations, organs and acts, characteristics of partners (clothes, birthmark, that guy with the one testicle or the slumped dick that tore), and what went down. Here was a perfect symbol of his generation, coming of age in the 1990s: a calendar tattooed by the traces of sex, paper flesh that memorialized details unable to capture the movement of bodies, fluids, energies—and all this playing into a political economy of risk. That was the erotic education of gay men before 1996. He did not keep such scrupulous records himself, but any fever or oddity in his love tool, his groin—a tingle in his pucker—prompted a run to a doctor and a battery of sexually transmitted infection (STI) tests from medical professionals, all of whom pretended to be cool when he disclosed being gay but then tested for everything. With HIV, he spent his twenties feeling like he filed taxes biannually, except that what could be in default could be his life.

This lusty dance with panic and fear was generalized in those years. There was the scared face of the tall black guy who revealed an HIV diagnosis, the benevolence barely masking the panic of his interlocutor, the agony of the test, the

142   CHAPTER SIX

matching of dates to partners and locations. All of this shaped the historicity of his fucking; his hunger for dick, cum, and burying his face in ass but having to look closely first, even in dark rooms when you could see nothing, for indications that something might go awry. The one day he met Hemphill's wolf eyes on a college campus? One missed opportunity to have their sex breed ancestral conocimiento for their tribe. That would have been a sex event for the history books.

What do we know as we fuck?

What do we fuck to know?

These are his questions.

Happy lived in the taste and smell of semen. He frequented the Roxy Theater in 1990s Philadelphia, where the film directors Marlon Riggs, Isaac Julien, and others taught their audiences not just about pride and affirmation, but also about how much belonging could be fostered in and through fucking. The pride stuff was nice, and some of it was fun, but he was clear from early on that (for him, at least) this was about dick/dejar la leche correr (bathe in rivers of semen). Before he ever knew who Hemphill was (let alone that he was a published poet), he had heard the chamber ensemble rapture of the poet reciting "Now we think" in Marlon Riggs's *Tongues Untied* against the *basso ostinato* "Now we think as we fuck," which works up in crescendo with Hemphill's voice (as in sex) to a final release (climax) and conclusion. The verses of this poem he heard before he ever laid eyes on the poet's words. *Community* was the most bandied, necessary, yet increasingly normative turn in gay male movements for liberation as they came to be institutionalized in the mid-1990s and the first decade of the twenty-first century. Community completed the movement of cis white male bodied gay men in couples into the fold of what the anthropologist Gayle Rubin called the "charmed circle" of normative sexualities. Indeed, Rubin was prophetic: she saw a homonormative horizon in the making at least one decade before it became clearer to many other observers. But there were collateral benefits proffered to bodies with proximal relation to those newly enfranchised gay white men, if they remained nominally committed to marriage and respectability. The time had come to leave aside trips to the sauna, glory holes, and phone-line hookups. The queers of Philly's Judy Garland Park knew that their days in the gutter, enjoying the occasional golden shower or gagging behind the bushes at least in that rapidly gentrifying section of the city, were numbered.

White men in the Philadelphia in which he came to be a young Dominican gay man taught him the ropes of homonormative selfhood with "skin the color of mocha," as Ricky Martin sang before the singer ever told everyone the obvious, though they also expected the dominicanito to wear condoms as a gesture of ethical community love. Under the whiteness of gayness, his latinidad was the racial cultural dehiscence expected, the bit of adobo of the almost the same but not white, the uncut meat and firecracker male version of Carmen Miranda, a declension from the big black dong worshiped by the fetishizing gaze of Mapplethorpe, and a distant cousin of the pornotrope.[38] That's the drift grid circuit of his travels through that side of the veil. Wearing a condom became hot not on its own but because it signaled how (mostly white) gay men affirmed their sex as the glue that held them together. For him, cumming in a condom became an affirmation of gay sex as loving loyalty. The love gesture that was needed was not the one directed at the partner, either; it was born out of fierce gratitude to the gay men who pioneered safe sex to ensure that life was in their (and his) future. He was so committed to this that he even sucked wrapped dick under bathroom stalls. The juxtaposition of "seedy" and "clean" could not have been more startling than this—prophylactic and hot.

But in the mid-1990s, community also exacted the price of foreclosing conversations about how sexual practices themselves (in all their varieties) held gay men together. What about cum, piss, shit, sweat, and saliva (especially in the porn he began to borrow from video stores)? What about the orgies structured around the grunting, the panting, the fisting, the anonymous force of the man sitting on his dick in the booth next door, the dick he salivated over for weeks in that bathroom until he mourned its disappearance, at that time and day and under that same shared wall between booths? Didn't he come out to enjoy that, too? The exhilaration of walking out of the bathroom or the park after having swallowed the load of the suit, the jogger whose inebriating sweat stayed with you a week after discovering his armpit? Sometimes he confided in his journals, but the gay men he knew and who were his friends (with few exceptions) exiled desire, perversion, and pleasure to the closets of privacy. None of them talked about *this*. Perhaps, like him, they played with themselves in the intoxication of that finger pushing in, the gagging reflex of the violent stranger, the sensation of opening to the cock in the booth next door, or the tart apple taste of the tongue that your tongue met on the train.

He once tried to talk at a dinner party hosted by his gay parents, two older white gay college professors, and other (mostly white) men. He was the youngest person in the room, maybe the only man of color, but he is not sure that is correct, being that his gay parents often had men of different backgrounds at their parties. Still, he was the young man listening for the wisdom of the elders. In the middle of a raunchy talk, he mentioned going to the local video store and finding vintage gay films, which he rented. In the early 1990s, some internet platforms featured gay porn from the 1970s. He described what he saw there, betraying his amazement at discovering a history of fucking that preceded him. The men were so hot. The sex was hot—sweaty, delirious, life-affirming, and messy.

He must have carried on for thirty seconds without noticing the energy shift in the room. "Remember that most of those guys are dead," one of his gay parents said. They had buried friends, fuck buddies, and partners; so had other men in the room. One man he knew (a man the couple had adopted decades earlier, just as they had adopted him) was HIV-positive; he died during those years. To them, this was not funny or hot.

Everyone else got up, putting an end to that phase of the conversation. He doesn't remember if this was during dessert, before or after the Sambuca. In the thicket of his memory is the recollection of shame. That was some fucked-up thing to say. But still, this scene dramatized a cross-generational and cross-racial rift among gay men, the coming apart of tectonic plates. As the scene aged in his mind, he considered it a perfect way to illustrate what Raymond Williams called "the residual" in social formations: "The residual, by definition, has been effectively formed in the past, but it is still active in the cultural process, not only and often not at all as an element of the past, but as an effective element of the present. Thus certain experiences, meanings, and values which cannot be expressed or substantively verified in terms of the dominant culture, are nevertheless lived and practised on the basis of the residue...of some previous social and cultural institution or formation."[39] The raunch of unbridled gay sex as residue, the remnants—these were the remains he venerated as he milked himself. The gap between his generation and that of older men was growing, but the depth of the hole that opened before his eyes was hard to imagine. How dare he salivate over men who were dead or dying? He could not afford to lose the gay family whom he came to know and love, so he fell in line, but the price exacted was that he now understood that some of his experience could not be spoken, even with fellow gay men.

A few years later, he joined the ranks of the HIV industry while pursuing a doctoral education. Glory holes began to disappear in New York, and this was tragic to him, especially because it was all turning during his first year in graduate school. I mean, he had a whole relationship of months with one large member, who met his mouth through a hole at a specific time and on specific days. Then that hole disappeared! People were more vigilant in parks and train stations. Bathrooms were being redesigned, even though one bold black guy with dreadlocks managed to eat his ass for several minutes while the door to the bathroom was fully open. The whole erotic geography of

New York for gay men was reengineered. He suspected that the institutions and buildings were so busy trying to eliminate traces of men like him that they hired professional homosexuals, or "dabblers" in these scenes, to provide native knowledge on how to interrupt the flow of body fluids. But it would take him years to recognize how he was implicated in large social-engineering processes that targeted gay men through the growing HIV research industry. He was part of the clan of credentialed "native experts" hired to figure out how best to perform the magic trick of steering and disciplining gay men's sexual behavior. When the Twin Towers fell (9/11), he shared in the shock and trauma that suddenly (and definitively) made him a New Yorker: the lives lost tragically before, during, and after the attacks. But he also quietly lamented that he would never get to know the tower bathrooms where hot sex happened. How could one mourn the loss of spaces of "stranger intimacy" without sounding completely heretical, inappropriate, or just dead wrong in that fractious moment of history?

It became clear that young men like him—educated, university-trained, upwardly mobile, professionally ambitious, light-skinned or white-presenting, and gender-conforming—would replace veteran workers of the organizations founded in response to the AIDS crisis as these organization became professionalized. The self-identified and trained black and brown gay "natives" were part of a broad and rich sexual landscape. They were a new class of experts and brokers, and professionalization demanded stability in sexual identifications, even if those enshrined to do the outreach, counseling, supporting, and so on were also less than forthcoming about the complexities of their intimacies. "Te quiero dar el culo, no mi vida" (I want to give you my ass, not my life), rang one HIV prevention message of this time, never mind the fact that some of those vocal activists dabbled with delight in bisexuality with men "on the DL" who began to overcrowd the public health imagination. It was like they designed studies right after reading the novels of E. Lynn Harris.[40] Never mind that some of them enjoyed their twists of sexual histories that were practiced but not uttered, let alone theorized. Some of them—professional black and brown hygienist homosexuals—were the ones looking at him in horror once at an event sponsored by the Centers for Disease Control, where he openly stated what seemed most obvious to him: men tend not to be consistent in their condom use because sex with condoms is not hot. They just glared at him with the outraged expression of hat-wearing churchgoing women learning that the pastor's dog ate his Sunday sermon. He kept asking himself why what he said seemed out of tune with the agenda at the meeting. Why were those scientific queens giggling behind his back? They were no doubt invested in curbing the infection rates and the "bisexual bridge" among African American and Latino men and their female partners—imagined usually as "Penelopes," with nothing better to do than knit and wait to spread their legs for their "Ulysses" while their men cavorted and stuck it into any and all holes available in their sexual journeys. But this zeal to instill the barely held drive to regulate intimacy cohabitated with the desire for transgression instilled by those projects of social engineering. In other words, some of those queens also longed for the condom break, to hold the load of the other in their cracks.

Cruising spots shrank, as did opportunities to have sex in public parks and alleys during the years Rudy Giuliani and Michael Bloomberg ran New York City. However, he was struck by the hunger one man brought to sucking him one early summer night in Central Park. He read about the policing of public sex in one of his first-year graduate seminars, but 1997 and 1998 were years when he was busy trying to put his body on the line of these fights. And here he was, in the park, on a walk with his roommate and the new friends he had made in New York. As the mouth worked and they approached the end and he knew he was about to shoot, the man held his hips and took in the full load. He was used to pulling out to finish by jerking himself; this move by the stranger took him by surprise. As they finished and rearranged themselves, he tried to bring up prevention in the brief conversation that followed. After all, he had just started working as an "assistant research scientist" in the HIV field, and he had slipped himself by allowing the encounter to finish the way it did. Something had to be said. The other man, whose silhouette could be made out in the darkness of the leafy rambles where they met, halted the conversation, no doubt smelling whiffs of safe-sex dogmatism instead of the "Thanks, man" that he had expected.

"I know the risks. I'm an HIV counselor myself."

Maybe one month later, in one of the bathrooms that were later to disappear in the Disneyfication of downtown New York City, he cruised a few guys. One encounter, which he initially expected to be only a circle jerk, soon shifted as the black man in the cubicle signaled to the older white man next to him. As he stood at the urinal, playing with himself and watching the scene unfold, the white man pulled his pants down and walked back into the cubicle of the man sitting at this urinal, cock erect and condomless, waiting for the visitor to sit on it. As the man did so and began to close the door to the cubicle, the professional HIV worker walked out. This time, he was the one in shock.

Probably jealous and envious, too. Loca celosa.

Closing Movement Open

Indecent saintliness, or the Queer kenosis of
God incarnate, needs to participate of a different
theological sense of knowing. It requires strategies
of critical bisexual interpretation, the encounter with
Queer traditions and the libertine body as sources of
theology, and new theological metaphors such as for
instance, orgies. These are all strategies of disaffiliation
and of the identification of the Queer nomadic subject
of theology. What sort of discoveries can be expected
from these new paths, or *via rupta*, of this Queer
kenosis of God? We can expect a God in dialogue
with amorous relationships, but from other sexually
transgressive epistemologies.

MARCELLA ALTHAUS-REID, *THE QUEER GOD*

The *Oxford English Dictionary* defines *kenosis* as "self-renunciation of the divine nature, at least in part, by Christ in the incarnation."[41] The turning away from the divine and toward the carnal, evacuating divinity to "become" human, belies recognition that it is in and through the erotic, the sexual, and the fleshy that one can access the mystical. The bliss of our flesh affords us access to hints of the plenitude of the divine, but how does kenosis negotiate relationality? One immediately notices that there is a potential analogical bridge to be built to link turning away from the divine toward the carnal, with the tension between the "captive" and "liberated" positions around which Hortense Spillers choreographs the dyad of body and flesh for black women and other subject positions located at the meeting points of "black" and "woman." Might we, then, consider that "queer kenosis" might not require orgies for subject positions already joined to perversity, bodily excess, and queerness through "the brush of discourse" (Spillers)? In centering bodies already marked as excessive under coloniality, our horizon of freedom cannot lose sight of the violent ontological markings of the conjunction of "black" and "woman" as already "too much," potentially held captive through chattel slavery and its afterlife in the eye of the master, the "marked woman" Spillers describes: "a meeting ground of investments and privations in the national treasury of rhetorical wealth."[42] As Zakiyyah Iman Jackson writes, "Black female flesh persistently functions as the limit case of 'the human' and is its matrix-figure."[43] When discussing what she terms "the aesthetics of excess" among mostly African American and Latinx female arts practitioners, Jillian Hernández captures the drift of the horizon outlined here: "To present aesthetic excess is to make oneself hypervisible, but not necessarily in an effort to gain legibility or legitimacy. . . . Aesthetics of excess are the targets of commodification, appropriation, cultural dismissal, and erasure—but they tend to spectacularly survive and morph, slipping through such attempts at capture."[44] The overflowing, morphing, kinesthetic saturation, slipping, spilling over the confining finitude, tearing, and lock of commodification in the gaze of the master is part of what we are after.

We need to multiply the "sense of knowing" to think the conjunction of sex with the divine, faggotological explications that derive their force from the intuition of libertine bodies that act as our instruments of contact with one another, as well as with that which we cannot name. But we don't all arrive at the scene of the kenotic in the same way. Some of us arrive through channels steeped in privilege built on violence that forecloses our access to the human (historical and contemporary; spectacular and banal), making the entanglements through which we make contact operations in pain/pleasure and in touch of the sentient animal thing at the threshold. The sections of this suite followed the threads of a sexy mysticism to elaborate on the boundaries; generational gaps; transnational dynamics; and workings of blackness, difference, and power that inform the quality of contact, as well as the pleasures that derive from it. In framing what brings together the movements of this suite, as I salute and ask for the blessings of Gloria and Marcella, my mind's eye puts me back in graduate school in the late 1990s in the New York University American Studies Program office on Mercer Street in New York City. Although I did not become his student, Professor José Esteban Muñoz taught courses that my fellow students took, and he hung out with my adviser. Little busybody that I was, I must have pretended to read or do fumbling stage business of clerical tasks related to coursework in the program office while remaining attentive to the repartee buzzing nearby, and I do not recall who his interlocutors were. I do remember that the conversation was about *This Bridge Called My Back*, and this writing also prompts me to recall that he visited a proseminar led by one of my professors. I was in such awe of Muñoz that I can't bring myself to remember anything other than his camp take on the title of Cherríe Moraga and Anzaldúa's groundbreaking anthology. "This bridge called *my crack* [italics added]," he said, punctuating the utterance with his signature wicked wit and charm. My mind goes to this phrase, and to the gift it was for me to witness, read, and walk with Muñoz's presence and words, even from afar, to underscore the degree to which one's ability to be open, vulnerable, and uncomfortable are preconditions for faggotology.[45] Thinking and feeling from the crack. Anzaldúa certainly insisted on the possibility of our wounds as sites of pain and trauma, as well as insight, with the Mexican accent to pronounce Gloria's word in Spanish for wound—*raja*—as itself a guttural tear in my ear drum. "Me raja" (It tears me).

Each movement in this suite performs a "conjuring," akin to what Herukhuti describes: "The present progressive tense of the verb conjure; to use desire, intentionality, and spiritual power to mix elements from the environment in a manner that produces a magical effect; to work roots; to trouble the waters; to call into physical reality that which is germinated in the loins, believed in the heart, and conceived in the mind."[46] Together, the movements in the suite generate something close to what Solimar Otero calls *archives of conjure*: "a set of spiritual, scholarly, and artistic practices based on an awareness of the dead as active agents that work through imaginative principles."[47] Some elements in this rasanblaj suite, and in this volume, arrived at disjointed times, anticipating the book and the suite in which they sit. "Adagio," for instance, was a cuento I wrote between 2012 and 2013 and submitted to creative journals for consideration. In the case of one creative writing journal, the piece sat in the submission platform for two years and was never reviewed. It was not published until now, though writer friends read it and offered feedback—one of them suggesting the story as the balancing ingredient in this suite. Other published writings anticipated this book and its leanings, even when I had no idea that I would arrive at what you now read.[48]

My friendly amendment to Herukhuti's formulation is to suggest that each section of the suite messes with what might present as heteronormative, as well as Cartesian figurations of how and where we map what we know. Much germination, belief, and thought happens when our bodies perform that opening to the stranger, when they cast away expectations of relationality and intimacy, pause or move away from relationality altogether and offer radical hospitality. Our loins need not "germinate," or cum, to get wet and warm, to open up the anus as a site for the "germination" of something other than reproductive futurity or excretion. As we think as we fuck that this nut we hold, the "babies" he dropped in our hole, the dick or fist that slides in and out, the tongue that moves into the folds of our sphincter, receiving us to make us feel alive. The gift we receive is the restoration of historical lines and swerving lineages that shape the form, path, and education of multitudes of queer black men. The first and second movements of this chapter perform this labor by recourse of memoir and ethnography, moving through critical analysis of film and creative writing in the second movement. The aim is to pry open imaginative possibilities to offer something like what Otero calls an "archive of conjure" while making the shape of the text itself and the movements of its narrators into maps to be navigated by the reader. The affective range traversed is wide, and the suite mobilizes viscerality as recourse, provoking reactions in readers that put pressure on what academic writing is supposed to be, as well as in how comfortable the reader should feel. Indeed, this writing insists on bringing you in through the gut as you simmer in the sensorial maps traced and analyzed.

Elaine Padilla draws from Althaus-Reid's provocations in conjunction with the theologian Otto Maduro to think of what she describes as the "impropriety" of "carnivalesque passion." Padilla proposes a different topography useful for a queer kenosis: "It's a 'dance' of flesh that descends to the depths of the underworld, even the anal and pubic regions, not as the site furthest removed from the divine enjoyment but as the very being of a God whose nature is love."[49] What if God is something like what Padilla describes: "a semideterritorialized body in love that, though shared by everyone, *wholly* belongs to no one"?[50] Padilla's theology performs a geopolitical repositioning of "impropriety" south of the US-Mexico border, and she marks the colonial, racial, and moral geographies that subtend the bodies and paths she presents to her readers: "These dark enthusiasts, people of passion, many of them from the Southern Hemisphere, with their bodies that have been considered too dark and dirty, too sensuous, and uncivilized to be of God, are also embodied by the God of the carnival."[51] Deepening the engagement of indecency with race and coloniality as she analyzes the meeting points between Fanon and Merleau-Ponty, Mayra Rivera offers the *poetics of the flesh*: "A poetics of the flesh thus entails not only rejecting the projection of a flesh conceived as depravity or weakness on certain bodies. . . . It also calls for a revaluing of the affective charge of flesh and beauty of the bodies on which it has been projected."[52] One might say, following Rivera, that the "revaluing" may begin by reveling in how one is beguiled or turned on by the depraved black faggotry one has been taught to despise in oneself, by the gutter of being black and queer and poor or (to play with the titles of books by Roderick Ferguson and Ginetta Candelario) to embrace the aberrations in the black behind one's ear.[53] It is not lost on this Dominican American maricón that the moments closest to bliss in being Dominican—the sexual, sensory, ludic, etc.—all implicate practices and relationalities marked explicitly or implicitly as "black." With implicit attunement to the value of the distinction articulated by Spillers, Rivera challenges us to cast a different light on desires of the flesh, more than violent bodily markings.

The various parts of the suite—through a dance with, around, and through the perverse and the improper—illustrate the shifting boundaries of bodily intimacy and the policing, as well as the crossing, of those boundaries. But together, these movements also highlight that the pursuit of libidinal mystical "freedom" is tied to collectives and disciplined work, provoking communal imaginations of futurity and sexy intimacies growing an ethics of entangled proximity with our others: Musser's brown jouissance. The stepping off the "body" to the "flesh," from the encasement or "captivity" under the gaze of coloniality to "liberation," can be pursued only through the accompaniment, mentorship, and labor of humans, spirits, nonhuman animals, and sentient elemental others. And it is not a "pure" pursuit, being that it often negotiates inequality and power, as well as the colonial and neocolonial dimensions of transnational capitalism.

We must insist on holding space for individual self-determination when it concerns decisions about how and when individuals experience bodies at their limit through the erotic, the sexual, and the mystical. Various sections of the suite also unpack the implications of individual decisions and actions for collectives. The crossings of the one might become the charge of "all" (if you will), except that the "all"—or the "we"—in question is unevenly structured. And the care, emotional, and embodied work involved in accompanying the one is usually carried out by those at bottom of existing gender, race, and power hierarchies. In several situations discussed in the suite, the labor of black people (and particularly of black women) sustains the infrastructures for the privileged pursuit of freedom as dissolution and as what gets called "ego shattering" in some lines of white bourgeois thought in psychoanalytic queer studies. This is perhaps illustrated most clearly in "¡No te montes!" as the discussion compares the party at which I was told to hold back from being possessed and the analysis of Brenda in *Vers le sud*. Consistent with a privileged and extractive touristic sensibility, I thought of my friend's interdiction as a call to pause in the pursuit of what I thought was in the offing in trance possession—a "self-shattering" analogous to that pursued by Brenda in her manic trance dance interrupted by Legba. When my friend whispered "¡No te montes!" in my ear, and when Legba goes to the director of the musical group and tells him to switch back to the music they had been playing to stop Brenda, these two figures were performing care for the individual, the collective, and the traditions at the center of the frame. One does not "dabble" or "slum" their way into the grace of Olodumare or Bondye. Love of the infinite flesh involves guidance, education, commitment, and work with others. And those "others" working to support the scaffolding of privileged realization of pleasure—those others, who are mostly black women—also have desires, pleasures, and wants in excess of the structures conditioning their working bodies in asymmetrical fields of power. Have some respect.

The movements of the suite describe different modalities of "stranger intimacies." A return to the cruising park, to the bareback sex party, to the dark room, to the dungeon, or the orgy as sites of "indecent conocimientos," with close kinship with spaces of trance possession and ritual initiation (the misa spiritual, el cuarto de santo) illustrates a sense of the divine that knows not to know it all. In his stunning reading of Tim Dean's book on barebacking, the theologian Luis Menéndez-Antuña extrapolates from Dean's text to offer a vision of sociality and intimacy consistent with the horizon of radical openness toward which the suite gestures. As Menéndez-Antuña writes, "Barebacking... is more than a good fuck; it crystalizes a transcendent intimacy, a touch of skin to skin that disavows the threat of being killed by crafting an impersonal closeness that barebackers experience as sacred. Barebacking and cruising blur physical, social, psychological boundaries by disavowing autonomy, delinking intimacy from the epistemological imperative to 'know' the other. Anonymous intimacy evokes a transcendent touch precisely because it does not match carnal intercourse. It encompasses a set of feelings, experience, and practices that involve contact with an anonymous and, under certain circumstances, total otherness."[54] I agree with critics such as Herukhuti and Marlon Bailey when they insist on the need to bolster the way black and Latinx men enter and engage "raw" sex from the vantage point of sexual autonomy and in how HIV prevention gets mobilized to intervene in the decisions men of color make about how to enjoy their bodies.[55] But my drift includes and goes beyond the raw scene. Faggotology sits under the sign of blackness, occasionally enjoying the gymnastics of toxic masculinity and phallicity recycled in barebacking subcultures and circuit parties, in clone cultures, etc. But the circuits with which I play hold space for bodies forbidden from entering these settings for being too black, poor, Latina crazy, or femme. Sucias are (1) the homeless, who are held back from entering the gym to take a shower next to the gym bunny that tenders chum change; (2) the creature not meeting fat or muscle or masculinity or class or age or ability quotients; or (3) the man who is uninterested in myopically genital choreographies and temporalities.

What is salient to me about the socialities and intimacies enacted in and through barebacking and anonymous sex has to do with openness and vulnerability. Raw, park, and glory-hole queens are looking to blow a good nut, but the touch of the other that you need or want to know is a quest for contact with the divine. In a sense, then, the vision sketched throughout this suite of texts is close to what the critic Nguyen Tan Hoang calls a "bottomhood" or "view from the bottom": "Instead of shoring up our sovereignty by conflating agency with mastery, adopting a view from the bottom reveals an inescapable exposure, vulnerability, and receptiveness in our reaching out to other people."[56] I find value in explorations of "bottoming" that link it to multiple and racialized nodes of abjection and debasement in the work of Amber Jamilla Musser, Darieck Scott, and Kathryn Bond Stockton, and I look forward to see how others follow Althaus-Reid in bringing BDSM into considerations of "indecent conocimientos." However, I dwell in Nguyen's framing.[57] To reach through Nguyen back to Menéndez-Antuña, what is intimate yet impersonal about this exposure, this vulnerability to touch, to bodies organs fluids? What in this connection consummates the sacred? The grace of Olodumare manifested in arms of the madrina, the truths about past-present-future articulated through oracles that are impersonal yet radically individual, and the breath saliva words of ceremony participants who bless the iyawo as a conduit to the divine object and channel—could all these analogies be more than a coincidence? Is this the goddess in the gutter that we want, the black (w)hole?

Consider the nonphallic and nonorgasmic pleasures of rimming, a practice that performs a reorientation of the cartographies of the erotic. You don't need a dick or fist to be a good rimmer. The partner who is at the receiving end of the act, the person whose hole is being eaten, offers their anal opening to the tongue that teases and moves in all directions, biting and brushing chin, lips, and teeth meeting in that point—the most intimate corner of the body, a corner that neighbors one's genitalia and meets the body's excretion needs. The partner whose tongue works the hole plays with that erotic site, tests the capacity and sensations of the other, and tastes their body—sweat, urine, soap, shit. One takes in the other through smell and taste—the density of smell and taste of Peach that assaults the narrator who remembers the lover's body and its humors, a receptivity and vulnerability that opens the senses to the other, not to consume that body but to perform something closer to *worship*.

Does it matter that, in the end, the narrator of the cuento mourns the loss of a lover whose name he may not know? Who "tops" and who "bottoms"? Or does it matter? Risking imbibing the smell and taste of the other through rimming and practices that explore erotic stranger intimacies affords us a sense of contact with the stranger as contact with the sacred. Faggotology proposes and performs an otherwise map of pilgrimage to rapture. The sense of a futurity available through "indecent conocimientos," for a faggotology, suggests that the touch of the divine in the gutter—a flower mapped on the asshole one licks—holds a disposition to reject the moral economies of coloniality, as well as respectability.

Werk.

Epístola al Futuro/
An Epistle to the Future

Dear J and J,

There is a picture of one of you when we first met—
after Bababa arrived in South Orange from a trip
to Santo Domingo, after a year of working through
state bureaucracies to become licensed to foster
and adopt. You looked lost. Papapa Alfredo got
emotional when he recalled that in those first seven
months of life as you lived with another family, you
were fed, cleaned, and provided for. But you needed
love.

    Our first trip to the farmer's market the next day
was, I thought, my first chance to practice being
your "Bababa" (as you called me later), as you took
in the world. But then we got there, and (as I put on the
harness I carried you in as centipede mama), I did
not know where to start.

    This was no practice.

    Do I talk about colors, shapes, smells?

    I held on to you—my two black baby boys, my
"suns" (as auntie Hyacinth loves to call you)—your
form vibrating and moving every which way, excited
and overstimulated. We had just met, but your

> My folk, in other words,
> have always been a race for
> theory—though more in the
> form of the hieroglyph, a
> written figure that is both
> sensual and abstract, both
> beautiful and communicative.
>
> BARBARA CHRISTIAN,
> "THE RACE FOR THEORY"

sentience, your being, inspired in me a different kind of love—one that is open, that gives and gives and gives and that delights in boundlessness. I had to stop for an extra beat to take in this realization, being that I had always told Alfredo that having children was his project and that I was in this as my gesture of love for him. But here I was, with you, experiencing an exuberant love I did not know before meeting you.

My family never owned anything in Santo Domingo, and abuelo reminded me that the house that great-grandfather Francisco allowed us to live in during my childhood stored coal. Era una carbonera. So much running away from blackness, and it turns out that the home in my other country was a coal house.

Simmer in that conmigo, mi hijo. Mis hijes.

I remember seeing carbón when my parents ran out of gas for the stove and Abuela Xiomara used an anafe to cook. Not only was it black to my eyes. Touch coal and it leaves a trace in your hands (or any body part that touched it).

How could it be that my I grew up in a house of coal and I don't remember?

The black stains that remain.

Papapa Alfredo and I agreed that we would be vigilant of the behavior we modeled for you, but over the first few years of our life together and as you hit two or three, one of you scratched your nose through breathing in roughly and loudly—the way I do. Like a trumpet. It is a horrible habit, and the moment we realized you had picked it up, your father and I noted that I passed along a gesture that had provoked much of Alfredo's eye-rolling throughout our decades together. I must have picked this up from my dad or brothers, being that we all do this, and that eruption of vibration courses through us the moment we come together.

It is impertinent. It is rude. It is embarrassing. It is low class, cafre, chopo. It is me.

Papapa thinks it a terrible idea that I passed this along to you. But like my mother when I first showed up at her house ogling over men on television after coming out in the late 1990s, I delight in knowing that something of me will remain in you. I read somewhere that the famous Cuban singer La Lupe was once asked about the commenting and extemporizing she performed while singing. Should they erase that from the recordings? Her answer was, "That's me!" The Canadian pianist Glenn Gould was famous for cultivating strangeness in playing, talking, and relentless humming in his recordings. That's him.

That's them. Scratching the nose: that's your Bababa, guided by Elegguá to walk with you.

I am the wails of La Lupe, the relentless hums of Glenn Gould, the coal that stains. It is in your form that my touch reaches the other mothers you have had and will have. And like Lyndon Gill as he witnessed the women who mothered him hug one another, my eyes turn misty at the thought of touching and hugging all your mothers in gratitude for the life we hold together.[1]

I fear for your black bodies in the world, but let me say this: hold on to your freak, your crazy, your queer.

Me despido como Gloria, from you and from the black queer children of the future: Con ustedes y suyo. Siempre.

Babá

You started writing this epistle, a freak letter from your Apostle Paul in fear of the suffering, sacrifice, violence, and promise of the persecuted early Christians, as gospel for the black queer children of the future, in and through your two black suns, the ibeyis and marassás of your heart, black futures for the faggots in all of us. The time has come to propose an amendment to Barbara Christian's observation regarding the hieroglyph. Like the pataki or the Christian parable, this faggotology salutes its ancestors and its progeny, praying for Elegguá to favor passage. This gathering of letters/syllables/words—your rasanblaj circuit—is a sensual figure (jeroglífico) that describes as it practices messages it cannot explain but that can be heard if you listen, like the secrets Rigoberta knows that not even anthropologists, or creatures like you, are supposed to know.

Notes

Introduction

1. See Vargas, "Ruminations on *Lo Sucio* as a Latino Queer Analytic."

2. The phrase "ancestors we want to be" comes from conversations with Carlos iro Burgos in spring 2021.

3. Mary Ann Clark defines *ori* as "head; personal destiny, one's personal Orisha": see Clark, *Where Men Are Wives and Mothers Rule*, 167. I have heard *ori* described as "what makes you who you are individually." One of my elders discusses it as one's "chip," living at the top center of your forehead, as the seat of your individual consciousness.

4. Beliso-De Jesús translates *iyawó* as "bride of the *oricha*; Santería initiate within first year of priesthood": Beliso-De Jesús, *Electric Santería*, 224. Strongman translates *iyáwó* as "bride of the Spirit": Strongman, *Queering Black Atlantic Religions*, 24. Apart from noticing the differences in punctuation, which suggest how these terms have traveled through languages of the black diaspora, the feminine casting of the newly initiated priest (irrespective of biological gender) as "wife" has prompted debate, particularly in its conjunction with gender politics and homosexuality. However, this is only one of several sites in Yoruba studies where gender and sexuality are politicized and are sources of acrimony. For a field-defining debate on the geopolitics of gender and sexuality in Afro-Atlantic traditions, see the account of the Oyěwùmí-Matory debate in Strongman, *Queering Atlantic Religions*, 22–24. Clark offers a useful elaboration of marriage imagery and its gendered dimensions. "Regardless of his actual sex, the iyawo assumes a female position in that household. He is addressed as 'iyawo' throughout his novitiate year and must prostrate himself to every member of the household and of the larger community whose initiation predates his own": Clark, *Where Men Are Wives and Mothers Rule*, 77.

5. Iya means "mother; also, title of any adult woman": see Clark, *Where Men Are Wives*, 165.

6. I'm thinking of the lines at the opening of *Borderlands/La Frontera*, where Anzaldúa writes about life on the US–Mexico border as being in the "1,950 mile-long open wound / dividing a pueblo, a culture, / running down the length of my body, / staking fence rods in my flesh, / splits me splits me / me raja me raja": Anzaldúa, *Borderlands/La Frontera*, 55, emphasis added. The idea comes from Hammonds, "Black (W)Holes and the Geometry of Black Female Sexuality."

7. Prescod-Weinstein, *The Disordered Cosmos*, 41.

8. Bataille, *Erotism*, 9; "movement," *Oxford English Dictionary Online*, accessed 30 May 2021, https://www-oed-com.proxy.libraries.rutgers.edu/view/Entry/123031?redirectedFrom=movement#eid.

9. Crawley, *Blackpentecostal Breath*, 3.

10. See Hanawa, "Circuits of Desire," viii.

11. The abbreviation BDSM encompasses bondage and discipline, dominance and submission, and sadomasochism.

12. Weiss, *Techniques of Pleasure*, 7.

13. Da Silva, *Toward a Global Idea of Race*, 7.

14. "Aché"—also spelled "ashé"—is "life force energy; spiritual power; blessings; breath, saliva, and touch of the santero who imparts blessings": Beliso-De Jesús, *Electric Santería*, 223.

15. "Electrify" and its implications are usefully conceptualized in Beliso-De Jesús, *Electric Santería*.

16. Walt Whitman, "Song of Myself," sec. 51, accessed 16 October 2022, https://www.poetryfoundation.org/poems/45477/song-of-myself-1892-version.

17. A valuable articulation and critique of the whiteness of latinidad comes in the work of Arlene Dávila: see Dávila, *Latino Spin*. But research in this area is shaping an emerging generation of scholars in Latinx studies. An important contribution is Hernández, *Racial Innocence*.

18. Figueroa-Vásquez, *Decolonizing Diasporas*, 9.

19. As the sociologist Ruth Enid Zambrana documents, "One of the major theorizing arguments is that study participants [scholars of color] are marked by coconstitutive and mutually reinforcing social status identities that shape life chances, opportunities, and, in turn, experiences of higher education institutions": Zambrana, *Toxic Ivory Towers*, 10.

20. Vizenor, *Survivance*, 1.

21. "Do a gathering, a ceremony, a protest": Ulysse, "Introduction," *Anthropology Now*, 125. I use the phrase "No escogemos de aquí y allá entre los desechos: debemos ensamblar todo junto" (roughly "We don't choose from here or there among the remains: we assemble everything together"). I called Ulysse to ask if the Spanish word for "remains" was intended, being that such a word did not appear in the French, Kreyòl, Portuguese, or English translations. She stated that *desechos* made it into the Spanish unintentionally. We agreed that it was a felicitous mistranslation: Gina Athena Ulysse, personal communication, March 2021. In Portuguese, *lixo* is translated

as "garbage, trash; refuse, waste, sweepings, rubbish." The Portuguese text reads, "Você não pode ficar escolhendo do lixo, deve recolher tudo": "lixo," in Michaelis, *Pequeno Dicionário Inglês-Português Português-Inglês*.

22. The literature on Dominican-Haitian relations, histories, and tensions, is voluminous. For some important and recent texts, see García Peña, *The Borders of Dominicanidad*; Mayes, *Mulatto Nation*; Paulino, *Dividing Hispaniola*. I echo the recent call of scholars in Dominican studies to continue to explore how anti-Haitianism structures Dominican identity but, also, how we need to open up space for a Dominican blackness as a formation that deserves its own focus and attention in relation but also independently from Haiti as signifier. For an text and group of essays addressing this problematic, see Chetty and Rodriguez, "The Challenge and Promise of Dominican Black Studies."

23. "Wretched refuse" draws from "Give me your tired, your poor, / Your huddled masses yearning to breathe free, / The wretched refuse of your teeming shore": Emma Lazarus, "The New Colossus," accessed 4 June 2021, https://poets.org/poem/new -colossus?gclid=CjoKCQjw—GFBhDeARIsACH_kdZdW9pGR-h8fu5tqTXVRnv TGycyu5VXWaI56dx4SraFt6vH-AmFZ4saAjIFEALw_wcB.

24. Alexander, *Pedagogies of Crossing*, 293.

25. Pérez, *Religion in the Kitchen*, 9.

26. Pérez, *Religion in the Kitchen*, 11.

27. See Gallop, *Anecdotal Theory*.

28. Howe, "Melville's Marginalia."

29. Howe, "Melville's Marginalia," 97.

30. Howe, "Melville's Marginalia," 99.

31. Howe, "Melville's Marginalia," 97.

32. Strongman, *Queering Black Atlantic Religions*, 252.

33. There is an archive of research discussing the nuances of mental health among Latinx populations and the "culturalist" and problematic readings of Latinx cultural excess as psychiatrically problematic. Two recent contributions to this literature are Gherovici, *The Puerto Rican Syndrome*, and Santiago-Irizarry, *Medicalizing Ethnicity*.

34. This makes the performance of critical exegesis as an act of radical black madness consistent with the creative impulses described and analyzed in Bruce, *How to Go Mad without Losing Your Mind*. It is also consistent with critique as "translocura," undertaken by Lawrence La Fountain-Stokes in his wonderful book. "Translocas, whether insane women, effeminate homosexuals, drag performers, or transgender subjects, are way too many things in an ever-expanding trans-geographic rhizomatic map that inhabits and pushes out from the tropics and engulfs other spaces and locales": La Fountain-Stokes, *Translocas*, 1–2.

35. Ochoa, *Society of the Dead*, 37.

36. Ochoa, *Society of the Dead*, 37.

37. As Haider explains, "In its contemporary ideological form, rather than its initial form as a theorization of a revolutionary political practice, identity politics is an individual method": Haider, *Mistaken Identity*, 23. In her trenchant critique of bourgeois conceits of queer critique, Hennessy writes, "The commodification of gay styles and

identities in corporate and academic marketplaces is integrally related to the formation of a postmodern gay/queer subjectivity.... To a great extent the construction of a new 'homosexual/queer spectacle' perpetuates a class-specific perspective that keeps invisible the capitalist divisions of labor that organize sexuality and in particular lesbian, gay, queer lives. In so doing, queer spectacles often participate in a long history of class-regulated visibility": Hennessy, *Profit and Pleasure*, 138. Hames-García emphasizes the complicity of some visible strands of queer theory with whiteness. As he explains, "Despite the failure of so many canonical works in queer theory to live up to their own promises to address race complexly and fully, queer theory clearly offers something useful to theorists, as it has continued to entrench itself in the academy. I suspect that the success of queer theory actually has much to do with that failure. Its disavowal of race (in the separatist guise) and its disavowal of identity (in either guise), in other words, offer theorists of sexuality a means whereby they might disavow whiteness": Hames-García, "Queer Theory Revisited," 32–33.

38. Savastano, "Gay Men as Virtuosi of the Holy Art of Bricolage and as Tricksters of the Sacred," 10n4.

39. Crawley, *Blackpentecostal Breath*, 17.

40. Saint, *Spells of a Voodoo Doll*, 9.

41. Called assotto, asotò, or asotor, this drum is described by Lois Wilcken as physically a "Rada drum, although its shape is more cylindrical than conical, and it has large orifices in the collar for the emission of sound.... Measuring no less than six feet of height, we might call it the giant of the drum pantheon." Wilcken cites Jacques Roumain's explanation of what makes the asotò particular: "They [the other drums] are servants, the instruments of the deity, whereas the Assôto(r), dressed in its sacrificial skin [kerchiefs], is also, and above all, the power Afro-Haitian god: Assoto Micho Tokodun Vodoun": Wilcken, *The Drums of Vodou*, 38. It is considered a rare drum. I am grateful to Elizabeth McAlister, Angel Lebrun King Agassouyemet, and Roberto Strongman for email exchanges in support of this brief description.

42. See Singh, *Unthinking Mastery*.

43. See Kusch, *América profunda*.

44. Taylor, *How We Get Free*.

45. Scholarship on Santería and other Afro-Cuban (as well as Afro-Atlantic Yoruba) traditions includes Carr, *A Year in White*; Gonzalez, *Afro-Cuban Theology*; Gregory, *Santería in New York City*; Matory, *Black Atlantic Religion*; Murphy, *Working the Spirit*; Palmié, *Wizards and Scientists*. The classic study of Haitian Vodou is McCarthy Brown, *Mama Lola*. A more recent addition is Beaubrun, *Nan Dòmi*. On Brazilian Candomblé and the broader field of Afro-Atlantic Yoruba traditions, J. Lorand Matory's work is pivotal. For a representative example, see Matory, *Black Atlantic Religion*.

46. See Vidal-Ortiz, "'Maricón,' 'Pájaro,' and 'Loca'"; Vidal-Ortiz, "Queering Sexuality and Doing Gender"; Vidal-Ortiz, "Sexuality Discussions in Santería,"

47. As the philosopher Mario Sáenz explains, "Descartes's dualism is unable to define the person in terms of fluid, changing, and ambiguous borders. That is, his definitions of corporeal and spiritual substances as things that require nothing but

their essential attributes to exist ... as well as his uncomplicated perception of the self as a solitary thing with thoughts, preclude any conceptualization or description of the self as existing with others and under the spell of social ideologies and relations that blur individual distinctions and de-essentialize selfhood; in short, the self *is not* in the flesh": Sáenz, "Cartesian Autobiography/Post-Cartesian Testimonials," 311.

48. This insight is elaborated in Matory, "Vessels of Power."

49. Strongman, *Queering Black Atlantic Religions*, 11.

50. Strongman, *Queering Black Atlantic Religions*, 17.

51. Beliso-De Jesús, *Electric Santería*, 194.

52. I take seriously Ulysse's urging queer feminist projects of the sacred to be clear about the distinction between (1) their engagement with the "idea" of Santería and sister traditions; and (2) the actual praxis, dogma, and theologies that inform the traditions. See the critique in Ulysse, "Vodou as Idea."

53. Throughout this study, I think of "conocimiento" as a form of knowledge closest to the word "wisdom" in English. This is partly inspired in the work of Anzaldúa discussed throughout the book, but it is also based in the frequent surfacing of "conocimiento" in the words of elders to account for inarticulable ancestral wisdom learned through imitation, accompaniment, and other interactions across generations.

54. In the vast literatures that have developed around US-bound Dominican migration, New York City figures centrally. For an extended historical treatment of this phenomenon, see Hoffnung-Garskof, *A Tale of Two Cities*.

55. In the case of Anzaldúa, much of the critique focuses on her use of the eugenicist-tinged text *La raza cósmica (The Cosmic Race)*, by the philosopher José Vasconcelos. Pointed critiques of the problems generated by Anzaldúa's use of Vasconcelos to her theory of "mestiza consciousness" include Sexton, *Amalgamation Schemes*, 198–202; and Smith, "Queer Theory and Native Studies." A trenchant critique of tendencies surfacing in the work of the late María Lugones appears in Terrefe, "The Pornotrope of Decolonial Feminism." Macharia's *Frottage* and Marriott's *Haunted Life* address the complexity of Frantz Fanon's thinking and its reception among feminist and queer critics and artists.

56. Rivera-Colón, *Love Comes in Knots*.

57. See Beliso-De Jesús, *Electrict Santería*, 12–14.

58. Barad, *Meeting the Universe Halfway*, 80.

59. Barad, *Meeting the Universe Halfway*, 81.

60. Beliso-De Jesús, *Electric Santería*, 13.

61. Barad, *Meeting the Universe Halfway*, 81.

62. Lugones, *Pilgrimages/Peregrinajes*, 1.

Chapter One. Re-membered Life

1. Coates, *Between the World and Me*.

2. A *tíguere* (literally, a "tiger") is a Dominican working-class figuration of racialized masculinity attempting to survive the multiple odds stacked up against them

through cunning and street savvy. Often cast as borderline "criminal" from the vantage point of the dominant class, *tígueres* might be best described as (mostly, though not exclusively) men with a street cunning threading on the edges of the licit. The classic text on *tigueraje* is Collado, *El tíguere dominicano*.

3. Fanon, *Black Skin, White Masks*, 1.

4. Fanon, *Black Skin, White Masks*, 91.

5. Here, I'm invoking my own definition of masculinity as "strai(gh)tjacket," following E. Antonio De Moya. See Decena, *Tacit Subjects*, 48, 60–61; and 122–26.

6. Fanon, *Black Skin, White Masks*, 91.

7. I suspect this remembrance of blackness and Dominican childhood would figure Haiti and blackness differently in the 1990s or early 2000s, as state and other actors promoted a metastasizing of anti-Haitianism into quotidian sentiment, and as increased Haitian migration to the Dominican Republic, the intensification of economic and political entanglements, and border disputes were weaponized for political expediency: see Ricourt, *The Dominican Racial Imaginary*.

8. In thinking of childhood as a country of its own, I recall the phrase "l'enfance est un pays en soi" from Laferrière, *Je suis fatigué*, 70.

9. Ulysse's line in Spanish, as quoted at the beginning of this book: "No escogemos de aquí y allá entre los desechos: debemos ensamblar todo junto" (We don't choose, from here or from there, among the leftovers. We assemble everything together): see Ulysse, "Introduction," *emisférica*.

Chapter Two. Bridge Crónica

1. "Path," in *Oxford English Dictionary* online, accessed 5 March 2021, https://www-oed-com.proxy.libraries.rutgers.edu/view/Entry/138770?rskey=7VraIU&result=1&isAdvanced=false#eid.

2. Antonio Machado, "Caminante, no hay camino/Traveler, There Is No Road," accessed 11 November 2021, https://www.favoritepoem.org/poem_CaminanteNoHayCamino.html. The famous version by Joan Manuel Serrrat was released in the 1969 track "Cantares," an homage to Machado's poems, combined with additional lyrics by Serrat: see "Joan Manuel Serrat: Cantares," accessed 11 November, 2021, https://www.youtube.com/watch?v=QHcypSLIp_A.

3. Beliso-De Jesús, *Electric Santería*, 80.

4. In his account of the distinction between *ser* (ontological being) and *estar* (to be somewhere), Kusch argues that, in transplanting European models to the building of their country, the architects of the Argentine nation missed the geopolitical conditions that make asking about ontological "being" something that cannot ignore its location in the American continent: see Kusch, *América profunda*.

5. See Candelario, *Black behind the Ears*.

6. Arnaldo Cruz-Malavé's work is an inspiration for this chapter, particularly as he recounts (1) the "life trails" that shaped his education and training as a literary scholar; and (2) interaction, friendship, and access to a connection (and eventual *testimonio*) from Juan Rivera, whose life and relationship to artist Keith Haring Cruz-Malavé engages,

transcribes, and narrates in experimental form: see Cruz-Malavé, *Queer Latino Testimonio, Keith Haring, and Juanito Xtravaganza*.

7. Kusch's trenchant critique of urban elites in Buenos Aires capitulates to a default narrative of Argentine whiteness. The historian Erika Denise Edwards describes the notion of absence of black people in Argentina as part of a "national narrative of Argentine exceptionalism." In *América profunda* and throughout his oeuvre, Kusch establishes a dyad of differentiation between Argentine "self" and "other" only through the figure of indigenous Argentines, thus reproducing and upholding black erasure: see Edwards, *Hiding in Plain Sight*, 1–2.

8. "Almost the same but not white" is from Bhabha, *The Location of Culture*, 89.

9. The phrasing of this question comes from Du Bois's line "How does it feel to be a problem?": see Du Bois, *The Souls of Black Folk*, 7. One of many recent meditations on this field-defining question is Moustafa Bayoumi's 2009 book, which bears the question as its title: see Bayoumi, *How Does It Feel to Be a Problem?*

10. Savage, "Penn Debates the Meaning of Water Buffalo."

11. I invoke the language of living under the sign of gayness in the work of Manolo Guzmán: see Guzmán, *Gay Hegemony/Latino Homosexualities*.

12. I am referencing the ambivalent readings of Mapplethorpe in Kobena Mercer's *Welcome to the Jungle*. The chapter "Reading Racial Fetishism: The Photographs of Robert Mapplethorpe" brings together two essays in which Mercer engages and revises his own perspectives on Mapplethorpe's photography to account for the ways his identification as a black gay man shapes his engagement and reception of the photographs. The pairing is necessary to account for the "inscription of major changes in the political and cultural context in which the reading and interpretation of Mapplethorpe's work has become a key site of struggle and contestation" (171). Nevertheless, Mercer also revises his interpretation of Mapplethorpe to account for his relationship with identifications produced by photographic images of black men. In his first reading of the photographer, Mercer presents a critique of racial fetishism that takes aim at Mapplethorpe's white gaze on the black body. In contrast, his second view of the matter attends to Mercer's erotic implication in the fetishization of black men's bodies. "I was also implicated in the fantasy scenario as a gay subject—a desiring subject . . . sharing the same desire to look, I am forced to confront the rather unwelcome fact that I would actually occupy the same position in the fantasy of mastery that I said was that of the white male subject!" (193).

13. The University of Medicine and Dentistry in New Jersey (UMDNJ) was founded in 1954 and dissolved in 2013. Many of its schools have merged with Rutgers.

14. My invocation of the "mirror stage" refers to the classic mother-child pairing in Lacan, "The Mirror Stage as Formative of the *I* Function as Revealed in Psychoanalytic Experience."

15. Du Bois, *The Souls of Black Folk*, 157.

16. See Rivera-Colón, "Getting Life in Two Worlds."

17. "Deracinate," in *Oxford English Dictionary* online, accessed 8 March 2021, https://www-oed-com.proxy.libraries.rutgers.edu/view/Entry/50532?redirectedFrom=deracinate#eid.

Chapter Three. Experiencing the Evidence

1. Menchú and Burgos-Debray, *Me llamo Rigoberta Menchú y así me nació la conciencia*, 271, my translation.

2. The question is formulated as what Joan W. Scott calls "the evidence of experience." Her essay with this title is the center of the discussion later in this chapter.

3. Ramón Grosfoguel defines the locus of enunciation as "the geo-political and body-political location of the subject that speaks": Grosfoguel, "Epistemic Decolonial Turn," 213.

4. It is not coincidental that the ensemble of codes and recollections are tethered to what I later discuss as *andrographic performatives of Dominican masculinity*, being that the moment before the tree recalls previous moments of identity formation. I have written about this previously: see Decena, *Tacit Subjects*, esp. chap. 4.

5. Here I am referencing my previous theorizing of masculinity as a strai(gh)tjacket, drawing on the work of the late Dominican social psychologist E. Antonio de Moya. In my take on de Moya's view of rules and conventions of masculinity as strict bodily codes, I suggest that "what is opposed to masculinity on the surface of this body is not femininity per se, but *locura* (craziness). An expansive interpretation of locura . . . illustrates the ways in which power and legitimacy . . . produce masculinity as cover, as a straightjacket, for bodies imagined as always already excessive, prone to break, and feminized": see Decena, *Tacit Subjects*, 125.

6. For an invaluable analysis of institutionalized religion and its relationship to the colonial project in the Dominican Republic, see Lara, *Streetwalking*.

7. I am thinking with the work of the anthropologist Martin Manalansan, whose scholarship explores "getting by" not as mindless survival existence but as traversing of the quotidian with pathos, pleasure, and fabulousness. A few of his publications highlight this feature of Manalansan's work among queer Filipinos. See Manalansan, "Queer Worldlings"; Manalansan, "The 'Stuff' of Archives."

8. This turn of phrase intentionally recalls the work of José Esteban Muñoz, particularly his book *Cruising Utopia*.

9. Hemphill, *Ceremonies*, 74–77.

10. Riggs, *Tongues Untied*.

11. Anzaldúa, *Borderlands/La Frontera*, 60.

12. Anzaldúa, *Borderlands/La Frontera*, 60–61.

13. Anzaldúa, *Borderlands/La Frontera*, 61.

14. My thinking here is aligned with Chandan Reddy's reading of "home" for queers of color. "Unaccounted for within both Marxist and liberal pluralist discussions of the home and the nation, queers of color *as people of color*, I argue, take up the critical task of both remembering and rejecting the model of the 'home' offered in the United States in two ways: first, by attending to the ways in which it was defined over and against people of color, and second, by expanding the locations and moments of that critique of the home to interrogate processes of group and self-formation from the experience of being expelled from their own dwellings and families for not conforming to the dictation of and demand for uniform gendered and sexual types": Reddy, "Home, Houses, Nonidentity," 356–57.

15. Harper, "The Evidence of Felt Intuition," 650.

16. Harper, "The Evidence of Felt Intuition," 643.

17. Hesford and Diedrich, "On 'The Evidence of Experience' and Its Reverberations," 197.

18. Hesford and Diedrich, "On 'The Evidence of Experience' and Its Reverberations," 199.

19. Hesford and Diedrich sketch out these connections in their comments introducing their interview with Scott: Hesford and Diedrich, "On 'The Evidence of Experience' and Its Reverberations," 197–98..

20. Scott, "The Evidence of Experience," 775.

21. Scott, "The Evidence of Experience," 776.

22. Scott, "The Evidence of Experience," 786.

23. I am thinking here with Austin, *How to Do Things with Words*.

24. Scott, "The Evidence of Experience," 775.

25. Scott, "The Evidence of Experience," 777.

26. Thompson, *The Making of the English Working Class*.

27. Scott, "The Evidence of Experience," 785, emphasis added.

28. Scott, "The Evidence of Experience," 785.

29. See Stone-Mediatore, *Reading across Borders*, 99.

30. Martínez, *On Making Sense*, 27.

31. Alcoff, "Phenomenology, Post-structuralism, and Feminist Theory on the Concept of Experience," 45.

32. Scott, "The Evidence of Experience," 794.

33. Scott, "The Evidence of Experience," 794.

34. Scott, "The Evidence of Experience," 794.

35. Karen Swann, quoted in Scott, "The Evidence of Experience," 794, fn45.

36. Stone-Mediatore, *Reading across Borders*, 104.

37. Daniel, *Dancing Wisdom*, 13.

38. Jeff Friedman, personal communication, 22 May 2020.

39. "Kinesthesis," *Oxford English Dictionary* online, accessed 22 May 2020, https://www-oed-com.proxy.libraries.rutgers.edu/view/Entry/103437?redirectedFrom=kinesthesis#eid.

40. Delany, *The Motion of Light in Water*, 173.

41. Delany, *The Motion of Light in Water*, 174.

42. Delany, *The Motion of Light in Water*, 174.

43. Daniel, *Dancing Wisdom*, 19.

Chapter Four. Loving Stones

1. Lugones, *Pilgrimages/Peregrinajes*, 1. The bracketed section includes snippets of the footnote on that page, which I have integrated into the narrative of the text.

2. Isasi-Díaz, "Lo Cotidiano," 13.

3. Alexander, *Pedagogies of Crossing*, 326.

4. Roughly translated as "spiritual mass," *misa espiritual* is a habitual event in the Caribbean tradition and a translation of the influence of nineteenth-century spiritualist

Allan Kardec. Misas are on a smaller scale than the traditional Catholic mass; they are held in family homes, and they often involve singing, prayer, dancing, and spirit invocation. Spirit possession, combined with the proffering of advice, critiques, and divination to all attendees, are part of the expected course of events, particularly in "combined" traditions that establish proximity between Santería and espiritismo. For a sustained engagement with misas with tremendous value, see Otero, *Archives of Conjure*. Although Otero accurately mobilizes the term *séance* to describe the misas, I hold on to *misa*/mass to also hold space for the loose and vernacular invocation of Catholic liturgy.

5. For an extended meditation of the spectral presence thought by Stephan Palmié's Cuban interlocutors to have guided him to study Afro-Cuban religion, see the prologue in Palmié, *Wizards and Scientists*.

6. Beliso-De Jesús explains, for instance, some of the challenges presented to "Santero Travelers" by levels of derecho payments expected depending on where ceremony is performed (in Cuba versus the United States) and on the place from which the initiate travels. This puts many Santeros from the United States and Europe in positions where, to work up the resources needed for their ceremonies, they take foreigners to Cuba for ritual: see Beliso-De Jesús, *Electric Santería*, 98–99.

7. Beliso-De Jesús, *Electric Santería*, 7, 102. Beliso-De Jesús further explains that, instead of utopia, Santería "assumes the terrors of violence and negotiations with negativities as part and parcel of the everyday. Copresences are haunting conjurings of seething imperfections, partialities that link injustice and marginality but also produce new problematic relationships": see Beliso-De Jesús, *Electric Santería*, 102.

8. As Beliso-De Jesús explains, "In the case of Santería and other African diaspora assemblages, ontologies actually shift transnationalism, where the 'trans' of transnationalism might be better understood through the 'trance' of copresence": see Beliso-De Jesús, *Electric Santería*, 98. The connection of "trans" and "trance" is also explored in the forthcoming work of Omaris Zamora.

9. Anzaldúa, *Light in the Dark/Luz en lo oscuro*, 116, my translation.

10. Beliso-De Jesús's *Electric Santería* is particularly instructive regarding the transnational complexity of this history.

11. The scholarship of Patricia de Santana Pinho maps the cartographies of desire for authenticity and blackness as they collide with ideas of African "authenticity" in transnational travel to Brazil, particularly by African American "roots travelers" to Brazil: see de Santana Pinho, *Mapping Diaspora*; de Santana Pinho and Langdon, *Mama Africa*.

12. Marx, *Capital, Volume 1*, 164–65, emphasis added.

13. Matory, *The Fetish Revisited*, 15.

14. Matory, *The Fetish Revisited*, 18.

15. Matory, *The Fetish Revisited*, xix–xx.

16. Matory, *The Fetish Revisited*, 192.

17. Matory, *The Fetish Revisited*, 193.

18. Beliso-De Jesús, *Electric Santería*, 121.

19. This is consistent with the findings in Beliso-De Jesús. See *Electric Santería*, 99.

20. Matory, *The Fetish Revisited*, 194.

21. Alexander, *Pedagogies of Crossing*, 297, emphasis added.

22. "Transpose," *Oxford English Dictionary* online, accessed 18 May 2021, https://www-oed-com.proxy.libraries.rutgers.edu/view/Entry/205034?rskey =MmN600&result=2&isAdvanced=false#eid.

23. Kumar, *Passport Photos*, 3.

Chapter Five. ¡Santo!

1. My use of "subject form" here subscribes to the conceptualization offered by Michel Pêcheux, citing Althusser. "No human, i.e. social individual, can be the agent of a practice if he does not take *the form of a subject*. The 'subject-form' is actually the historical form of existence of every individual, of every agent of social practices:" Althusser, cited in Pêcheux, *Language, Semantics and Ideology*, 114n12.

2. Muñoz, *Cruising Utopia*.

3. See Spillers, "Mama's Baby, Papa's Maybe."

4. Spillers, "Mama's Baby, Papa's Maybe," 67.

5. Spillers, "Mama's Baby, Papa's Maybe," 67.

6. Spillers, "Mama's Baby, Papa's Maybe," 67.

7. Stephens, *Skin Acts*, 3.

8. Stephens, *Skin Acts*, 24.

9. Fanon, *Black Skin, White Masks*, 111.

10. Here, like in my theorization of *la loca* as a "gynographic performative," I am indebted to the work of Ben Sifuentes-Jáuregui. See his *Transvestism, Masculinity, and Latin American Literature*. As I explained in previous work, la loca is a form of femininity "staged as excess on a male body." By contrast, an andrographic performative represents codes that comport with what legible and legitimate masculinity looks like. Though in appearance stable, these codes are unstable and subject to debate, observation, and the validations of more than one person. They are also intensely calibrated and nuanced codes that are racialized and classed. For my discussion of la loca as "gynographic performative," see Decena, *Tacit Subjects*, chap. 4.

11. The Caribbean cultural nuances of this dance lesson can be appreciated with the stark contrast presented between Pepe's masculinity "with hips" in the cuento versus what Erica Rand describes as the distinction between manuals of ice skating (which discuss women's hips) and the absence of discussions of skating men as having hips at all—in ice hockey, for instance. As she explains, "'Laterally projecting prominence' is precisely what men are no supposed to have, either by bone or movement.... The default for men who rule in contact sports doesn't include that option": Rand, *The Small Book of Hip Checks*, 24. We might comment further that Pepe at least *has* hips, but his possible slide into womanhood and Matilde's quest for a partner who can shield her from unwanted touch suggest that in both cases the sway of the hip into femininity also produces vulnerability and risk of unwanted intimacy. If not "on the same boat," the cousins are linked by a proximity to the implications of femininity as vulnerability. For productive interpretations of racialized working of butts in the

coverage, embodiments, and styles of Jennifer López and Ricky Martin, see Negrón-Muntaner, *Boricua Pop*.

12. "Transcendent erotics and politics," Allen writes, "insists on creation of a new space, which may become a political organization or a heretical theoretical paradigm, but also may be a new name that defies, reappropriates or refuses old labels, or a complex of acts beyond what is interpellated within prevailing ideologies": Allen, *¡Venceremos?*, 95.

13. Rand's discussion of spine alignment in dance, yoga, and figure skating shows that gender bodily training also taps racialized and classed repertoire of how one carries one's body, not only achieving a bigger- or smaller-looking butt but also indexing moral economies of racial and class difference. "Straight spines and tucked butts," she writes, "enable certain movements but they also signal a racialized version of classy": Rand, *Red Nails, Black Skates*, 131.

14. The *pariguayo* is seen, in Dominican street culture, as an inept form of heterosexual masculinity, diametrically opposed to the *tíguere*, the prototype of street savvy. For a useful discussion of Dominican *tigueraje*, see Krohn-Hansen, "Masculinity and the Political among Dominicans."

15. The essay by Althusser that I reference here is "Ideology and Ideological State Apparatuses."

16. Tinsley, *Ezili's Mirrors*, 4.

17. Tinsley, *Ezili's Mirrors*, 12–13.

18. L. H. Stallings writings stand as some of the most clear-headed, sex-affirmative, and just straight-up badass on blackness, women, and sexuality: see Stallings, *A Dirty South Manifesto*; Stalling, *Funk the Erotic*.

Chapter Six. Indecent Conocimientos

1. In invoking the phrase "stranger intimacy," I draw on the work of Nayan Shah on alternative male socialities in the North American West. He explains, "Stranger intimacy is an avenue for analyzing a 'public world of belonging' in which the verbal and gestural cues, ethical codes, and cultural frames that transient men exchanged and elaborated generated a vibrant public culture for participating in and 'witnessing intense and personal affect.'" Drawing from the work of the cultural critic Michael Warner, Shah argues that "intimacy among strangers points to how 'strangerhood' is a crucial ingredient for public meeting. Even as conventional status may determine the basis of trust, civility, and conviviality for many, both participants and observers of migrant social worlds professed fluency in alternative habits and codes of erotic sociability." See Shah, *Stranger Intimacy*, 55.

2. See Allen, *¡Venceremos?*, 3.

3. Gill, "In the Realm of Our Lorde," 182.

4. In thinking with the black, divine, and the queer, my work throughout this book in general, and in this chapter in particular, joins that of Ashon Crawley (among other thinkers) on these questions. As he explains in his discussion of Black Study as a collective project, "Black Study is the force of belief that blackness is but one critical

and urgently necessary disruption to the epistemology, the theology-philosophy, that produces the world, a set of protocols, wherein black flesh cannot easily breathe": Crawley, *Blackpentecostal Breath*, 3. Crawley goes on to explain that "Blackpentecostalism" is made up of a set of aesthetic practices that "constitute a performative critique of normative theology and philosophy": Crawley, *Blackpentecostal Breath*, 7. I join Crawley in engaging analogous practices and questions from the vantage point of Regla de Ocha, and I concur with Crawley's assertion that "as life and love, these performative dances, songs, noises, and tongues illustrate how enjoyment, desire, and joy are important for the tradition that antiphonally speaks back against aversion, embarrassment, and abandonment, against the debasement and denigration of blackness": Crawley, *Blackpentecostal Breath*, 7–8.

5. Griffin, *If You Can't Be Free, Be a Mystery*, 88.

6. Griffin, *If You Can't Be Free, Be a Mystery*, 89.

7. Griffin, *If You Can't Be Free, Be a Mystery*, 90.

8. "Tumultuous derangement" comes from the work of Fred Moten, in a section where he is meditating on language in relationship to how black people narrate their own historical experience. The phrase reads, "That critical celebration of tumultuous derangement, of the constitutive force of dehiscence, of the improvisations of imagining things, is written in the name of blackness": Moten, *Stolen Life*, xii.

9. Though my work is indebted to activism and theoretical interventions carried out by queers of color, my initial engagement with the questions throughout this chapter was prompted and informed by Elaine Padilla's theology. Her capaciously open and crucial book *Divine Enjoyment* proposes a vision of a God who lives in flesh and experiences not only joy but even impropriety: see Padilla, *Divine Enjoyment*, esp. chap. 5.

10. Musser, *Sensual Excess*, 13.

11. As Savastano further explains, "Few gay men that I have met can fully embrace their religious tradition without having to draw from other sources, intellectual, devotional or ritualistic, in order to locate themselves within their chosen tradition and still remain fully attentive to who they are as psycho-spiritual-sexual beings": Savastano, "Gay Men as Virtuosi of the Holy Art of Bricolage and as Tricksters of the Sacred," 12.

12. Michael Bernard Kelly's *Christian Mysticism's Queer Flame* is an important contribution to this line of work in dialogue with gay men's lived experiences, perspectives, and theology. For more information on circuit parties and spirituality, see Gorrell, "Rite to Party." For information on nonmonogamy, group sex, and spirituality, see Rudy, "Where Two or More Are Gathered."

13. See Gill, *Erotic Islands*; Hernández, *Aesthetics of Excess*; Miller-Young, *A Taste for Brown Sugar*; Nash, *The Black Body in Ecstasy*; Pérez, *Eros Ideologies*; Rodríguez, *Sexual Futures, Queer Gestures, and Other Latina Longings*; Stallings, *A Dirty South Manifesto*; Stallings, *Funk the Erotic*.

14. The phrase "charmed circle" references the work of Gayle Rubin and specifically describes hierarchies of sexual pairings and practices in relation to propriety, legibility, and respectability. Sketched in the essay "Thinking Sex," this and other visionary formulations of Rubin set the agenda for holding space for a critique of sexuality as a

related yet distinct site of the intellectual activist struggle within feminism: see Rubin, "Thinking Sex."

15. Martínez, "¿Con quién, dónde, y por qué te dejas?," 237.

16. Althaus-Reid, *Indecent Theology*, 2.

17. Althaus-Reid, *The Queer God*, 173, chap. 1, n1.

18. Althaus-Reid, *Indecent Theology*, 3.

19. See Weismantel, *Cholas and Pishtacos*, 261.

20. Holland et al., "Introduction," 394.

21. Holland et al., "Introduction," 395.

22. See the introduction to *América profunda*, where Kusch explicitly discusses the *hedor* in relation to cross-racial and cross-class contact and mixing.

23. I thank Santiago Slabodsky and PJ DiPietro for our conversations over Zoom in April 2021 on questions of hedor in the philosophies of Althaus-Reid and Kusch.

24. Vallone, "The Wound as Bridge."

25. Anzaldúa, *Light in the Dark/Luz en lo oscuro*, 118.

26. "Avoid," *Oxford English Dictionary Online*, accessed 15 July 2019, https://www.oed-com.proxy.libraries.rutgers.edu/view/Entry/13796?rskey=ruEJuo&result=3&isAdvanced=false#eid.

27. "Desconocer," *Diccionario de la Real Academia de la Lengua Española*, accessed 15 July 2019, https://dle.rae.es/, my translations.

28. Vargas, "Ruminations on *Lo Sucio* as a Latino Queer Analytic," 718.

29. Vargas, *Dissonant Divas in Chicana Music*, 56.

30. Cantet, *Vers le sud/Heading South*.

31. My analysis of this scene draws from information exchanged with the artist Irka Mateo on 1 July 2019.

32. Jenkins, *Moonlight*.

33. Crawley, cited in Sexton, "Shadow and Myth," 189.

34. Sexton, "Shadow and Myth," 189.

35. Musser, *Sensual Excess*, 5.

36. The line is a response and paraphrase to Hemphill's poem "Now We Think": "Now we think / as we fuck / this nut / might kill us." See Hemphill, *Ceremonies*, 155.

37. Perry Halkitis describes the AIDS generation as that of men who came of age in the 1980s and who "witnessed the emergence and evolution of HIV/AIDS, the robust scientific literature on the disease, and the media and other artistic reactions to the epidemic": Halkitis, *The AIDS Generation*, xiv.

38. My thinking here is similar to that of Allan Bérubé in "How Gay Stays White and What Kind of White It Stay."

39. Williams, *Marxism and Literature*, 122.

40. E. Lynn Harris (1955–2009) was an openly gay African American author of novels such as *Invisible Life* (1994) and *Just as I Am* (1995), among others, that address the lives of closeted and bisexual African American men. His novels played an important role in early conversations about of men "on the down low." Though one might argue that his novels participated in the more reductive view of these men as "closeted"

black gay men, Harris's work thematized masculinity, sexuality, and the politics of respectability in ways that were sensitive, empathetic, and complex.

41. "Kenosis," *Oxford English Dictionary Online*, accessed 16 July 2019, https://www-oed-com.proxy.libraries.rutgers.edu/view/Entry/102927?redirectedFrom=kenosis#eid.

42. Spillers, "Mama's Baby, Papa's Maybe," 65.

43. Jackson, *Becoming Human*, 4.

44. Hernández, *Aesthetics of Excess*, 11.

45. Muñoz deploys the phrase in his reading of the work of Ricardo Bracho. The phrase "is a play on the classic 1981 anthology of writing by radical women of color, *This Bridge Called My Back*. I chose the word 'crack' as part of a playful attempt to highlight the thematics of anal eroticism and recreational drug use. . . . I am interested in calling attention to the continuation of the radical women of color project by gay men": Muñoz et al., *The Sense of Brown*, 15.

46. Herukhuti, *Conjuring Black Funk*, v.

47. Otero, *Archives of Conjure*, 6.

48. See Decena, "Fè yon rasanblaj"; Decena, "Tostones, Madeleines."

49. Padilla, *Divine Enjoyment*, 184.

50. Padilla, *Divine Enjoyment*, 189–90.

51. Padilla, *Divine Enjoyment*, 189.

52. Rivera, *Poetics of the Flesh*, 119.

53. Candelario, *Black behind the Ears*; Ferguson, *Aberrations in Black*.

54. Menéndez-Antuña, "Is Caravaggio a Queer Theologian?," 136.

55. See Herukhuti, "Whose Booty Is This?" See also Bailey, "Black Gay (Raw) Sex."

56. See Nguyen, *A View from the Bottom*.

57. See Scott, *Extravagant Abjection*; Stockton, *Beautiful Bottom, Beautiful Shame*. Recent work on bondage and sadomasochism (BDSM) also suggests ways forward and challenging horizons for queer spiritological work: see Cruz, *The Color of Kink*; Weiss, *Techniques of Pleasure*.

Epístola/Epistle

1. I am thinking here of Gill's moving account of the recorded moment when he witnesses a hug between the two women who have "reared" him as biological mother and mentor in an event celebrating of the life and work of Audre Lorde. "What might it mean for these two women who have mothered me—in different ways most certainly—to embrace? What might it mean to witness that loving embrace without standing in its way?" See Gill, "In the Realm of Our Lorde," 171.

Bibliography

Alcoff, Linda Martín. "Phenomenology, Post-structuralism, and Feminist Theory on the Concept of Experience." In *Feminist Phenomenology*, edited by Linda Fisher and Lester Embree, 39–56. Dordrecht, Netherlands: Kluwer Academic, 2000.

Alexander, M. Jacqui. *Pedagogies of Crossing: Meditations on Feminism, Sexual Politics, Memory, and the Sacred*. Durham, NC: Duke University Press, 2005.

Allen, Jafari S. *¡Venceremos? The Erotics of Black Self-Making in Cuba*. Durham, NC: Duke University Press, 2011.

Althaus-Reid, Marcella. *Indecent Theology: Theological Perversions in Sex, Gender and Politics*. Oxford: Routledge, 2000.

Althaus-Reid, Marcella. *The Queer God*. London: Routledge, 2003.

Althusser, Louis. "Ideology and Ideological State Apparatuses: Notes towards an Investigation." In *Lenin and Philosophy and Other Essays*, 127–86. New York: Monthly Review, 1971.

Anzaldúa, Gloria E. *Borderlands/La Frontera: The New Mestiza*. San Francisco: Aunt Lute, [1987] 2021.

Anzaldúa, Gloria E. *Light in the Dark/Luz en lo oscuro: Rewriting Identity, Spirituality, Reality*. Edited by Analouise Keating. Durham, NC: Duke University Press, 2015.

Austin, J. L. *How to Do Things with Words*. Cambridge, MA: Harvard University Press, 1962.

Bailey, Marlon M. "Black Gay (Raw) Sex." In *No Tea, No Shade: New Writings in Black Queer Studies*, edited by E. Patrick Johnson, 239–61. Durham, NC: Duke University Press, 2016.

Barad, Karen. *Meeting the Universe Halfway: Quantum Physics and the Entanglement of Matter and Meaning*. Durham, NC: Duke University Press, 2007.

Bataille, Georges. *Erotism: Death and Sensuality*. San Francisco: City Lights, 1986.

Bayoumi, Moustafa. *How Does It Feel to Be a Problem? Being Young and Arab in America*. New York: Penguin, 2008.

Beaubrun, Mimerose. *Nan Dòmi, le récit d'une initiation vodou*. La Roque d'Anthéron, France: Vents d'Ailleurs, 2010.

Beliso-De Jesús, Aisha M. *Electric Santería: Racial and Sexual Assemblages of Transnational Religion*. New York: Columbia University Press, 2015.

Bérubé, Allan. "How Gay Stays White and What Kind of White It Stays." In *The Making and Unmaking of Whiteness*, edited by Birgit Brander Rasmussen, Eric Klinenberg, Irene J. Nexica, and Matt Wray. Durham, NC: Duke University Press, 2001.

Bhabha, Homi K. *The Location of Culture*. London: Routledge, 1994.

Bruce, La Marr Jurelle. *How to Go Mad without Losing Your Mind: Madness and Black Radical Creativity*. Durham, NC: Duke University Press, 2021.

Butler, Judith P. *Gender Trouble: Feminism and the Subversion of Identity*. New York: Routledge, 1990.

Candelario, Ginetta E. B. *Black behind the Ears: Dominican Racial Identity from Museums to Beauty Shops*. Durham, NC: Duke University Press, 2007.

Cantet, Laurent, dir. *Vers le sud/Heading South*. Film. Haut et Court, Paris, 2006.

Carr, C. Lynn. *A Year in White: Cultural Newcomers to Lukumi and Santería in the United States*. New Brunswick, NJ: Rutgers University Press, 2016.

Chetty, Raj, and Amaury Rodriguez. "The Challenge and Promise of Dominican Black Studies." *Black Scholar* 45, no. 2 (2015): 1–9.

Christian, Barbara. "The Race for Theory." *Feminist Studies* 14, no. 1 (1988): 67–79.

Clark, Mary Ann. *Where Men Are Wives and Mothers Rule: Santería Ritual Practices and Their Gender Implications*. Gainesville: University Press of Florida, 2005.

Coates, Ta-Nehisi. *Between the World and Me*. New York: Penguin, 2015.

Collado, Lipe. *El tíguere dominicano: Ensayo*. Santo Domingo: Panamericana, 1992.

Crawley, Ashon T. *Blackpentecostal Breath: The Aesthetics of Possibility*. New York: Fordham University Press, 2017.

Cruz, Ariane. *The Color of Kink: Black Women, BDSM, and Pornography*. New York: New York University Press, 2016.

Cruz-Malavé, Arnaldo. *Queer Latino Testimonio, Keith Haring, and Juanito Xtravaganza: Hard Trails*. New York: Palgrave Macmillan, 2007.

Daniel, Yvonne. *Dancing Wisdom: Embodied Knowledge in Haitian Vodou, Cuban Yoruba, and Bahian Candomblé*. Urbana: University of Illinois Press, 2005.

da Silva, Denise Ferreira. *Toward a Global Idea of Race*. Minneapolis: University of Minnesota Press, 2007.

Dávila, Arlene M. *Latino Spin: Public Image and the Whitewashing of Race*. New York: New York University Press, 2008.

Decena, Carlos Ulises. "Fè Yon Rasanblaj: A Body Portal Fantasy Book." *emisférica: Caribbean Rasanblaj* 12, no. 1 (2015). http://archive.hemisphericinstitute.org/hemi/en/emisferica-121-caribbean-rasanblaj/decena.

Decena, Carlos Ulises. *Tacit Subjects: Belonging and Same-Sex Desire among Dominican Immigrant Men*. Durham, NC: Duke University Press, 2011.

Decena, Carlos Ulises. "Tostones, Madeleines: Dominicanidad and Other Useless Pleasures." *On the Visceral: A Special Issue of GLQ*, 25 February 2015. http:// onthevisceral.tumblr.com.

Delany, Samuel R. *The Motion of Light in Water: Sex and Science Fiction Writing in the East Village, 1957–1965*. New York: Arbor House, 1988.

de Santana Pinho, Patricia. *Mapping Diaspora: African American Roots Tourism in Brazil*. Chapel Hill: University of North Carolina Press, 2018.

de Santana Pinho, Patricia, and Elena Langdon. *Mama Africa: Reinventing Blackness in Bahia*. Durham, NC: Duke University Press, 2010.

Du Bois, W. E. B. *The Souls of Black Folk*. New York: Oxford University Press, 2007.

Edwards, Erika Denise. *Hiding in Plain Sight: Black Women, the Law, and the Making of a White Argentine Republic*. Tuscaloosa: University of Alabama Press, 2020.

Fanon, Frantz. *Black Skin, White Masks*. New York: Grove, 1967.

Fanon, Frantz. *Peau noire, masques blancs*. Points. Essais; 26. Paris: Seuil, 2008.

Ferguson, Roderick A. *Aberrations in Black: Toward a Queer of Color Critique*. Minneapolis: University of Minnesota Press, 2004.

Figueroa-Vásquez, Yomaira. *Decolonizing Diasporas: Radical Mappings of Afro-Atlantic Literature*. Evanston, IL: Northwestern University Press, 2020.

Gallop, Jane. *Anecdotal Theory*. Durham, NC: Duke University Press, 2002.

García-Peña, Lorgia. *The Borders of Dominicanidad: Race, Nation, and Archives of Contradiction*. Durham, NC: Duke University Press, 2016.

Gherovici, Patricia. *The Puerto Rican Syndrome*. New York: Other, 2003.

Gill, Lyndon K. *Erotic Islands: Art and Activism in the Queer Caribbean*. Durham, NC: Duke University Press, 2018.

Gill, Lyndon K. "In the Realm of Our Lorde: Eros and the Poet Philosopher." *Feminist Studies* 40, no. 1 (2014): 169–89. https://doi.org/10.1353/fem.2014.0028.

Gonzalez, Michelle A. *Afro-Cuban Theology: Religion, Culture, and Identity*. Gainesville: University Press of Florida, 2006.

González, Octavio. "Eucharist." *Lambda Literary*, 2019. https://lambdaliterary.org /2019/01/octavio-r-gonzalez.

Gorrell, Paul J. "Rite to Party: Circuit Parties and Religious Experience." In *Gay Religion*, edited by Scott Thumma and Edward R. Gray, 313–26. Walnut Creek, CA: Altamira, 2004.

Gregory, Steven. *Santería in New York City: A Study in Cultural Resistance*. New York: Garland, 1999.

Griffin, Farah Jasmine. *If You Can't Be Free, Be a Mystery: In Search of Billie Holiday*. New York: Free Press, 2001.

Grosfoguel, Ramón. "The Epistemic Decolonial Turn." *Cultural Studies* 21, no. 2 (2007): 211–23. http://www.informaworld.com/10.1080/09502380601162514.

Guzmán, Manolo. *Gay Hegemony/Latino Homosexualities*. New York: Routledge, 2006.

Haider, Asad. *Mistaken Identity: Race and Class in the Age of Trump*. London: Verso, 2018.

Halkitis, Perry N. *The AIDS Generation: Stories of Survival and Resilience*. New York: Oxford University Press, 2014.

Hames-García, Michael. "Queer Theory Revisited." In *Gay Latino Studies: A Critical Reader*, edited by Michael Hames-García and Ernesto Javier Martínez, 19–45. Durham, NC: Duke University Press, 2020.

Hames-García, Michael, and Ernesto Javier Martínez. "Introduction: Re-membering Gay Latino Studies." In *Gay Latino Studies: A Critical Reader*, edited by Michael Hames-García and Ernesto Javier Martínez, 1–18. Durham, NC: Duke University Press, 2020.

Hammonds, Evelynn. "Black (W)Holes and the Geometry of Black Female Sexuality." *differences* 6, nos. 2–3 (1994): 126–45.

Hanawa, Yukiko. "Circuits of Desire: Introduction." *positions: east asia cultures critique* 2, no. 1 (Spring 1994): v–xi.

Harper, Phillip Brian. "The Evidence of Felt Intuition: Minority Experience, Everyday Life, and Critical Speculative Knowledge." *GLQ* 6, no. 4 (2000): 641–57.

Harris, E. Lynn. *Invisible Life*. New York: Anchor, 1994.

Harris, E. Lynn. *Just as I Am: A Novel*. New York: Anchor, 1995.

Hemphill, Essex. *Ceremonies: Prose and Poetry*. New York: Plume, 1992.

Hennessy, Rosemary. *Profit and Pleasure: Sexual Identities in Late Capitalism*. New York: Routledge, 2000.

Hernández, Jillian. *Aesthetics of Excess: The Art and Politics of Black and Latina Embodiment*. Durham, NC: Duke University Press, 2020.

Hernández, Tanya Katerí. *Racial Innocence: Unmasking Latino Anti-black Bias and the Struggle for Equality*. Boston: Beacon, 2022.

Herukhuti (H. Sharif Williams). *Conjuring Black Funk: Notes on Culture, Sexuality, and Spirituality*, vol. 1. New York: Vintage Entity, 2007.

Herukhuti. "Whose Booty Is This? Barebacking, Advocacy, and the Right to Fuck." In *Conjuring Black Funk: Notes on Culture, Sexuality, and Spirituality*, edited by Herukhuti, 99–102. New York: Vintage Entity, 2007.

Hesford, Victoria, and Lisa Diedrich. "On 'The Evidence of Experience' and Its Reverberations: An Interview with Joan W. Scott." *Feminist Theory* 15, no. 2 (2014): 197–207.

Hoffnung-Garskof, Jesse. *A Tale of Two Cities: Santo Domingo and New York after 1950*. Princeton, NJ: Princeton University Press, 2008.

Holland, Sharon P., Marcia Ochoa, and Kyla Wazana Tompkins. "Introduction: On the Visceral." *GLQ* 20, no. 4 (2014): 391–406.

Howe, Susan. "Melville's Marginalia." In *The Nonconformist's Memorial: Poems by Susan Howe*. New York: New Directions, 1989.

Isasi-Díaz, Ada María. "Lo Cotidiano: A Key Element of Mujerista Theology." *Journal of Hispanic/Latino Theology* 10, no. 1 (2002): 5–17.

Jackson, Zakiyyah Iman. *Becoming Human: Matter and Meaning in an Antiblack World*. New York: New York University Press, 2020.

Jenkins, Barry, dir. *Moonlight*. Film. Plan B, Los Angeles, 2016.

Kelly, Michael Bernard. *Christian Mysticism's Queer Flame: Spirituality in the Lives of Contemporary Gay Men*. Milton Park, UK: Routledge, 2019.

Khan-Cullors, Patrisse, and Asha Bandele. *When They Call You a Terrorist: A Black Lives Matter Memoir*. New York: St. Martin's, 2018.

Krohn-Hansen, Christian. "Masculinity and the Political among Dominicans: 'The Dominican Tiger.'" In *Machos, Mistresses, Madonnas: Contesting the Power of Latin American Gender Imagery,* edited by Marit Melthuus and Kristi Anne Stolen, 108–33. London: Verso, 1996.

Kumar, Amitava. *Passport Photos.* Berkeley: University of California Press, 2000.

Kusch, Rodolfo. "América profunda" (1963). In *Obras completas,* vol. 2, 3–254. Rosario, Argentina: Editorial Fundación Ross, 1999.

Lacan, Jacques. "The Mirror Stage as Formative of the *I* Function as Revealed in Psychoanalytic Experience." In *Écrits: The First Complete Edition in English,* 94–100. New York: W. W. Norton, 2006.

Laferrière, Dany. *Je suis fatigué.* Outremont, Québec: Lanctôt, 2001.

La Fountain-Stokes, Lawrence. *Translocas: The Politics of Puerto Rican Drag and Trans Performance.* Ann Arbor: University of Michigan Press, 2021.

Lara, Ana-Maurine. *Streetwalking: LGBTQ Lives and Protest in the Dominican Republic.* New Brunswick, NJ: Rutgers University Press, 2020.

Lhermitte, Jean. *L'image de notre corps.* Paris: Edition de la Nouvelle Revue Critique, 1939.

Lorde, Audre. "Uses of the Erotic: The Erotic as Power." In *Sister Outsider: Essays and Speeches by Audre Lorde,* 53–59. Freedom, CA: Crossing, 1984.

Lugones, María. *Pilgrimages/Peregrinajes: Theorizing Coalition against Multiple Oppressions.* Lanham, MD: Rowman and Littlefield, 2003.

Macharia, Keguro. *Frottage: Frictions of Intimacy across the Black Diaspora.* New York: New York University Press, 2019.

Manalansan, Martin F. "Queer Worldings: The Messy Art of Being Global in Manila and New York." *Antipode* 47, no. 3 (2015). https://doi.org/10.1111/anti.12061.

Manalansan, Martin F. "The 'Stuff' of Archives: Mess, Migration, and Queer Lives." *Radical History Review* 120 (2014): 94–107. https://doi.org/10.1215/01636545 -2703742.

Marriott, David. *Haunted Life: Visual Culture and Black Modernity.* New Brunswick, NJ: Rutgers University Press, 2007.

Martínez, Ernesto Javier. "¿Con quién, dónde, y por qué te dejas? Reflections on Joto Passivity." *Aztlán* 39, no. 1 (2014): 237–46.

Martínez, Ernesto Javier. *On Making Sense: Queer Race Narratives of Intelligibility.* Palo Alto, CA: Stanford University Press, 2012.

Marx, Karl. *Capital, Volume 1: A Critique of Political Economy.* London: Penguin, [1976] 1990.

Matory, J. Lorand. *Black Atlantic Religion: Tradition, Transnationalism, and Matriarchy in the Afro-Brazilian Candomblé.* Princeton, NJ: Princeton University Press, 2005.

Matory, J. Lorand. *The Fetish Revisited: Marx, Freud, and the Gods Black People Make.* Durham, NC: Duke University Press, 2018.

Matory, J. Lorand. "Vessels of Power: The Dialectical Symbolism of Power in Yoruba Religion and Polity." Master's thesis, University of Chicago, 1986, https:// dukespace.lib.duke.edu/dspace/handle/10161/10715.

Mayes, April J. *The Mulatto Republic: Class, Race, and Dominican National Identity.* Gainesville: University Press of Florida, 2015.

McCarthy Brown, Karen. *Mama Lola: A Vodou Priestess in Brooklyn.* Berkeley: University of California Press, 2011.

Menchú, Rigoberta, and Elisabeth Burgos-Debray. *Me llamo Rigoberta Menchú y así me nació la conciencia.* Historia Inmediata. Mexico City: Siglo Veintiuno, 1985.

Menéndez-Antuña, Luis. "Is Caravaggio a Queer Theologian? Paul's Conversion on the Way to Damascus." *Critical Research on Religion* 6, no. 2 (2018): 132–50.

Mercer, Kobena. *Welcome to the Jungle: New Positions in Black Cultural Studies.* New York: Routledge, 1994.

Michaelis Pequeno Dicionário Inglês-Português Português-Inglês. Sao Paulo: Companhia Melhoramentos DE SAO Paulo Industrias DE PAPEL, 1996.

Miller-Young, Mireille. *A Taste for Brown Sugar: Black Women in Pornography.* Durham, NC: Duke University Press, 2014.

Moten, Fred. *Stolen Life (Consent Not to Be a Single Being),* vol. 2. Durham, NC: Duke University Press, 2018.

Muñoz, José Esteban. *Cruising Utopia: The Then and There of Queer Futurity.* New York: New York University Press, 2009.

Muñoz, José Esteban, Joshua Chambers-Letson, and Tavia Nyong'o. *The Sense of Brown.* Perverse Modernities. Durham, NC: Duke University Press, 2020.

Murphy, Joseph M. *Working the Spirit: Ceremonies of the African Diaspora.* Boston: Beacon, 1995.

Musser, Amber Jamila. *Sensual Excess: Queer Femininity and Brown Jouissance.* New York: New York University Press, 2018.

Nash, Jennifer C. *The Black Body in Ecstasy: Reading Race, Reading Pornography.* Next Wave. Durham, NC: Duke University Press, 2014.

Negrón-Muntaner, Frances. *Boricua Pop: Puerto Ricans and American Culture from "West Side Story" to Jennifer Lopez.* New York: New York University Press, 2003.

Nguyen, Tan Hoang. *A View from the Bottom: Asian American Masculinity and Sexual Representation.* Durham, NC: Duke University Press, 2014.

Ochoa, Todd Ramón. *Society of the Dead: Quita Manaquita and Palo Praise in Cuba.* Berkeley: University of California Press, 2010.

Otero, Solimar. *Archives of Conjure: Stories of the Dead in Afrolatinx Cultures.* New York: Columbia University Press, 2020.

Padilla, Elaine. *Divine Enjoyment: A Theology of Passion and Exuberance.* New York: Fordham University Press, 2014.

Palmié, Stephan. *Wizards and Scientists: Explorations in Afro-Cuban Modernity and Tradition.* Durham, NC: Duke University Press, 2002.

Paulino, Edward. *Dividing Hispaniola: The Dominican Republic's Border Campaign against Haiti, 1930–1961.* Pittsburgh: University of Pittsburgh Press, 2016.

Pêcheux, Michel. *Language, Semantics and Ideology.* New York: St. Martin's, 1982.

Pérez, Elizabeth. *Religion in the Kitchen: Cooking, Talking, and the Making of Black Atlantic Traditions.* New York City: New York University Press, 2016.

Pérez, Laura Elisa. *Eros Ideologies: Writings on Art, Spirituality, and the Decolonial.* Durham, NC: Duke University Press, 2019.

Prescod-Weinstein, Chanda. *The Disordered Cosmos: A Journey into Dark Matter, Spacetime, and Dreams Deferred.* New York: Bold Type, 2021.

Rand, Erica. *Red Nails, Black Skates: Gender, Cash, and Pleasure on and off the Ice.* Durham, NC: Duke University Press, 2012.

Rand, Erica. *The Small Book of Hip Checks: On Queer Gender, Race, and Writing.* Durham, NC: Duke University Press, 2021.

Reddy, Chandan C. "Home, Houses, Nonidentity: Paris Is Burning." In *Burning Down the House: Recycling Domesticity*, edited by Rosemary Marangoly George, 355–79. Boulder, CO: Westview, 1998.

Ricourt, Milagros. *The Dominican Racial Imaginary: Surveying the Landscape of Race and Nation in Hispaniola.* Critical Caribbean Studies. New Brunswick, NJ: Rutgers University Press, 2016.

Riggs, Marlon, dir. *Tongues Untied.* Film. Frameline, California Newsreel, 1989.

Riley, Denise. 1988. *Am I That Name? Feminism and the Category of "Women" in History.* Minneapolis: University of Minnesota Press.

Rivera, Mayra. *Poetics of the Flesh.* Durham, NC: Duke University Press, 2015.

Rivera-Colón, Edgar. "Getting Life in Two Worlds: Power and Prevention in the New York City House Ball Community." PhD diss., Rutgers University, 2009.

Rivera-Colón, Edgar. *Love Comes in Knots: Meditations in the American Labyrinth.* Forthcoming.

Rodríguez, Juana Maria. *Sexual Futures, Queer Gestures, and Other Latina Longings.* Sexual Cultures. New York: New York University Press, 2014.

Rubin, Gayle. "Thinking Sex: Notes for a Radical Theory of the Politics of Sexuality" (1984). In *Pleasure and Danger: Exploring Female Sexuality*, edited by Carole Vance, 267–319. New York: Routledge, 1984.

Rudy, Kathy. "'Where Two or More Are Gathered': Using Gay Communities as a Model for Christian Sexual Ethics." *Theology and Sexuality*, no. 4 (1996): 81–99. https://doi.org/10.1177/135583589600200406.

Sáenz, Mario. "Cartesian Autobiography/Post-Cartesian Testimonials." In *Feminist Interpretations of René Descartes*, edited by Susan Bordo, 305–27. University Park: Pennsylvania State University Press, 1999.

Saint, Assotto. *Spells of a Voodoo Doll: The Poems, Fiction, Essays and Plays of Assotto Saint.* New York: Masquerade, 1996.

Santiago-Irizarry, Vilma. *Medicalizing Ethnicity: The Construction of Latino Identity in Psychiatric Settings.* Ithaca, NY: Cornell University Press, 2001.

Savage, David G. "Penn Debates the Meaning of Water Buffalo." *Los Angeles Times,* 10 May 1993. https://www.latimes.com/archives/la-xpm-1993-05-10-mn-33609 -story.html.

Savastano, Peter. "Gay Men as Virtuosi of the Holy Art of Bricolage and as Tricksters of the Sacred." *Theology and Sexuality* 14, no. 1 (2007): 9–28.

Scott, Darieck. *Extravagant Abjection: Blackness, Power, and Sexuality in the African American Literary Imagination.* New York: New York University Press, 2010.

Scott, Joan Wallach. "The Evidence of Experience." *Critical Inquiry* 17, no. 4 (1991): 773–97.

Scott, Joan Wallach. *Gender and the Politics of History*. New York: Columbia University Press, 1988.

Sexton, Jared. *Amalgamation Schemes: Antiblackness and the Critique of Multiracialism*. Minneapolis: University of Minnesota Press, 2008.

Sexton, Jared Yates. "Shadow and Myth." In *Black Masculinity and the Cinema of Policing*, 161–94. Cham, Switzerland: Palgrave Macmillan, 2017.

Shah, Nayan. *Stranger Intimacy: Contesting Race, Sexuality, and the Law in the North American West*. Berkeley: University of California Press, 2011.

Sifuentes-Jáuregui, Ben. *Transvestism, Masculinity, and Latin American Literature: Genders Share Flesh*. New York: Palgrave, 2002.

Singh, Julietta. *Unthinking Mastery: Dehumanism and Decolonial Entanglements*. Durham, NC: Duke University Press, 2018.

Smith, Andrea. "Queer Theory and Native Studies: The Heteronormativity of Settler Colonialism." *GLQ* 16, no. 1 (2010): 42–68.

Spillers, Hortense J. "Mama's Baby, Papa's Maybe: An American Grammar Book." *Diacritics* 17, no. 2 (1984): 64–81.

Stallings, L. H. *A Dirty South Manifesto: Sexual Resistance and Imagination in the New South*. Berkeley: University of California Press, 2019. doi:10.2307/j.ctvqr1b92.

Stallings, L. H. *Funk the Erotic: Transaesthetics and Black Sexual Cultures*. Urbana: University of Illinois Press, 2015.

Stephens, Michelle Ann. *Skin Acts: Race, Psychoanalysis, and the Black Male Performer*. Durham, NC: Duke University Press, 2014.

Stockton, Kathryn Bond. *Beautiful Bottom, Beautiful Shame: Where "Black" Meets "Queer."* Durham, NC: Duke University Press, 2006.

Stone-Mediatore, Shari. *Reading across Borders: Storytelling and Knowledges of Resistance*. New York: Palgrave Macmillan, 2003.

Strongman, Roberto. *Queering Black Atlantic Religions: Transcorporeality in Candomblé, Santería, and Vodou*. Durham, NC: Duke University Press, 2019.

Taylor, Keeanga-Yamatha, ed. *How We Get Free: Black Feminism and the Combahee River Collective*. Chicago: Haymarket, 2017.

Terrefe, Selamawit D. "The Pornotrope of Decolonial Feminism." *Critical Philosophy of Race* 8, nos. 1–2 (2020): 134–64. https://www.jstor.org/stable/10.5325/critphilrace.8.1-2.0134.

Thompson, E. P. *The Making of the English Working Class*. New York: Vintage, 1966.

Tinsley, Omise'eke Natasha. *Ezili's Mirrors: Imagining Black Queer Genders*. Durham, NC: Duke University Press, 2018. https://doi.org/10.1215/9780822372080.

Ulysse, Gina Athena. "Introduction." *Anthropology Now* 8, no. 1 (2016): 125–27. https://doi.org/10.1080/19428200.2016.1154772.

Ulysse, Gina Athena. "Introduction." *emisférica: The Hemispheric Institute* 12, nos. 1–2 (2015). https://hemisphericinstitute.org/en/emisferica-121-caribbean-rasanblaj/121-introduction.

Ulysse, Gina Athena. "Vodou as Idea: On Omise'eke Natasha Tinsley's 'Ezili's Mirrors.'" *Los Angeles Review of Books*, September 28, 2018. https://lareviewofbooks.org /article/vodou-as-idea-on-omiseeke-natasha-tinsleys-ezilis-mirrors.

Vallone, Mirella. "The Wound as Bridge: The Path of *Conocimiento* in Gloria Anzaldúa's Work." *Revue Électronique d'Études sur le Monde Anglophone* 12, no. 1 (2014). https://doi.org/10.4000/erea.4135.

Vargas, Deborah R. *Dissonant Divas in Chicana Music: The Limits of La Onda*. Minneapolis: University of Minnesota Press, 2012.

Vargas, Deborah R. "Ruminations on *Lo Sucio* as a Latino Queer Analytic." *American Quarterly* 66, no. 3 (2014): 715–26.

Vidal-Ortiz, Salvador. "'Maricón,' 'Pájaro,' and 'Loca': Cuban and Puerto Rican Linguistic Practices, and Sexual Minority Participation, in U.S. Santería." *Journal of Homosexuality*, no. 58 (2011): 901–18.

Vidal-Ortiz, Salvador. "Queering Sexuality and Doing Gender: Transgender Men's Identification with Gender and Sexuality." *Gender Sexualities* 6 (2002): 181–233.

Vidal-Ortiz, Salvador. "Sexuality Discussions in Santería: A Case Study of Religion and Sexuality Negotiation." *Sexuality Research and Social Policy* 3, no. 3 (2006): 52–66.

Vizenor, Gerald Robert. *Survivance: Narratives of Native Presence*. Lincoln: University of Nebraska Press, 2008.

Weismantel, Mary J. *Cholas and Pishtacos: Stories of Race and Sex in the Andes*. Chicago: University of Chicago Press, 2001.

Weiss, Margot. *Techniques of Pleasure: BDSM and the Circuits of Sexuality*. Durham, NC: Duke University Press, 2011.

Wilcken, Lois. *The Drums of Vodou*. Tempe, AZ: White Cliffs Media, 1992.

Williams, Raymond. *Marxism and Literature*. Oxford: Oxford University Press, 1977.

Zambrana, Ruth Enid. *Toxic Ivory Towers: The Consequences of Work Stress on Underrepresented Minority Faculty*. New Brunswick, NJ: Rutgers University Press, 2018.

Index

experiencing the evidence of being Chip, 74–78

Ezili, 119–20

Ezili's Mirrors (Tinsley), 17

facultades, 33, 65, 75, 130

faggotological rasanblaj, 102

faggotology (pensar maricón), 34, 64–67, 125; blackness and, 34, 153; convergences related to, 100; Decena's "arrival" to, 16; features of, 87; functions of, 20, 57–58, 78, 154; nature of, 3, 11–13, 15, 126; neighborhoods and, 27; origin of the term, xii; path toward, 29, 57, 127, 153; preconditions for, 149; repurposing, 57–58. *See also* maricón; *individual topics*

Fanon, Frantz, 24, 25, 79, 105; schemas and, 105, 116; "somewhere else and something else," 79, 82

femininity, 116, 117; morphology and, 115, 117; as vulnerability, 24, 115, 169n11 (*see also* vulnerability). *See also* sissy

feminisms: of color, 10–12, 58, 72; queer, 3, 10–12, 72; Joan Scott and, 58, 67, 68, 70–73; white, 58, 70, 71

fè yon rasanblaj (gather everything), 5, 8

Figueroa-Vásquez, Yomaira, 7

flesh, 103, 142, 148, 151; vs. body, 104, 148, 152; meaning of the term, 104; poetics of the, 151; vs. self, 163n47

foundationalist history and foundationalist historians, 68, 69

fractured locus, 127

freedom, 29, 121, 132, 152

Friedman, Jeff, 75, 76

funk, 11, 16

funking the erotic, 120

gathering (fè yon rasanblaj), 5, 8

gender training and religious initiation, 105

getting through, 64

Gill, Lyndon K., 125, 173n1

God, 15, 16, 148, 151. *See also* divine

gods, 4; making of, 93

González, Octavio, 123

Griffin, Farah Jasmine, 126

"gynographic performative," la loca as, 169n10

habits and habituation, 95–98, 130

Haider, Asad, 11, 161n37

Haiti, 119–20, 132–33, 164n7. *See also* anti-Haitianism

Halkitis, Perry N., 172n37

Hames-García, Michael, 11, 24, 162n37

Hanawa, Yukiko, 6

Harper, Phillip Brian, 65–66

Harris, E. Lynn, 172n40

Havana, 118; Decena in, 10, 67, 82, 85, 93, 118

Heading South/Vers le sud (film), 132–33, 152

Hemphill, Essex, 65, 142, 143; looking for, 142–47

Henry (college friend in "Looking for Essex"), 142

Hernández, Jillian, 148–49

Herukhuti (H. Sharif Williams), 150, 153

historical foundationalism, 68, 69

historical-racial schema, 105

HIV, 142, 145–47

Hoang, Nguyen Tan, 153–54

holding space, 63–64

holes, 5, 22, 81, 145, 147. *See also* anus; black (w)hole; raja (opening/tearing/rupture/wound)

Holiday, Billie, 126

Holland, Sharon P., 129

Holocaust, 42

"home" and peoples of color, 166n14

homonormativity, 130, 143

homophobia, 36, 37

homosexuality, 76. *See also individual topics*

Howe, Susan, 9–10

"I," transparent, 5, 7, 13, 70–72, 126

identity, proof of, 86. *See also* passport

identity essentialisms, 72

identity politics, 11, 72, 161n37; dissing, 71–72

identity work, 68–71

Ilé de Abbebe Oshún, 58–61, 63

indecency, 128, 148, 151

ritual markings/inscriptions, 95, 96

rituals, 34, 92–94, 97, 98, 118; economics/finance and, 91–94; intentionality in, 94; orishas and, 7; otases and, 83, 90, 91. *See also individual topics*

ritual trance possession. *See* trance possession

Rivera, Mayra, 151

Rubin, Gayle, 12, 143, 171n14

sacred, the, 7, 9, 81–82, 98; sexuality and the, 153, 154

sacred bodies, 98

sacred objects, 82, 126

sacred stones, 7. *See also* otases (ritual stones)

sacred (w)hole, touching the, 81

Sade, Marquis de, 140, 141

Sáenz, Mario, 162n47

Saint, Assotto (Yves F. Lubin), 12

sainthood, 12, 117; desire and quest for, 107, 109, 117. *See also* santo

Santería initiation, 98, 103, 109, 112–14, 118, 120; Decena's, 67, 83–84, 91–94; gender training and, 105; nature of, 117, 119; orishas and, 117, 119; preparation for, 118; priests and, 4, 67, 84, 92–94, 96, 98, 114, 117, 159n4; suspension of mirror in, 105–7, 109, 110, 112–18, 120–21. *See also* initiation

Santería/Lucumi, 88, 93–95, 98; Aisha Beliso-De Jesús on, 15, 33; Blacks and, 93; Decena's early encounters with, 15, 109; famous people in, 13–14; LGBTQ and, 14, 15; nature of, 15. *See also individual topics*

santo: becoming of, 126; looking for, 105–14, 117–20

Savastano, Peter, 11, 127, 171n11

schemas: conjunction of, 116; corporeal, 53, 105; racial, 41, 105, 116–17

Scott, Joan Wallach, 75, 76; Linda Martin Alcoff on, 73; criticisms of, 71, 73; dawdling with, 67–74; Samuel Delany and, 67–68, 73, 74, 76, 77; feminism and, 58, 67, 68, 70–73; and foundationalist history and historians, 68–70; on

historical writing, 69–70; language and, 73; Karen Swann and, 73, 77; on E. P. Thompson, 69–70; transparent "I" and, 70–72; transparent vision and, 68; writings, 67–74

séance. *See* misas

self, 14, 25, 105, 163n47

ser alguien (to be someone), 13, 34, 38, 39

shadow, 56, 130

Shah, Nayan, 170n1

sissy, 19, 23, 29, 108, 115

slavery, 93

socio-political order of the New World, 103–4

soul work, 75, 126; sex as, 22, 120; visual metaphors for, 17

space holding, 63–64

speculative, the, 65–66

spheres of relationality (Marx), 89

Spillers, Hortense J., 103–4, 148, 151

spirit, life of, 107, 119, 120

spiritology, 11

spiritscapes, 82

spiritualism/spiritism, 167n4

spirituality, 16, 33, 85, 94–96, 132; money and, 92; sexuality and, 125, 127. *See also individual topics*

spiritual mass. *See* misa espiritual (spiritual mass)

Stephens, Michelle Ann, 104, 105

Stone-Mediatore, Shari, 70, 74

stones, ritual: befriending, 84; consecration, 84, 85, 98; initiation and, 84; loving your, 83, 96; orishas and, 7; touching, 83. *See also* otases (ritual stones)

strai(gh)tjacket, 25, 104; masculinity as, 59, 164n5, 166n5

stranger intimacy, 11, 22, 125, 131, 146, 153, 170n1

Strongman, Roberto, 10, 14

substitution of relations (Marx), 88–89, 94, 96, 97

sucias, 130, 153

surrender, 111

survivance, 8

Swann, Karen, 73, 77

tactility, 83, 102

tantear, 18, 121; uses and meanings of the term, 19, 81

tanteo, 19, 21, 82, 121

Tatica, Doña, 110–12, 116

theft, 45; of the body, 45–46, 104

theology, 11, 129, 151; liberation, 12, 81, 128; queerness, queer theory, and, 11–12, 128, 148; spiritology and, 11

thinking sex, 12

"Thinking Sex" (Rubin), 171n14

third eye (ori), 4

Thompson, E. P., 69–70

Tinsley, Omise'eke Natasha, 17, 119–20

touch, 4, 5, 19, 134, 136, 137, 153; of Pepe Aguilar and Matilde, 109, 114, 115; sense of, 74. *See also* tantear; tanteo

trance possession, 118, 125, 131, 132, 152, 153

trances, 10

transcendent erotics, 115, 170n12

transcorporeal Afro-diasporic self, 14

transcorporeal body, 17

transcripturality, 10

Transnational Black Feminist Retreat, 16, 58, 131

transparent "I," 5, 7, 13, 70–72, 126

transparent vision, 68

transposition, 95–99; meanings of the term, 96–97

triple consciousness, 105, 116

tumultuous derangement, 126, 171n8

Ulysse, Gina Athena, 3, 160n21, 163n52, 164n9

Vallone, Mirella, 129–30

Vargas, Deborah R., 130, 131

Vers le sud/Heading South (film), 132–33, 152

view from the bottom, 153–54

visceral, the, 58, 128, 129; and the visual, 68

visual, the, 68, 115

vulnerability, 129, 132, 153, 154; and the erotic, 125; femininity as, 24, 115, 169n11. *See also* boyar

"water buffalo" incident, 40–41

Weiss, Margot, 6

whiteness, 162n37; of gayness, 34, 144; identity work of, 71 (*see also* identity work); liberal, 40; protocols of, 42; sentimental education in, 34

(w)hole. *See* black (w)hole; holes; sacred (w)hole, touching the

wholeness, 4

Wilcken, Lois, 162n41

Williams, H. Sharif (Herukhuti), 150, 153

wounds, 127, 150

yellows and greens, 61–63

Yoruba, 14, 15, 58, 59, 77

Zambrana, Ruth Enid, 160n19